Climate Change and Industry Structure in China

In order to effectively address global warming, many countries have significantly reduced the amount of carbon dioxide emissions that are put into the atmosphere. From the perspective of industrial structure, this volume examines the emission reduction potentials and abatement costs in China. By making an empirical analysis of the emission reduction, the author proposes some practical strategies.

The book comprehensively summarizes related theories and research of contaminant disposal modeling, and estimates the shadow price of interprovincial CO_2 emissions, the emission reduction potential of different regions, and the marginal emission reduction cost based on the parametric model. It finally puts forward the strategy to adjust the industrial structure in China.

The book hence provides solid evidence for policy-makers to help mitigate CO_2 emissions through industrial restructuring strategy.

Wei Chu is a professor at Renmin University of China. His research focuses on the analysis of energy efficiency, evaluation of abatement cost of pollutants, and the residential energy demand.

China Perspectives

The *China Perspectives* series focuses on translating and publishing works by leading Chinese scholars, writing about both global topics and China-related themes. It covers Humanities & Social Sciences, Education, Media and Psychology, as well as many interdisciplinary themes.

This is the first time any of these books have been published in English for international readers. The series aims to put forward a Chinese perspective, give insights into cutting-edge academic thinking in China, and inspire researchers globally.

Titles in economics partly include:

The Chinese Path to Economic Dual Transformation
Li Yining

Hyperinflation
A World History
Liping He

Game Theory and Society
Weiying Zhang

China's Fiscal Policy
Theoretical and Situation Analysis
Gao Peiyong

Trade Openness and China's Economic Development
Miaojie YU

Perceiving Truth and Ceasing Doubts
What Can We Learn from 40 Years of China's Reform and Opening-Up?
Cai Fang

For more information, please visit https://www.routledge.com/series/CPH

Climate Change and Industry Structure in China

Mitigation Strategy

Wei Chu

LONDON AND NEW YORK

First published 2020 by Routledge

2 Park Square, Milton Park, Abingdon, Oxon OX14 4RN
605 Third Avenue, New York, NY 10017

Routledge is an imprint of the Taylor & Francis Group, an informa business

First issued in paperback 2021

Copyright © 2020 Wei Chu

The right of Wei Chu to be identified as author of this work has been asserted by him in accordance with sections 77 and 78 of the Copyright, Designs and Patents Act 1988.

All rights reserved. No part of this book may be reprinted or reproduced or utilised in any form or by any electronic, mechanical, or other means, now known or hereafter invented, including photocopying and recording, or in any information storage or retrieval system, without permission in writing from the publishers.

Notice:
Product or corporate names may be trademarks or registered trademarks, and are used only for identification and explanation without intent to infringe.

Publisher's Note

The publisher has gone to great lengths to ensure the quality of this reprint but points out that some imperfections in the original copies may be apparent.

English Version by permission of China Renmin University Press.

British Library Cataloguing-in-Publication Data
A catalogue record for this book is available from the British Library

Library of Congress Cataloging-in-Publication Data
A catalog record has been requested for this book

ISBN: 978-0-367-43577-6 (hbk)
ISBN: 978-1-03-217393-1 (pbk)
DOI: 10.4324/9781003004455

Typeset in Times New Roman
by Newgen Publishing UK

Contents

List of figures	vi
List of tables	vii
Preface	ix

PART I
Emission reduction analysis 1

1 Literature review of contaminant disposal modeling
 under the productivity framework 3

2 Interprovincial CO_2 shadow price research based on the
 parametric model 30

3 Regional decomposition of CO_2 emission reduction
 potential and emission reduction targets 42

4 Research on CO_2 marginal abatement cost in Chinese cities 69

PART II
Strategic response 117

5 Industrial restructuring strategy to mitigate and control
 CO_2 emissions 119

References	142
Index	154

Figures

1.1	Schematic diagram of directional distance function and output distance function	7
3.1	CO_2 emission reductions in the eastern, central, and western regions (1995–2007)	53
3.2	CO_2 emission reduction potential in the eastern, central, and western regions (1995–2007)	53
3.3	CO_2 marginal abatement costs in the eastern, central, and western regions (1995–2007)	56
3.4	Distribution of Equity Index and Efficiency Index of emission reduction in each province (1995–2007)	59
3.5	Emission reduction priority	60
3.6	Preferred emission reduction efficiency	61
4.1	Directional distance function and shadow price	78
4.2	Trends of input and output variables (2001–2008)	88
4.3	Shadow price comparison in the eastern, middle, and western regions (2001–2008)	92
4.4	Provincial shadow price ranking (2001–2008)	93
4.5	Fifteen cities with the highest marginal abatement costs and the lowest 15 cities (2001–2008)	93
4.6	City shadow price coefficient of variation (2001–2008)	94
5.1	China's GDP, fiscal revenue and expenditure and local energy conservation protection expenditure trends (2000–2012)	125

Tables

1.1	Summary of evidence-based literature on studies about environmentally sensitive productivity	16
2.1	Descriptive statistics of various variables	37
2.2	Average productivity and average CO_2 shadow price of provinces (cities, districts) in China (1995–2007)	37
3.1	Descriptive statistics of various variables (1995–2007)	50
3.2	CO_2 emission reductions by province, accounting for the national proportion and emission reduction potential (1995–2007)	51
3.3	CO_2 shadow price estimates by province (1995–2007)	55
3.4	Fairness Index, Efficiency Index, and Capacity Index (average between 1995 and 2007)	58
3.5	CO_2 emission reduction capacity of major provinces under different principles (1995–2007)	62
3.6	Regression analysis of emission reduction potential (1995–2007)	64
3.7	EKC test of CO_2 shadow price	64
4.1	Results of China's 2010 marginal carbon abatement costs	75
4.2	Comparison of literature based on the parametric model for directional distance function at home and abroad	82
4.3	Various energy standard coal conversion factors and carbon emission factors	86
4.4	Descriptive statistics of input–output variables (2001–2008)	87
4.5	Comparison of output and input in terms of regions (2001–2008)	87
4.6	Comparison of sample representativeness (2008)	89
4.7	Direction distance function parameter estimates	90
4.8	Descriptive statistics of eight direction distance functions and shadow prices	90
4.9	Comparison of the results of CO_2 shadow price calculation in different literatures	91
4.10	Summary of factors affecting marginal abatement costs	97
4.11	Descriptive statistics for explanatory variables	98
4.12	Initial regression analysis results	100

viii *Tables*

4.13	Further study of pollutants	101
4.14	Comparison table of sample cities	104
4.15	Individual cities' effect parameters	108
4.16	Provincial marginal emission reduction cost (2001–2008)	109
4.17	Marginal emission reduction cost of cities (2001–2008)	110
4.18	Relative coefficients of variables (relative coefficient and significance of Spearman)	114
4.19	Multicollinearity of explanatory variables	115

Preface

The low-carbon transformation of the industrial structure is not only an inevitable choice for dealing with climate change, but also an important embodiment of the transformation of the economic development mode. This book starts from the perspective of industrial structure and quantifies the main characteristics of China's carbon dioxide emissions, and proposes corresponding emission reduction strategies and countermeasures based on the analysis results.

The book consists of two volumes. In volume one, this book reviews the current status of greenhouse gas (GHG) emissions and challenges that China faces; sorts out the theoretical literature on the mechanism of industrial structure CO_2 emissions, and the conductive effects based on the perspective of industrial structure and systematically summarizes the corresponding analysis model; estimates and predicts regional CO_2 emissions in China at the interprovincial level and uses the econometric model to identify the influencing factors of per capita CO_2 emissions; measures and disintegrates CO_2 emissions from industrial sectors in China on industrial basis; taking Zhejiang industry as the research object, investigates and compares the differences of industrial CO_2 emissions between Zhejiang and other developed provinces.

In volume two, interdisciplinary/urban CO_2 reduction potentials and costs are assessed by further examining the regions, using a combination of econometric analysis, linear programming, and scenario analysis and looking into the preference problem in the decomposition of emission constraint target; finally, based on the perspective of industrial structure, key areas and links for controlling and slowing carbon emissions are identified and four strategic concepts of "increasing productivity," "reducing emissions," "proposing solutions," and "transforming production" are proposed. This volume has the following main findings.

First, this volume quantitatively evaluates China's CO_2 emission reduction potential and marginal abatement cost, and further examines the relationship between industrial structure and CO_2 emission reduction. The average emission reduction potential of China's CO_2 is about 40%, and it shows the regional differences in the eastern < central < western; the level x *Preface*

of economic development and proportion of the tertiary industry is negatively correlated with the relative emission reduction potential, while the energy intensity, coal weight, and technological progress as well as capital deepening are positively correlated with emission reduction potential. The industrial structure, energy intensity, and energy consumption structure have a greater impact on emission reduction potential. The interprovincial level of CO_2 marginal abatement costs in China is 94.4–139.5 yuan/ton, and the average marginal abatement cost at the urban level is 967 yuan/ton, both of which are characterized by the eastern > central > western, and the heterogeneity between the regions/cities is still expanding. There is a U-shaped relationship between marginal abatement costs and income, and the level of urbanization is positively related to marginal abatement costs, while the proportion of secondary industry, degree of openness, and per-capita transportation infrastructure are significantly negatively correlated with marginal abatement costs.

Second, based on the principles of fairness and efficiency, this volume simulates the regional emission quota allocation scheme and proposes two market instruments that can be adopted in the future. If only the principle of fairness is considered, then regions with higher per-capita CO_2 emissions and higher economic development levels should bear more emission reduction obligations; if only efficiency principles are considered, then they have greater emission reduction potential and lower marginal abatement costs. The provinces should undertake more emission reduction tasks; if both dimensions of equity and efficiency are considered, the provinces that need to be focused on, including Inner Mongolia, Shanxi, and Hebei, can be identified. In the future, the cost of mandatory emission reduction will become higher and higher. The characteristics of emission reduction between provinces/urban cities should be fully considered, and the total cost of emission reduction should be reduced through market mechanisms. One possible solution is the emission trading system, which reduces the cost of abatement through transactions between regions with higher marginal abatement costs and those with lower marginal abatement costs; or a tax system with unilateral payments, i.e., the central government imposes a tax on carbon emissions in areas with higher marginal abatement costs, and transfers some of the tax payments to areas with lower marginal abatement costs to compensate for their emission reductions.

There are three major innovations in this book: first, the theoretical model is used to define the mechanism of the industrial structure's contribution to GHG emissions; second, a large number of quantitative analyses are used to identify key areas and essential drivers of GHG emissions in different industries/regions in China. The specific direction and size of the industrial structure for GHG emissions were examined. Third, based on the dimensions of fairness and efficiency, China's GHG emission reduction potential and decomposition goals were evaluated and simulated. In addition, based on the aforementioned theoretical and conclusions of empirical research, four industrial structure adjustment strategies of "increasing productivity," "reducing emissions," "proposing solutions," and "transforming production" were proposed.

This book also has many deficiencies. First, limited by the availability of data and relatively rough selection of industry, no microscopic analysis was conducted to further subdivide industry categories to the four-digit level; second, the calculation of carbon emissions of different sectors is mainly based on the burning of terminal fossil fuels without considering the release of GHGs during the production process. Due to the lack of more detailed data, carbon sequestration of special sectors (such as forestry) is not considered. Besides, in terms of the calculation of GHG emission, existing studies on GHG emission accounting are based on the coefficients given in the IPCC's emission accounting checklist. Actually, differences in the quality of energy products in various regions and industries and degree of oxidation in combustion process will result in differences between the calculated data and actual emissions, which can only be improved through further refinement of data and development of accounting methods. Finally, the adjustment of industrial structure may affect the situation as a whole, and changes in the structure of a certain sector will be transmitted to other related departments, therefore further influencing the development of entire national economy. The analysis of the impact of different industrial structure adjustment policies on macroeconomic or sectoral economy should be based on the input–output table for the Computable General Equilibrium (CGE) analysis. Constrained by time and effort, this book is less involved in this direction, which needs to be further studied.

The relevant research of this book comes from the National Social Science Fund Project I hosted, "Climate Change and the Strategic Study of China's Industrial Structure Adjustment during the Twelfth Five-Year Plan Period" (10CJY002), and the National Natural Science Foundation Project "Regarding Regional Carbon Equity with Equity and Efficiency." The research results in the Design and Comparison of the Right Allocation Plan (41201582), and the research also received the "Beijing Municipality's Household Energy Consumption Model and Energy-saving Approaches" (9152011) and the Mingde Young Scholar Program of Renmin University of China Support for Carbon Dioxide Abatement Cost Curve (13XNJ016). Some of the chapter content has been published in journals, and comments are given at the beginning of each chapter. During the study, President Shen Manhong of Ningbo University, Associate Professor Ni Jinlan from the University of Nebraska, Associate Professor Du Limin from Zhejiang University, Associate Professor Cai Shenghua from the Chinese Academy of Sciences, Dr. Yu Dongzheng, Student Huang Wenruo, and Student Su Xiaolong participated in some of the collaborative research, or participated in the writing and revision of some chapters, or provided a large number of research assistants, and I express my sincere gratitude to them for their contributions. In addition, we would also

xii *Preface*

like to sincerely thank the people's publishing house Zhai Yanhong for his efforts in publishing the book.

Due to the limited research energy and the lack of experience of the authors, the errors or defects in this book sincerely welcome criticism and correction from experts and readers.

Part I
Emission reduction analysis

1 Literature review of contaminant disposal modeling under the productivity framework[1]

In order to quantitatively study carbon dioxide emission reduction, it is necessary to model the pollutant disposal. Therefore, it is necessary to first review the relevant models in the form of a literature review and select the corresponding modeling tools. This book will be modeled in the subsequent quantitative analysis based on environmental production techniques under the productivity framework.

Traditional productivity analysis tends to focus on the ratio of companies using various valuable input factors to valuable saleable products. The efficiency boundary means that the output is unchanged and the input factors are the least, or the output is fixed under the condition of fixed input factors. This method of measurement ignores the "undesirable output"[2] of pollution, thereby underestimating the true productivity of firms under stronger environmental controls. Because the company needs to invest extra cost to reduce pollutants under the stronger environmental control, or reduce the output correspondingly to reduce pollution emissions, the cost (or reduced output) used to reduce pollution is included in the calculation. The input (or output) of the production of the enterprise are not included in their productivity calculations but not the positive social effects of reducing pollutants, thus underestimating the true productivity of these enterprises, which will further affect the decision-makers' environmental regulation policy formulation.[3]

The "undesirable output" of pollutants is not included in the classical production theory and productivity measurement. The main reason for this is that the market price of pollutants cannot be determined. Traditional accounting methods and production theories cannot directly deal with them, so they cannot be weighted.[4] To measure its true productivity, the latest theoretical research has integrated environmental pollution as an "undesirable output" into the production framework to measure "environmental sensitive productivity."[5] This chapter is a review of the development of this theory.

The structure of this chapter is organized as follows. The first part introduces the existing main research ideas and theoretical models; the second part introduces the specific estimation methods of each model; the third section summarizes and compares the existing empirical research, and the existing research deficiency comment; the final part is the conclusion.

4 *Emission reduction analysis*

1.1 Research ideas and theoretical development

In the existing environmental sensitivity productivity analysis, there are three main ideas: index method, distance function, and directional distance function.

1.1.1 Index method

Traditional productivity indices include Fisher, Tornqvist, and Malmquist. These productivity indices are built by weighting different input or output factors[6] to construct a multifactor efficiency measurement index. If "non-consensus output" is considered, the price of undesirable output needs to be set by means of polluting emissions trading price or estimated shadow price, and is added to each productivity index based on the same weighting method.

Pittman (1983) first explored this issue.[7] He pointed out: "The biggest difficulty and challenge is how to allocate shadow prices for undesired outputs," although the shadow price of pollutants can be estimated based on survey data on manufacturers' abatement costs (Pittman, 1983), or by evaluating unintended production. The external damage price (Repetto et al., 1996)[8] is used for calculation, but in practice, it is often impossible to pass research because it is difficult to distinguish between capital and other inputs used for production and for pollutant emission reduction (de Boo, 1993). Obtaining the real emission reduction amount and emission reduction expenditure of the manufacturer and the external damage of pollutants to society cannot be accurately calculated due to the transfer of time and space.[9] In addition, the accuracy of existing evaluation methods is also controversial (Hailu & Veeman, 2000).

The Malmquist index does not require price information on input and output factors, but as Chung et al. (1997) pointed out, the traditional Malmquist index cannot be calculated when including undesired outputs, and then they moved to the directional distance function (directional distance). Based on the function, the Malmquist–Luenberger Productivity Index (hereinafter referred to as the ML Index) is proposed, which can measure the total factor productivity when there is unintended output, and at the same time consider the increase of desirable output. The reduction in unsatisfactory output has the good nature of the Malmquist index. Therefore, the ML index has been widely used in subsequent studies.

1.1.2 Distance function

Beginning in the 1990s, theorists began to use distance functions to include undesired outputs and to derive shadow prices for environmentally sensitive productivity and undesired output (Färe et al., 1993; Ball et al., 1994;

Yaisawarng & Klein, 1994; Coggin & Swinton, 1996; Hetemäki, 1996; Hailu & Veeman, 2000). The distance function is essentially an application of the frontier production function. The biggest difference between the frontier production function and the traditional production function is that the former considers the inefficiency term of the decision-making unit (DMU), that is, in the actual economic operation, the basic under the given input conditions, the unit is affected by external uncontrollable factors, and there will be a certain efficiency loss, so the potential maximum output may not be achieved. This is more in line with the actual situation, because production inefficiency is ubiquitous, and fully effective economic operations are rare (Yue Shujing et al., 2009). The distance function actually depicts the efficiency of the previous edge efficiency, the distance from each unit in the production set to the production front.

Färe et al. (1993) used the distance function to conduct environmental sensitivity productivity research earlier. The basic theoretical model of the distance function based on output is as follows.

Suppose the input vector $x \in R\_+^N$, the output vector $u \in R\_+^M$, the production technique $P(x)=\{u: x \text{ can produce } u\}$, allowing the output for weak disposability instead of strong one,[10] according to Shepard and Chipman (1970), the output distance function is defined as:

$$D_o(x, u) = \inf \{\theta: (u/\theta) \in P(x)\} \tag{1.1}$$

Under this definition, a minimum threshold is required to achieve the goal of expanding output to the frontier. $\theta \leq 1$, when and only $\theta = 1$, the unit efficiency is on the leading edge.

In the same way, the input distance function is to fix the output and minimize the input. Let the input vector $x \in R\_+^N$, the output vector $u \in R\_+^M$, the production technique $L(u)=\{x: x \text{ can produce } u\}$, then the input distance function is defined as:

$$D_I(x, u) = \sup \{\rho: (x/\rho) \in L(u)\} \tag{1.2}$$

The maximum value of ρ is required here to minimize the input under fixed output. When $\rho = 1$, the efficiency of the point is at the leading edge.

In addition, based on the distance function of the input or output direction, the shadow price of the undesired output can be further derived, and the output price $r = (r_1, ..., r_M)$, assuming $r \neq 0$,[11] the income function can be defined as

$$R(x, r) = \sup \{ru: D_o(x, u) \leq 1\} \tag{1.3}$$

For the convex output set $P(x)$, the relationship between $R(x, r)$ and $Do(x, u)$ (Shepard & Chipman, 1970; Färe, 1988), constructing the Lagrange function

6 Emission reduction analysis

and finding the first order of output guide, you can get the shadow price of undesired output relative to the desired output:

$$r_{m'} = R \cdot \pm r_{m'}^{*}(x,u) = R \cdot \left[\frac{\partial D_o(x,u)}{\partial u_{m'}} \right] = r_m^o \cdot \frac{\partial D_o(x,u)/\partial u_{m'}}{\partial D_o(x,u)/\partial u_m} \qquad (1.4)$$

Here, the observed price of the desired output r_m^o is used as the standardized price, because the desired output has an observable and market-oriented price, and $r_{m'}$ is the absolute shadow price of the undesired output, so the output/ input distance.[12] The function can also be used to calculate the contaminant shadow price.

1.1.3 Directional distance function

Chung et al. (1997) first proposed a directional distance function for environmental sensitivity productivity analysis. The difference between the directional distance function and the ordinary distance function is that the assumptions for the joint production of desirable and undesired outputs are different. The distance function only considers the maximum expansion of the desired output, while the directional distance function examines the decrease in the undesired output while examining the increase in desirable output, only if the desired output cannot continue to expand and is unsatisfactory. When the output cannot continue to decrease, the observation point is at the forefront of efficiency. Its model is as follows.

Suppose the input vector $x \in \mathfrak{R}_+^N$, the desirable output vector $y \in \mathfrak{R}_+^M$, the undesired output $b \in \mathfrak{R}_+^J$, and the production technique is defined as $P(x) = \{(y, b): x \ can \ produce \ (y, b)\}$, which has two characteristics:

(i) Consensus output is freely dispositioned, undesired output is weakly disposed of

$$(y, b) \in P(x), \quad if \ y' \le y, (y', b) \in P(x) \qquad (1.5)$$

$$(y, b) \in P(x), \quad if \ 0 \le \theta \le 1, (\theta y, \theta b) \in P(x) \qquad (1.6)$$

(ii) Joint production:

$$(y, b) \in P(x), \quad if \ b = 0, \ then \ y = 0 \qquad (1.7)$$

The directional distance function first needs to construct a direction vector of $g=(g_y, -g_b)$ and $g \in \mathfrak{R}^M \times \mathfrak{R}^J$, which is used to constrain the direction of change of the desired output and the undesired output. The size of the change, that is, the increase (decrease) of the desired (unintended) output on the path specified by the direction vector, the specific choice of the direction vector depends on factors such as research needs or policy orientation preferences. The directional output distance function can be defined as:

$$\vec{D}_o(x, y, b; g_y, g_b) = sup\{\beta:(y+\beta g_y, b-\beta g_b) \in P(x)\} \quad (1.8)$$

β represents the degree to which a given unit's desirable output (unsatisfactory output) can be expanded (reduced) compared to the most efficient unit on the leading edge production surface. If β = 0, it means that this decision unit is on the leading-edge production side, which is the most efficient. The larger the value of β, the greater the potential for the desired output of the decision-making unit to continue to increase, and the smaller the space for the reduction of undesired output, so the lower the efficiency.

The directional distance function is a general form of Shephard's output distance function (Chung et al., 1997). When the direction vector **g** = (1, 0), the Shephard yield distance function is a special case of the directional distance function. The main relationships and differences between them can be illustrated by Figure 1.1.

In Figure 1.1, $P(x^t)$ is the production possible set, and the output distance function is extended along the ray defined by the origin and the observation point A, and the desired output y^t is expanded to the front edge in the same proportion as the undesired output b^t. The point C of the directional output function is: the path of the given direction vector $g = (g_y, -g_b)$, the expansion of the desired output y^t and the reduction of the undesired output b^t, thereby go to point B at the front of the output. Obviously, for the distance function, moving from the invalid point A to the C point on the leading edge, there is either an excessive undesired output, or a desirable output insufficiency, while the directional distance function is not only considered. The expansion of desirable output, and the minimization of undesired output, can more

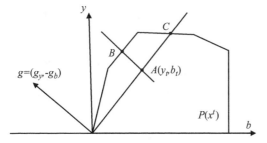

Figure 1.1 Schematic diagram of directional distance function and output distance function

8 *Emission reduction analysis*

accurately describe its real productivity. In recent years, the use of directional distance function model to measure environmental sensitivity productivity has been increasing.

1.2 Model solving method

Whether it is the distance function or the directional distance function developed in the later stage, the production boundary they use to construct is to use the multiple sets of input–output data to derive the production front, and to make the decision-making units in the sample and the production frontier. The best advantages are compared to solve the relative efficiency values of each decision unit. At present, the solution to the model can be generally divided into two types: parameterized and non-parametric. The parametric solution mainly includes: Parametric Line Program (PLP) and Stochastic Frontier Analysis (SFA). Here, translog, quadratic, and hyperbolic functions are adopted for the parameterized distance function form; nonparametric solutions mainly refer to Data Envelopment Analysis (DEA). The following mainly introduces four widely used solving methods.

1.2.1 Parametric distance function solution based on translog function

The parameterized output/input distance function method can overcome the shortcomings of the exponential method. Färe et al. (1993) first used the parameterized distance function to study environmental sensitivity productivity. The idea is to select the super-logarithm function to parameterize the output distance function $D_o(x,u)$[13] and to minimize the distance between all samples and the production front by linear programming constraints, and the value of the output distance function is environmentally sensitive productivity. Its super-logarithmic function is set to:

$$
\begin{aligned}
lnD_o(x,u) = {} & \alpha_0 + \sum_{n=1}^{N}\beta_n lnx_n + \sum_{m=1}^{M}\alpha_m lnu_m + \frac{1}{2}\sum_{n=1}^{N}\sum_{n=1}^{N}\beta_{nn}\left(lnx_n\right)\ln\left(x_n\right) \\
& + \frac{1}{2}\sum_{m=1}^{M}\sum_{m=1}^{M}\alpha_{mm}\left(lnu_m\right)\ln\left(u_m\right) + \sum_{n=1}^{N}\sum_{m=1}^{M}\gamma_{nm}\left(lnx_n\right)\ln\left(u_m\right)
\end{aligned}
\tag{1.9}
$$

Assuming that the function of equation (1.9) has general symmetry and homogeneous constraints, the method of Aigner and Chu (1968) is used to minimize the deviation of the sample from the leading edge, that is, to solve the following linear programming problem:

$$
Max\sum_{k=1}^{K}\left[lnD_o\left(x^k,u^k\right) - ln1\right]
\tag{1.10}
$$

s.t.

(i) $\quad lnD_o\left(x^k, u^k\right) \leq 0, \qquad k = 1, \ldots, K$

(ii) $\quad \dfrac{lnD_o\left(x^k, u^k\right)}{lnu_m^k} \geq 0, \quad m = 1, \ldots, i, \quad k = 1, \ldots, K$

(iii) $\quad \dfrac{lnD_o\left(x^k, u^k\right)}{\partial lnu_m^k} \leq 0, \quad m = i+1, \ldots, M, \quad k = 1, \ldots, K$

(iv) $\quad \displaystyle\sum_{m=1}^{M} \alpha_m = 1, \quad n = 1, \ldots, N$

$$\sum_{m'=1}^{M} \alpha_{mm'} = \sum_{m=1}^{M} r_{nm} = 0, \quad m = 1, \ldots, M, \quad n = 1, \ldots, N$$

(v) $\quad \alpha_{mm'} = \alpha_{m'm}, \quad m = 1, \ldots, M, \quad m' = 1, \ldots, M$

$\quad \beta_{nn'} = \beta_{n'n}, \quad n = 1, \ldots, N, \quad n' = 1, \ldots, N$

where $k = 1, \ldots, K$ represents different observational samples, the first i outputs are desirable outputs, and the later $(m - i)$ outputs are undesired outputs. The objective function in equation (1.10) is to minimize the deviation of all samples from the optimal leading edge. Constraints (i) ensure that each sample is at the leading edge or below the leading edge; constraint (ii) guarantees that the shadow price of the desired output is non-negative; constraint (iii) guarantees that the non-conforming output shadow price is not positive; constraint (iv) pairs the output, which is applied once in a row to ensure that the production technology meets the output weak disposal assumption; constraint (v) is a symmetry constraint. Once the values of the parameters in the distance function are solved using (1.10), the environmental sensitivity productivity of the sample and the shadow price of the undesired output can be calculated.

1.2.2 Solution of directional distance function based on quadratic function

If the directional distance function is set instead of the distance function, the super-logarithmic function is generally not used, and the quadratic function is used, because the quadratic function satisfies the constraints required for the directional distance function characteristic (Färe & Grosskopf, 2006). Generally, the direction vector $\mathbf{g} = (1, -1)^{14}$ can be set. Assuming $k = 1, \ldots, K$ represents a different observation sample, the quadratic direction distance function can be expressed as:

10   *Emission reduction analysis*

$$\bar{D}_o(x,g,b;1,-1) = \alpha_0 + \sum_{n=1}^{N}\alpha_n x_n + \sum_{m=1}^{M}\beta_m g_m + \sum_{j=1}^{J}\gamma_j b_j$$
$$+\frac{1}{2}\sum_{n=1}^{N}\sum_{n'=1}^{N}\alpha_{nn'}(x_n)(x_{n'})$$
$$+\frac{1}{2}\sum_{m=1}^{M}\sum_{m'=1}^{M}\beta_{mm'}(u_m)(u_{m'})$$
$$+\frac{1}{2}\sum_{j=1}^{J}\sum_{j'=1}^{J}\gamma_{mm'}(b_j)(b_{j'})$$
$$\sum_{n=1}^{N}\sum_{m=1}^{m}\delta_{nm}(x_n)(g_m)+\sum_{n=1}^{N}\sum_{j=1}^{J}\eta_{nj}(x_n)(b_j)$$
$$+\sum_{m=1}^{m}\sum_{j=1}^{J}\mu_{nm}(g_n)(b_m)$$

(1.11)

The parameter solution is also based on the idea of linear programming, which minimizes the sum of the distances of the observations to the boundary.

$$Min\sum_{k=1}^{K}\left[\bar{D}_o(x_k,g_k,b_k;1,-1)-ln1\right]$$

(1.12)

s.t.

(i) $\bar{D}_o(x_k,g_k,b_k;1,-1)\geq 0,\quad k=1,\dots,K$

(ii) $\dfrac{\partial \bar{D}_o(x_k,g_k,b_k;1,-1)}{\partial g_m^{k}}\leq 0,\quad m=1,\dots,i,\quad k=1,\dots,K$

(iii) $\dfrac{\partial \bar{D}_o(x_k,g_k,b_k;1,-1)}{\partial b_j^{k}}\geq 0,\quad j=1,\dots,J,\quad k=1,\dots,K$

(iv) $\dfrac{\partial \bar{D}_o(x_k,g_k,b_k;1,-1)}{\partial x_n^{k}}\geq 0,\quad n=1,\dots,N,\quad k=1,\dots,K$

(v) $\sum_{m=1}^{M}\beta_m - \sum_{j=1}^{J}\gamma_j = -1,$

$$\sum_{m'=1}^{M}\beta_{mm'} - \sum_{j=1}^{J}\mu_{mj} = 0,\quad m=1,\dots,M$$

$$\sum_{j'=1}^{J}\gamma_{jj'} - \sum_{m=1}^{M}\mu_{mj} = 0,\quad j=1,\dots,J$$

$$\sum_{m=1}^{M}\delta_{nm} - \sum_{j=1}^{J}\eta_{nj} = 0,\quad n=1,\dots,N$$

(vi) $\beta_{mm'} = \beta_{m'm}, \quad m = 1,\ldots,M, \quad m' = 1,\ldots,M$

$\alpha_{nn'} = \alpha_{n'n}, \quad n = 1,\ldots,N, \quad n' = 1,\ldots,N$

$\gamma_{jj'} = \gamma_{j'j}, \quad j = 1,\ldots,N, \quad j' = 1,\ldots,N$

Constraints (i) ensure that each sample is at the leading edge or below the leading edge; constraints (ii) and (iii) ensure monotonicity of desirable and undesired outputs, respectively, while constraints (iv) also apply to inputs The monotonic constraint, constraint (v), satisfies the transformation property of the direction distance function, and the constraint (vi) is the symmetry constraint. Using (1.12) to solve the values of each parameter in the direction distance function, the environmental sensitivity productivity of different samples can be obtained, and the shadow price of the undesired output can be calculated.

1.2.3 Stochastic Frontier Analysis (SFA)

The stochastic frontier production function was first proposed by Aigner et al. (1977). In the study of environmental sensitivity productivity, it is also used as a parameter estimation method. Compared with the deterministic parameter estimation method, it will be caused by uncertain factors. The impact is taken into consideration, from the aspects of technical inefficiency or random error, to find out why the sample production is inefficient and deviating from the production boundary. More importantly, the SFA method can give the statistics of the variables to be estimated. Its conclusions are more robust in terms of other parameter estimation methods.

Murty and Kumar (2003) used SFA and output distance functions to evaluate production efficiency. The stochastic output distance function is defined as follows:

$$D_o = F(X,Y,\alpha,\beta) + \varepsilon \tag{1.13}$$

D_o is the distance function value, $F(.)$ represents the production technique, X and Y are the input and output vectors, α and β are the parameters to be estimated, and ε is the error term. Because the data of the dependent variable D_o cannot be directly obtained,[15] in order to solve this problem, Ferrier and Lovell (1990), Grosskopf and Hayes (1993), Coelli and Perelman (1996), and Kumar (1999) use the output distance function once. The subfeatures are transformed, and in the case of ignoring the perturbation term, equation (1.13) is transformed into:

$$D_0(X,\lambda Y) = \lambda D_0(X,Y), \quad \lambda > 0. \tag{1.14}$$

12   *Emission reduction analysis*

Generally, a scaling variable can be arbitrarily selected. For example, if the Mth output is selected, let $\lambda = \dfrac{1}{Y_M}$, then (1.14) becomes:

$$D_0(X,Y/Y_M) = D_0(x,Y)/Y_M \tag{1.15}$$

Take the logarithm of the above formula (1.15) and become

$$ln(D_0/Y_M) = f\left(X, \frac{Y}{Y_M}, \alpha, \beta\right), \tag{1.16}$$

f can be expressed as a logarithmic form of a function expression, further transformed into:

$$-ln(Y_M) = f\left(X, \frac{Y}{Y_M}, \alpha, \beta\right) - ln(D_0) \tag{1.17}$$

After adding the random error v and the production inefficiency error u (i.e., the $-ln(D_0)$ term), the stochastic boundary yield distance function is expressed as:

$$-ln(Y_M) = f\left(X, \frac{Y}{Y_M}, \alpha, \beta\right) + v + \mu \tag{1.18}$$

Estimating the (1.18) formula gives the parameter values to be estimated and their statistics.

In addition, the directional distance function can also be estimated using a random frontier function method. Färe et al. (2005) used Kumbhakar and Lovell (2000) to set the random frontier function. Using the directional distance function to calculate, the definition of production technology is:
$T = \left\{(x, y, b)\mathfrak{R}_+^{N+M+J}, \ (y,b)P(x), \ xL(y,b)\right\}$, and its function is as follows[16]:

$$0 = \bar{D}_0\left(x^k, y^k, b^k, 1, -1\right) + \varepsilon^k, \quad k = 1, 2 \ldots K \tag{1.19}$$

where $\varepsilon^k = v^k - u^k$, v^k is a random statistical error, $v^k \sim N\,(0, \sigma_v^2$ and u^k is due to technology. The error caused by inefficiency, $u^k \sim N\,(0, \sigma_u^2)$, v^k and u^k are independent and identical, and independent of each other, and then use g The conversion of the directional distance function at $g = (1, -1)$ is:

$$\bar{D}_o\left(x^k, y^k + \alpha^k, b^k - \alpha^k, 1, -1\right) + \alpha^k = \bar{D}_o\left(x^k, y^k, b^k, 1, -1\right) \qquad (1.20)$$

If we put the figure into (1.19):

$$-\alpha^k = \bar{D}_o\left(x^k \ y^k + \alpha^k, b^k - \alpha^k, 1, -1\right) + \varepsilon^k \qquad (1.21)$$

Generally, $\alpha^k = b^k$ is used, and then the equation (1.21) is estimated by OLS or maximum likelihood methods to calculate the environmental sensitivity productivity, and the method can also estimate the statistic of each coefficient.

1.2.4 Solution based on non-parametric data envelope analysis (DEA) method

The DEA method has a large number of applications in the production environment frontier function. In recent years, with the deepening of the distance function and directional distance function research, research on measuring the environmental sensitivity productivity by DEA method has emerged (Färe et al., 1989; Ball et al., 1994; Yaisawarng & Klein, 1994; Chung et al., 1997; Tyteca, 1997; Lee et al., 2002; Kumar, 2006; Hu Angang et al., 2008; Tu Zhengge, 2009).

Suppose there are input and output data for k samples (yk, bk, xk), $k = 1$, ..., K. When production activities are subject to environmental regulations, the environmental production equation for the kth sample is expressed as follows:

$$F\left(x^{k'}; b^{k'}\right) = max \sum_{k=1}^{K} z_k y_k \qquad (1.22)$$

s.t.

$$\sum_{k=1}^{K} z_k b_{kj} = b_{k'j}, j = 1, \ldots, J$$

$$\sum_{k=1}^{K} z_k x_{kn} \leq x_{k'n}, n = 1, \ldots, N$$

$$\sum_{k=1}^{K} z_k \geq 0, \quad k = 1, \ldots, K$$

where zk ($k = 1, \ldots, K$) is the intensity variable, the purpose is to give each observation sample point weight when establishing the production boundary.

14 *Emission reduction analysis*

If the zk is not accumulated and limited, the model is fixed-scale compensation, and vice versa remuneration for scale. On the basis of the establishment of the boundary, the objective equation maximizes the desired output, and the constraint on the undesired output reflects its weak disposition, that is, the reduction of undesired output will inevitably lead to the reduction of desirable output. The right side of the second constraint inequality represents the input in actual production, and the left side represents the most efficient production input in theory. The inequality indicates that the theoretical input must be less than or equal to the actual production input, and also indicates the free disposal of the input.

However, the shortcoming of the above method is that it does not take into account the reduction of undesired output, but only the pursuit of the maximization of desirable output. Chung (1997) considers the development of the directional distance function and uses the DEA method while considering research on productivity issues under the premise of an increase in desirable output and a decrease in undesired output.

If producer $[\![k'(x_{k'}^t, y_{k'}^t, b_{k'}^t)$ is defined, the directional environment production frontier function under the reference technique $P^t(x^t)$ can be expressed as:

$$\vec{D}_o\left(x_{k'}^t, y_{k'}^t, b_{k'}^t; y_{k'}^t, -b_{k'}^t\right) = \max \beta \tag{1.23}$$

s.t.

$$\sum_{k=1}^{K} z_k^t y_{k,m}^t \geq (1+\beta) y_{k',m}^t, m = 1, \ldots, M$$

$$\sum_{k=1}^{K} z_k^t b_{k,j}^t = (1-\beta) b_{k',j}^t, j = 1, \ldots, J$$

$$\sum_{k=1}^{K} z_k^t x_{k,n}^t \leq x_{k',n}^t, n = 1, \ldots N$$

$$z_k^t \geq 0, k = 1, \ldots, K$$

Compared with model (1.22), model (1.23) imposes constraints on the desired output, thereby increasing the desired output while minimizing the unintended output. It is possible to reflect the connotation of environmentally sensitive productivity by considering the expansion and reduction of output in two different dimensions.

Parametric estimation and non-parametric estimation have their own advantages. In general, the parametric method needs to preset the distance function as a certain function expression. The advantage is that the parameter

Literature review 15

expression can be differentiated and algebraic (Hailu & Veeman, 2000). By means of linear programming, stochastic frontier analysis, etc., the parameter values in the distance function can be estimated, and the environmental sensitivity productivity values of each decision unit and the shadow price of the undesired output are calculated. However, if linear programming is used to solve the parameters, the relevant statistics are often not available (Hailu & Veeman, 2000)[17]; if the random frontier rule is used, the parameter values and corresponding statistics can be calculated, and the inefficiency can be further decomposed into techniques. Inefficiency, allocation inefficiency and random error, but the method also requires a preset function form, and the distribution of error terms is assumed to be strong.

When non-parametric DEA is used to estimate the production front, as there is no need to make a priori assumptions on the production function structure, no parameters need to be estimated, no inefficient behavior is allowed, and total factor productivity (TFP changes) can be decomposed, so there is more attention and application (Färe et al., 1998). In addition, the non-parametric DEA approach avoids residual autocorrelation when using time series or panel data (Färe et al., 1989; Yaisawarng & Klein, 1994). However, the non-parametric DEA method is sensitive to the sample data. The error of the abnormal sample value will affect the position of the production frontier, and then affect the value of the environmental sensitivity productivity. Therefore, the accuracy of the sample data is high. In addition, the non-parametric DEA method can generally only be used for productivity measures and is rarely used to estimate shadow prices for undesired outputs (Färe et al., 1998).

1.3 Review of existing empirical studies

The development of theoretical research is inseparable from the continuous verification of empirical research. Table 1.1 lists some important empirical documents. Through combining and summarizing these documents, the following conclusions can be drawn.

1.3.1 In terms of research objects, foreign countries focus on micro-scale research, and domestic focus on macro-level analysis

The research objects of most foreign literatures are mainly based on the production activities of micro-enterprises. In the selection of micro-enterprises, it is important to consider industrial production-oriented enterprises that are heavily invested or dependent on certain polluting raw materials in the production process, such as thermal power stations, which use fossil energy to burn and emit a lot of pollution. Gases, such as SO_2, not only cause greater pollution to the atmosphere, but also affect human health. Therefore, in the existing literature, research on environmentally sensitive productivity studies using SO_2 emitted from power stations as undesired outputs is dominant

Table 1.1 Summary of evidence-based literature on studies about environmentally sensitive productivity

Authors	Evidence-based methods			Data	Variables			Main results	
	Model	Functions	Assessment		Input	Desirable Output	Undesirable Output	Productivity	Shadow price
Gallop and Roberts (1985)	Cost function	–	Minimum cost method	56 power plants in the US from 1973 to 1979	Labor/capital/ low-sulfur fuels/high-sulfur fuels	Electricity generated	SO_2	–	SO_2: 0.195 (US$/pounds, 1979 price)
Färe et al. (1993)	DF(O)	Translog	Parameter method	30 paper-making factories in the US in 1976	Paper pulp/ energy/ capital/ labor	Paper	BOD/TSS/PART/ SO_x	Efficiency: 0.9182	BOD: 1,043.4, TSS: 0, PART: 25,270, SO_x: 3,696 (US$/ton, 1976 price)
Coggins and Swinton (1996)	DF(O)	Translog	Parameter method	14 heating and power plants in Wisconsin in 1990–1992	Sulfide/energy/ labor/ capital	Electricity generated	SO_2	Efficiency: 0.946	SO_2: 305 (1990), 251.6 (1991), 322.9 (1992), Average 292.7 (US$/ton, 1992 price)
Boyd et al. (1996)	DDF	–	DEA	Coal-fueled power plants in the US Yaisawarng and Klein 1994 data	Fuel/labor/ capital (fixed input)/sulfur (undesirable output)	Net electricity	SO_2	Average efficiency: 0.933	SO_2: 1,703 (US$/ton, 1973 price)
Chung et al. (1997)	DDF	–	DEA	30 Swedish paper-making factories in 1986–1990	Labor/wood fiber/energy/ capital	Pulp	BOD/COD/TSS	M index:0.997 (improved efficiency:0.977; technological progress:1.02)	–

									ML index: 1.039 (improved efficiency: 0.955; technological progress:1.088)	
Kolstad and Turnovsky (1998)	–	Quadric form	–	51 coal-generated power plants in eastern America in 1970–1979	Sulfur/ash/ capital/ thermal energy	Electricity generated	SO_2		–	SO_2: 0.071; Ash: 0.121 (US$/pounds, price in 1976)
Swinton (1998)	DF(O)	Translog	Parameter method	Coal-fueled power plants in 1990–1998 Florida	Energy/labor/ capital/ sulfur	Electricity generated	SO_2		Efficiency: 0.978	SO_2: 157.10 (US$/ton, 1996 price)
Murty and Kumar (2003)	DF(O)	Translog	Parameter method SFA	Industries with water pollution issues in India (samples from 60 companies)	Capital/labor/ energy/ materials	Turnover	BOD/COD/TSS		Efficiency: 0.899	BOD: 0.246, COD: 0.0775 (million Rupee/ ton, 1994/95 price)
Hailu and Veeman (2000)	DF(I)	Translog	Parameter method	Aggregated data of Canadian paper-making sector for 36 years between 1959 and 1994	Energy/wood residue/ wood pulp/ other raw materials/ production labor/ managerial labor/ capital	Wood pulp/ newsprint/ paper board/ other types of paper	BOD/TSS		TE: 0.996, M Index: 0.878, ML Index: 1.044	BOD: 123, TSS: 286 (US$/million ton, 1986 price)

(*continued*)

Table 1.1 (Cont.)

Authors	Evidence-based methods			Data	Variables			Main results	
	Model	Functions	Assessment		Input	Desirable Output	Undesirable Output	Productivity	Shadow price
Reig-Martinez et al. (2001)	DF(O)	Translog	Parameter method	18 pottery factories in Spain	Raw materials/ capital/ labor	Ceramic pavement	Cement/waste oil	Average efficiency: 0.927	Cement: 336.6 (euro/ton), waste oil: 125.5 (euro/kg)
Lee et al. (2002)	DDF	—	DEA	43 Korean power plants of 1990–1995	Installed capacity/ fuels/labor	Power generation	$SO_x/NO_x/TSP$	—	SO_x: 3,107, NO_x: 17,393, TSP: 51,093 (US$/ton)
Salnykov and Zelenyuk (2005)	DDF	Translog	Parameter method	50 countries	Labor/arable land/energy/ capital/	GNP	$CO_2/SO_2/NO_x$	Efficiency: 0.8433	CO_2: 331.89, SO_2: 59,997.95 NO_x: 154,583.63 (US$/ton)
Atkinson and Dorfman (2005)	DF(I)	Translog	Parameter method	43 US private for-profit power plants in 1980, 1985, 1990, 1995	Energy/labor/ capital	Power generation	SO_2	Classical efficiency: 0.564277 LIBS efficiency: 0.553187	1980 SO_2: 395.3; 1985 SO_2: 1,871.7; 1990 SO_2: 556.8; 1995 SO_2: 486.7 (US$/ton)
Lee (2005)	DF(I)	Translog	Parameter method	51 US thermal power generating units in 1977–1986	Capital/heat/ sulfide/ash	Power generation	Sulfur/ash	TE: 0.945	SO_2: 167.4, Ash: 127.7 (US$/pounds, 1976 price)
Färe et al. (2005)	DDF	Quadric form	Deterministic parameters	209 US thermal power plants in 1993/1997	Labor/ installed capacity/ fuel	Power generation	SO_2	1993: 0.814, 1997: 0.785	1993 SO_2: 1,117; 1997 SO_2: 1,974 (US$/ton)

			SFA					1993: 0.798, 1997:0.804	1993 SO_2: 76, 1997 SO_2: 142 (US$/ ton,1982–1984 price)
Kumar (2006)	DDF	–	DEA	41 countries in 1971–1992	Labor /capital/ energy	GDP	CO_2	M index: 0.9998 (Improved efficiency: 1.0019; technological progress:0.9981) ML index: 1.0002 (Improved efficiency: 0.9997; Technological progress: 1.0006)	–
Färe et al. (2007)	DDF	–	DEA	92 thermal power plants in the US in 1995	Capital/labor/ fuel heat (coal, oil and gas)	Power generation	SO_2 NO_x	–	–
Ke et al. (2008)	DF(O)	Translog	Parameters method	30 provinces in China from 1996 to 2002	Capital/labor	GDP	SO_2	East: 0.831, Middle: 0.706, West: 0.682	East: 0.516, Middle: 0.508, West: 0.529 (hundred million yuan/ ton, 1996 price)
Van Ha et al. (2008)	DF(O)	Translog	Parameter/ measurement assessment	63 papermaking workshops in Vietnam in 2003	Capital/labor/ energy/ waste paper/other materials/ social capital	Paper	BOD/COD/TSS	Efficiency: 0.72	BOD: 575.2, COD: 1,429.7, TSS: 3,354.8 (US$/ton, 2003 price)

(continued)

Table 1.1 (Cont.)

Authors	Evidence-based methods			Data	Variables			Main results	
	Model	Functions	Assessment		Input	Desirable Output	Undesirable Output	Productivity	Shadow price
Ghorbani and Motallebi (2009)	DF(O)	Translog	Parameters method	85 dairy farms in Iran in 2006	Farm area/ energy/ labor/feed	milk	$CH_4/CO_2/N_2O$	–	CH_4: 0.61, CO_2: 0.058, N_2O: 0.59 (price ratio against milk)
Hu et al. (2008)	DDF		DEA	30 provinces in China from 1999 to 2005	Capital/labor	GDP	CO_2/COD/SO_2/ waste water/ solid waste	Highest in the east and lowest in the west (specific value depends on the type of undesirable output)	
Tu (2008)	DDF		DEA	Industrial enterprises above a designated size in 30 provinces from 1998 to 2005	Capital/ energy/ labor	Industrial added value	SO_2	East: relatively harmonious relationship between industry and environment Middle and west: imbalances between environmental protection and industrial growth	
Wang et al. (2008)	DDF	–	DEA	1980–2004 APEC 17 countries and regions	Capital/labor	GDP	CO_2	ML: 1.0056 (Technological progress:0.76%)	–

Author										
Tu (2009)	DDF	–	DEA	Industrial enterprises above a designated size in 30 provinces from 1998 to 2005	Capital/ energy/ labor	Industrial added value	SO2	–	–	SO: 2.09 (RMB, hundred million yuan/ ten thousand tons, 1998 price unchanged)
Wu (2009)	DDF	–	DEA	1998–2007 China's 31 provinces industrial sector	Capital/labor	Industrial added value	COD/ SO_2		National average ML: 1.085 (contribution of technological progress 95.29%)	–
Yue & Liu (2009)	Inversed output Reciprocal method DDF	–	DEA	36 industrial sectors in China between 2001 and 2006	Capital/labor	Industrial added value	SO_2		Efficiency value: inverse algorithm: 0.55; reciprocal approach: 0.49; directional distance function: 0.68	–
Yang & Shao (2009)	DDF	–	DEA	30 provincial industrial sectors from 1998 to 2007	Capital/labor	Industrial added value	SO_2		East: 0.886, Middle: 0.703, West: 0.686	–
Zhou & Gu (2009)	DDF	–	DEA	Industry data of large and medium-sized industrial enterprises in Shanghai from 1997 to 2004	Capital/labor/ energy	Total industry	SO_2		2006 technological efficiency index: 0.6437 (heavy industry); 0.7396 (light industry)	–

(continued)

Table 1.1 (Cont.)

Authors	Evidence-based methods			Data	Variables			Main results	
	Model	Functions	Assessment		Input	Desirable Output	Undesirable Output	Productivity	Shadow price
Chen et al. (2010)	DDF	–	DEA	Industrial enterprises above a designated size in 11 provinces in the east of China from 2000 to 2007	Capital/labor	Output value	SO$_2$	ML: 0.902 (2007)	–
Wang et al. (2010)	DDF	–	DEA	30 provinces in China from 1998 to 2007	Capital/labor/ energy	Industrial added value	COD/ SO$_2$	National average:0.712 (VRS); 0.657 (CRS)	–
Dong et al. (2010)	–	–	DEA	29 provinces, 1995–2006	Capital/labor/ sown area/ energy	Actual regional GDP	Reciprocal of environmental pollution index	ML: 1.008	–
Wu et al. (2010)	DDF	–	DEA	East/Central/ Western region, 2000–2007	Capital/labor/ human capital	GDP	COD/ SO2	–	–

Note: price shown is the price of the year unless there is special explanation.

DF(O): Output distance function; DF(I): input distance function; DDF: directional distance function; DEA: Data Envelope Analysis method; SFA: stochastic frontier approach; M index: Malmquist productivity index; ML index: Malmquist–Luenberger productivity index; VRS: variable scale; CRS: invariant scale; BOD: biochemical oxygen demand; COD: chemical oxygen demand; TSS: total suspended solids; PART: particles; SO$_x$ sulfur oxides:

Literature review 23

(Gallop & Roberts, 1985; Coggins & Swinton, 1996; Lee et al., 2002; Färe et al., 2005, 2007); in addition, some industrial producers whose emissions are easily metered, such as BOD/COD emissions from paper mills, water pollutants (Färe et al., 1993; Chung et al., 1997; Hailu & Veeman, 2000; Van Ha et al., 2008), waste oils discharged from ceramic plants (Reig-Martinez et al., 2001) are also used in the environment.

As countries continue to pay attention to greenhouse gas (GHG) emissions issues, some scholars have begun to shift their perspectives to macro-level research. They usually measure and compare the environmental sensitivity productivity of major GHG emissions such as CO_2 and NO_x, which are equivalent in economic development level (such as OECD, transition economies) or geographically similar countries (such as APEC, EU) (Salnykov & Zelenyuk, 2005; Kumar, 2006; Wang Bing et al., 2008).

Limited by the lack of data at the domestic enterprise level, especially the pollutant data is difficult to obtain. Most of the research on China is based on the macro-level, mainly to measure the environmental sensitivity productivity and the marginal abatement cost of pollutants in different provinces or industries. For example, Ke et al. (2008) used the output distance function and the super-logarithmic function form to measure the environmental sensitivity productivity of 30 provinces in mainland China from 1996 to 2002, and estimated the shadow of SO_2 pollutants. Hu Angang et al. (2008) used the directional distance function earlier, using CO_2, COD, SO_2, total wastewater discharge and total solid waste discharge as indicators of undesired output, measuring 30 provinces in mainland China environmentally sensitive productivity during 1999–2005. At the industry level, there are mainly Tu Zhengge (2008, 2009), Wu Jun (2009), Yue Shujing and Liu Fuhua (2009), Yang Jun and Shao Hanhua (2009), Zhou Jian and Gu Liuliu (2009), Chen Ru et al. (2010). Based on the SO_2 data of China's provincial industrial sector, the scholars used the directional distance function to measure the environmental sensitivity productivity of the industrial sectors in various provinces; at the regional level, Wang Bing et al. (2010), Dong Feng et al. (2010), Wu Jun (2010) adopts provincial input–output data. In addition to capital and labor, the input includes energy consumption, human capital and other factors. The output end includes two Eleventh Five-Year Plan of COD and SO_2. The pollutants required to be forced to reduce emissions use the directional distance function to calculate the environmentally sensitive productivity at the provincial level. In addition, in the study of Tu Zhenge (2008), Wang Bing et al. (2010) scholars, the factors affecting environmentally sensitive productivity were further analyzed and the environmental Kuznets curve and pollution paradise hypothesis have been empirically tested. These studies have important implications for understanding the differences in environmentally sensitive productivity between industries and regions, but they are limited by data factors, and their microscopic mechanisms are often not revealed.

24 *Emission reduction analysis*

1.3.2 *In the theoretical hypothesis, the original part of the hypothesis needs to be relaxed, but the difficulty of the model is increased*

This is mainly reflected in two aspects. The first is the assumption of the shadow price symbol. In the existing theoretical model, in order to ensure that the solution of the model has economic significance, the shadow price of the unsatisfactory output is generally set to be non-positive, especially in the process of solving the parameterized function. The monotonicity of the undesired output to the distance function equation is specified. There are also some literatures that use the DEA method to solve the problem. After the shadow price is obtained, the shadow prices of different positive and negative symbols are interpreted or rejected. However, as discussed by Van Ha et al. (2008), some pollutants, such as suspended particles (mostly wood residue) in wastewater in the paper industry process, although appearing to be "unwanted" pollutants, It can be recycled as raw materials through different processes, thus turning "sub-output" into "positive output," and its shadow price becomes positive. Therefore, it is necessary to relax the existing shadow price of undesired output.

Second is the assumption of "complete efficiency" and "no redundancy." As pointed out by Lee et al. (2002), previous literature have assumed that the production front is completely efficient, but under the premise of certain technology, the unit inputs, outputs, or unit-desired outputs of each decision-making unit are not desirable. Outputs are all different. If imperfect efficiency is considered, the results of environmentally sensitive productivity will necessarily differ. Therefore, the shadow price of pollutants calculated based on the assumption of full efficiency will be different from the result of incomplete efficiency when other conditions are the same. As pointed out by Boyd et al. (1996), there is a gap between the theoretically estimated shadow price of pollutants and the actual observed price of pollutant emission trading in the trading market, possibly due to the imperfect efficiency.[18] In addition, Fukuyama and Weber (2009) further pointed out that most of the existing directional distance function studies do not take into account the possible redundancy (slacks), and redundancy will also lead to imperfect efficiency, resulting in biased environmental sensitive productivity.

1.3.3 *In the algorithm implementation, the function form setting is quite different, and the calculation process is still complicated*

First of all, the function form and estimation method are quite different, and each has its own advantages and disadvantages. Although there are two kinds of distance function and directional distance function in the theoretical model, the setting and solving methods of the function form are very different. As has been summarized above, the parametric method solution includes two main forms: deterministic function analysis and SFA. The deterministic function can be set to super-logarithm, quadratic or hyperbolic; DEA

Literature review 25

requires the use of a set of linear programming equations (inequalities) to find the optimal solution.

The commonly used method in the empirical estimation of the distance function is the method of deterministic linear programming, which needs to set the function form, and only a small number of methods using measurement estimation (Hetemäki, 1996).[19] The advantage of linear programming is that it is relatively simple to use without any distribution assumptions, even in the case of small samples, a large number of parameters can be calculated; the disadvantage is that the parameters are calculated rather than estimated (Kumbhakar & Lovell, 2000), so provide statistical criteria for consistency of conclusions, which may lead to bias in evaluations, as outputs may be affected by random disturbances. Some documents adopt a two-step analysis method to solve this problem; that is, first use the linear programming method to calculate the distance function, and then use the distance function value as the explanatory variable, and use the parameter random distance function to estimate the parameters.[20] Although the non-parametric method has the advantage of not having to set the function form, when calculating the shadow price of the contaminant, the shadow price cannot be obtained by differential calculation, and the statistic cannot be provided. In addition, the production frontier boundary is easily interfered by the error points, causing the result to deviate significantly from the actual situation.

In addition, when the directional distance function is applied, the selection of the directional vector is relatively simple. In the general theoretical research, a relatively neutral attitude is adopted, which is determined as (1, −1); that is, the ratio of expansion and contraction of desirable output and undesired output is 1. However, not all governments have a neutral preference. According to different research needs and policy preferences, the specific choice of directional vector should not be fixed as (1, −1), but so far no scholars have conducted research on the selection of non-neutral vectors, so the theoretical results that are more focused on the expansion of desirable output or more biased towards the unsatisfactory output remain to be explored.

Calculation process is more complicated and generally requires programming. Because the number of selected research objects is often large, more than 100 decision-making units, plus the model itself has several constraints on each unit, the calculation process is more complicated. At the same time, because the directional distance function is still a relatively new research field, there is no relevant solving software and program at present, which generally requires the researcher to implement it by himself,[21] which also hinders the popularization of related research to some extent.

1.3.4 *In the conclusion of the study, there is a certain gap with the reality, and it is still necessary to strengthen its policy significance*

Because the models, data, and calculation methods used by many research institutes are different, the differences in their research conclusions are also

26 *Emission reduction analysis*

large, and there is a certain gap between theoretical expectations and actual observations. For example, in the study of SO_2 emissions from power plants, the average environmental sensitivity productivity is about 0.9, and the variance is small, indicating that although these power plants may have different production equipment and technical levels, they are "close to the best frontier of production." This is in contrast to the intuition in practice; in addition, the SO_2 shadow price estimated from environmental sensitivity productivity ranges from $167/ton to $1,703/ton, while the market price of US SO_2 license transactions is $64–200/ton (Ellerman et al., 2000). The large differences between these research findings and reality indicate that the existing model settings may require further revision and improvement, as the full efficiency assumptions mentioned above may need to be further relaxed.

The practical application and policy significance of the conclusions of environmental sensitivity productivity research can be summarized into three aspects. First, quantitative evaluation of environmental performance and environmental productivity of economic units producing "unintended outputs" to verify whether "environmental regulation" it affects the productivity of enterprises and the competitiveness of enterprises. Second, with the analysis of environmental sensitivity productivity, the marginal abatement cost of pollution of different enterprises and departments can be measured, so as to set the initial price and environment of the pollutant trading market. Taxes and fees are provided as a basis; in addition, the findings of environmentally sensitive productivity can be further extended to the estimation of environmental control costs, thus providing a reference for the formulation of pollutant control policies. The investigation of environmental performance in different industries and different regions can guide low-efficiency units to promote high-efficiency production. The measurement of environmental control costs will guide policy-makers to make appropriate environmental control policies under the predetermined policy objectives. The determination of the shadow price can help the regulator to set the penalty for the discharge of different pollutants, and the manufacturer can also use this information to determine whether it is cost-effective to purchase the emission right, so as to carry out the most efficient production activities. Of course, all of this is based on the results of theoretical research with reference and reproducibility.

1.4 Conclusion

Through the introduction and evaluation of the above-mentioned environmental sensitivity productivity research, it can be seen that with attention to environmental issues, more and more scholars are investigating other factors such as pollutants when examining the productivity of enterprises (regions and countries). Based on the original productivity theory, theoretical models such as distance function and directional distance function are developed, and the parametric and non-parametric methods are used to solve and simulate the possible effects of desirability on real productivity. Although great progress has been made in theory, there is still a certain gap between the reality and policy guidance. In the future, more in-depth and detailed research is needed.

First of all, it is necessary to further improve and relax the existing assumptions in theory, especially considering how to determine the optimal production frontier under the conditions of incomplete efficiency and redundancy, and to develop appropriate criteria to select the appropriate directionality vector, which determines the path that each decision unit approaches toward the production front.

Secondly, the model itself and its implementation need to be further simplified. The current research on environmental sensitivity productivity requires the integration of economics, management operations research, mathematics and other related knowledge, and also needs to be realized by computer programming, which hinders the degree of integration to some extent. If you develop the corresponding software package, or the general program code, I believe it will attract more researchers.

In addition, in the empirical application, more open microdata support is needed. On the one hand, microdata are helpful to reveal the real behavior preference and technology of the enterprise, which can better reveal its mechanism of action. At the same time, it is easy to open the data and repeat the experiment. The mutual testing of different models makes the theoretical results closer to real problems and more effectively applied to policy formulation and production practices.

Notes

1 This chapter is based on the revision of Research Summary of Environment Sensitive Productivity, World Economy, 2011, vol. 5, co-published by Wei Chu, Huang Ruowen, and Shen Manhong.
2 It is referred to as "Bad Output" in the published journal by Färe et al. Here, it is translated into "Undesirable Output" from the study by Hu et al. (2008).
3 This is also where another argument that "environmental regulations will reduce the productivity (competitiveness) of firms" emerges.
4 The direct approach is mostly adopted at the beginning to address this issue, or shifting undesirable output through monotone decreasing function so that the resulting data can be included in the normal production formula when technical production conditions remain unchanged. Detailed methods include changing undesirable output into input elements (Liu & Sharp, 1999), or apply additive inversion to undesirable output (Berg et al., 1992; Ali & Seliford, 1990) or multiplication inversion (Golany & Roll, 1989; Lovell et al., 1995). Refer to Scheel (2001) for detailed illustration.
5 Environmentally sensitive productivity, environmental productivity, environmental performance, environmental efficiency are mostly adopted expressions for productivity measurement scale of "undesirable output." Here, we use the term employed by Hailu and Veeman (2000) and Kumar (2006) as environmentally sensitive productivity.

28 *Emission reduction analysis*

6   The weight of input or output is generally confirmed by the proportion of input in cost or output in profits.

7   Pittman (1983) extended the multiproductivity index proposed by Caves, Christensen and Diewert (1982). By taking 30 paper-making factories in Wisconsin and Michigan as the research target, he used his measurement assessment of marginal cost and assessment of pollution control cost in 1977 by the EPA as well as the census data retrieved from the reduction in pollution control cost by companies between 1976 and 1977 by US Census, respectively, to add the pollution reduction cost as the shadow price of undesirable output, constructing a multiproductivity index of undesirable output and comparing it with traditional productivity index.

8   Repetto et al. (1996) used market assessment of adjusted marginal pollution damage cost to calculate adjusted productivity index and calculated the productivity of three industries in the US, including the paper-making industry.

9   A typical example is air pollution. Apart from the influence of pollution on nearby residents, it also affects the health of residents in other areas. Likewise, some of the health impact cannot be revealed immediately, thus making it difficult to evaluate the damage cost of a certain region or in a specific year exactly.

10 Weak disposability: if $u \in P(x)$, $\theta \in [0,1]$, then $\theta u \in P(x)$; free/strong disposability: if $v \leq u \in P(x)$, then $v \in P(x)$. When it is weakly disposed, reducing undesirable output will only proportionately reduce desirable output, or reducing undesirable output means that it is imperative to abandon valuable desirable output. This is also means the negative shadow price of undesirable output. When it is strongly disposed, undesirable output can be freely dealt with to maintain desirable output unchanged.

11 It is not assumed here that r is non-negative, but partial prices are allowed to be non-positive.

12 It is not assumed here that r is non-negative, but partial prices are allowed to be non-positive.

13 The advantage of the output distance function: first, it can fully express the technique, it is a scalar value (combined with the multi-output feature compared to the scalar production function); second, it satisfies the output weak deal; finally, the output of the distance function and the income function are dual relationships, from which the shadow price can be found. Because the output distance function is less than or equal to 1, its natural logarithm is less than or equal to 0, so the value is "maximum."

14 This setting is in line with the regulative intentions, or proportionately increase desirable output and reduce undesirable output.

15 If D_o is set to the boundary efficiency point 1, the left side of the equation is non-variable, the intercept cannot be calculated, and the parameter estimation is biased. It is useless to take the logarithm to the left of the equation to make it zero.

16 When considering the productivity of undesired output factors, because the directional distance function is a vector, when the manufacturer reaches the production boundary, the technical inefficiency value is 0, so the dependent variable on the left side is set to zero.

17 Bootstrapping is employed by Grosskopf, Hayes and Hirschberg (1995) to overcome this deficiency.

18 Based on Lee et al. (2002)'s measurement, shadow price of the pollutant assessed with imperfect efficiency may lower than that with the perfect efficiency by 10%.

19 Vardanyan and Noh (2006) argued about the possible dependence of environment-resulted shadow price on the choice of the form of distance function and parameterization which is found better than any other methods.
20 General random parameter distance functions can refer to Aigner et al. (1977) and Meenusen and Broeck (1977).
21 Popular programming software includes Mathmatics, GAMS, LINDO/LINGO, MatLab, etc. In addition, Excel can be used for general linear planning problems. However, due to the limit to its solver, professional software like Solver should be used.

2 Interprovincial CO$_2$ shadow price research based on the parametric model[1]

The global warming caused by greenhouse gas (GHG) emissions has become an international consensus. Without mandatory carbon emissions interventions, climate change will worsen the Earth's ecological environment and affect human survival and development. As the largest country in terms of total carbon emissions, China is under heavy international pressure. Western developed countries, led by Europe and the USA, have put forward the requirement of "incorporating China into the world carbon emission reduction indicator system." If this requirement is implemented, the impact on China's future economic development will be extremely large. Therefore, in the special period of China's vigorous construction of an environment-friendly society, it is necessary to actively incorporate carbon emissions into the development indicators of the economic environment. Before the international community's emission reduction targets have been imposed on China, it is urgent to propose carbon in line with China's national policy recommendations for emissions reductions.

After implementing carbon emission control, enterprises will gradually assume GHG control and abatement costs, and may even reduce industrial output, which will lead to a reduction in economic profits and an impact on the economic growth of the entire society. If the carbon tax imposes a decline in carbon emissions and energy consumption, it will also cause different degrees of decline in economic growth rate, employment rate, consumption and investment levels (He Juhuang et al., 2002; Wei Taoyuan & Romslod, 2002; Gao Pengfei & Chen Wenying, 2002; Cao Jing, 2009; Su Ming et al., 2009; Zhang Mingxi, 2010), which caused suppression of economic growth, and the higher the carbon tax level, the higher the GDP loss. Therefore, measuring the economic cost of reducing the marginal output caused by carbon emissions is a very important practical issue. This has important reference value for determining the carbon tax rate level and will provide a reliable theoretical basis for policy-makers.

The economic cost of carbon emission reduction is often described by "shadow price." However, because the carbon dioxide emitted in the production process does not have the nature of market transactions, it is difficult to obtain its price information directly from the market. Therefore, this chapter adopts an international comparison. The general environmental directional distance function method is used to estimate the potential price of carbon dioxide, thereby obtaining the economic cost of unit carbon emission reduction. Due to the imbalance of economic development level in various regions of China, the environmental cost for economic growth is not the same. Therefore, the estimation of CO_2 shadow price for each province (city, district) in China will help to fully understand China's actual situation.

The structure of this chapter is as follows. The first part will explain the concept of shadow price and literature review; the second section gives the research method of this chapter – the environmental directional distance function; the third and fourth parts are the data variable description and the empirical result analysis; the final part is the conclusions of this chapter.

2.1 Shadow price concept and literature review

Under the pure market economy conditions, enterprises discharge waste in the production process, and there is an inconsistency between the private cost and social cost of the enterprise, thus generating negative externalities. Once the government regulates and restricts the discharge behavior of enterprises, the enterprise will assume the "external cost" of pollution control, which will reduce its output value and profits. If there is no environmental control, enterprises will not have to consider the external cost of pollution control, and will produce more products, increasing production value. The difference in output between the two can be called the cost of pollutants.

Therefore, the pollutant emissions and economic output of the production activities of the enterprise are taken as two kinds of outputs: the former is the undesired output, and the latter is the desirable output, also called the "bad" output and the "good" output, respectively. Then the shadow price of the pollutant is the output increased by abandoning one unit of pollution, or the output reduced by one unit of pollution (taking into account the cost of treatment caused by the production of unit pollutants). In other words, the shadow price of pollutants is the marginal cost of reducing unit pollution. By using the shadow price of pollutants, the marginal effect of pollutant emissions changes on economic output can be measured, thus providing a basis for formulating appropriate environmental control policies and guiding enterprises to carry out low-pollution production activities.

Because there is no real market price for contaminants, measuring the shadow price requires special methods. There are two main methods commonly used in the existing literature to solve the shadow price of pollutants. One is based on the parametric model: it can estimate the specific parameter form of the environmental production function including the pollution factor and then the environmental output. The function seeks partial derivatives to obtain the marginal effect of pollution (Färe et al., 1993, 2006); or uses the duality between the output distance function and the income function to derive the shadow of pollutant emissions in the form of parameter price

32   *Emission reduction analysis*

(Coggins & Swinton, 1996). The other is to use a non-parametric method, which relies less on the assumption of the function form, but calculates the environmental production frontier function through mathematical linear programming techniques (such as DEA), and further based on the intertemporal environment production frontier function. To measure the marginal effect of pollution emissions on cutting-edge output (Boyd et al., 1996; Lee et al., 2002; Tu Zhengge, 2009, etc.). Chen Shiyi (2010) uses both parametric and non-parametric methods to measure the shadow price of carbon dioxide. The two methods of measurement yield similar results.

The development of the model of the parametric approach has gone through two phases. Beginning in the 1990s, the academic community began to use distance functions to contain environmental output and derive shadow prices for undesired outputs (Färe et al., 1993; Ball et al., 1994; Yaisawarng & Klein, 1994; Coggin & Swinton, 1996; Hetemäki, 1996; Hailu & Veeman, 2000). Based on the parameterized output distance function model, Färe et al. (1993) used Pittman's (1983) data to evaluate the efficiency of 30 paper mills in Wisconsin and Michigan in 1976, and to produce biochemical oxygen demand in production. The shadow prices of undesired outputs such as (BOD) and total suspended particulate matter (TSS) were measured. Coggins and Swinton (1996) also used the output distance function to calculate the technical efficiency and SO_2 shadow price of 14 thermal power plants in Wisconsin. Hailu and Veeman (2000) used a parametric input distance function including desirable and undesired outputs to build productivity including environmentally sensitive factors, and built a Malmquist index based on the input angle, in addition to building a shadow price model and empirical studies using time-series data from the 1959–1994 paper industry in Canada. Shadow price estimates indicate that the marginal cost of vendor pollution control continues to rise over time.

The directional distance function developed since then has deepened the research in this field. Chung et al. (1997) specified the determination of the optimal boundary when the directional distance function reduces the undesired output while increasing the desired output and built the Malmquist–Luenberger index to provide new ideas for productivity research under environmental control. Many scholars have followed this new approach. Lee et al. (2002) used the panel data, directional distance function, and DEA method of 43 power plants in Korea in 1990–1995 to deal with various pollution caused by power generation: sulfide (SO_x), nitrogen oxides (NO_x). The shadow price of total suspended particulate matter (TSP) is measured. Färe et al. (2005) used the directional distance function to calculate the SO_2 shadow price of 207 thermal power plants in the USA in 1993 and 1997 using the deterministic parameter method and the stochastic frontier method, respectively.

The parameter estimation method has many advantages in model estimation and interpretation, especially the environmental production function in the form of directional distance function. By solving the unknown parameters in the preset function, the environmental production function can be obtained intuitively and the function can be utilized. The mathematical method calculates the shadow price information and is widely used in the calculation of shadow prices and the determination of environmental productivity. Therefore, the use of directional distance function is of great significance for building environmental production frontier functions.

2.2 Derivation of directional distance function and shadow price

The theoretical model of the directional distance function was proposed by Chung et al. (1997), who elaborated on how to use the directional distance function to study productivity when studying Swedish pulp mills. The difference between the directional distance function and the ordinary distance function is that the assumptions for the joint production of good and bad outputs are different. The ordinary distance function only considers the expansion of output, while the directional environmental distance function considers the increase in output while reducing the bad output. By deriving the partial production of the environmental production function based on the directional distance function, the shadow price of the pollutant (i.e., bad output) can be solved.

Assume the input vector of each production department, good and bad output vector, under certain production technology conditions: $P(x) = \{(y, b):$ x can produce $(y, b)\}$, has the following two characteristics:

(i) Weak disposition of bad output: when $(y, b) \in P(x)$, $0 \leq \epsilon \leq 1$, $(\epsilon y, \epsilon b)$ $\in P(x)$;
Free disposition of good output: when $(y, b) \in P(x)$, $y' \leq y$, $(y', b) \in P(x)$;
(ii) Co-production (good-output null-joint): when $(y, b) \in P(x)$, if $b = 0$, then $y = 0$.

The directional distance function needs to construct a direction vector of $g = (gy, gb)$, and this vector will be used to constrain the direction and variation of the M good output and the J bad output, that is, increase the constraint-specified path good output and reduce the bad output. Thus, the directional output distance function can be defined as:

$$\overrightarrow{D_O}(x, y, b; g_y, g_b) = sup\left\{\beta: (y + \beta g_y, b - \beta g_b) \in P(x)\right\} \tag{2.1}$$

where β indicates the degree to which a given good product (bad product) can be enlarged (reduced) compared to the most efficient unit on the leading edge production surface. If β is equal to 0, it means that this decision unit is on the leading edge production side, which is the most efficient. The larger the β value, the greater the potential for the decision-making unit to continue to

34 Emission reduction analysis

increase in output, and the greater the room for further reduction of the bad output, indicating that the efficiency is lower.

Regarding the method of solving the directional distance function, a parameter or non-parametric method can be employed. Here we use the parameterized hyperlog function (translog) method proposed by Chung (1996) to select the direction vector $g = (1, -1)$. This is in line with the intention of complying with neutral policy control, that is, scaling up the desired output and reducing the number of undesired outputs. Assuming $k = 1, ..., K$ represents a different observation sample, so the parameter form of the directional distance function is:

$$
\begin{aligned}
\ln[1+\bar{D}_0(x,y,b;1,1)] = {} & \alpha_0 + \sum_{n=1}^{N} \alpha_n x_n + \sum_{m=1}^{M} \beta_m y_m + \sum_{j=1}^{J} \gamma_j b_j + \frac{1}{2}\sum_{n=1}^{N}\sum_{n'=1}^{N} \alpha_{nn'}(x_n)(x_{n'}) \\
& + \frac{1}{2}\sum_{m=1}^{M}\sum_{m'=1}^{M} \beta_{nn'}(y_m)(y_{m'}) + \frac{1}{2}\sum_{j=1}^{J}\sum_{j'=1}^{J} \gamma_{mm'}(b_j)(b_{j'}) \\
& + \frac{1}{2}\sum_{n=1}^{N}\sum_{m=1}^{M} \delta_{nm}(x_n)(y_m) + \frac{1}{2}\sum_{n=1}^{N}\sum_{j=1}^{J} \eta_{nj}(x_n)(b_j) \\
& + \frac{1}{2}\sum_{m=1}^{M}\sum_{j=1}^{J} \mu_{nm}(y_n)(b_m)
\end{aligned}
\tag{2.2}
$$

The parametric equation solving is based on the idea of linear programming, which minimizes the distance between each observation and the boundary:

$$
\min \sum_{k=1}^{K} \left\{ \ln[1+\bar{D}_0(x,y,b;1,1)] - \ln(1+0) \right\}
\tag{2.3}
$$

s.t.

(i) $\ln[1+\vec{D}_0(x,y,b,1,-1)] \geq 0, k = 1,..., K$

(ii) $\dfrac{\delta\{\ln[1+\bar{D}_0(x_k,y_k,b_k;1,1)]\}}{\delta \ln g_m^k} \leq, \quad m = 1,...,i, \quad k = 1,...,K$

(iii) $\dfrac{\delta\{\ln[1+\bar{D}_0(x_k,y_k,b_k;1,1)]\}}{\delta \ln b_j^k} \geq 0, \quad j = 1,...,J, \quad k = 1,...,K$

(iv) $\dfrac{\delta\{\ln[1+\bar{D}_0(x_k,y_k,b_k;1,1)]\}}{\delta \ln x_n^k} \geq 0, \quad n = 1,...,N, \quad k = 1,...,K$

(v) $\sum_{m=1}^{M} \beta_m - \sum_{j=1}^{J} \gamma_j = -1,$

$$\sum_{m'=1}^{M} \beta_{mm'} - \sum_{j=1}^{J} \mu_{mj} = 0, \quad m = 1,\ldots,M$$

$$\sum_{j'=1}^{J} \gamma_{jj'} - \sum_{m=1}^{M} \mu_{mj} = 0, \quad j = 1,\ldots,J$$

$$\sum_{m=1}^{M} \delta_{nm} - \sum_{j=1}^{J} \eta_{nj} = 0, \quad n = 1,\ldots,N$$

(vi) $\beta_{mm'} = \beta_{m'm}, \quad m = 1,\ldots,M, \quad m' = 1,\ldots,M$

$\alpha_{nn'} = \alpha_{n'n}, \quad n = 1,\ldots,N, \quad n' = 1,\ldots,N$

$\gamma_{jj'} = \gamma_{j'j}, \quad j = 1,\ldots,N, \quad j' = 1,\ldots,N$

The objective function is to minimize the deviation of all sample points to the boundary line. Constraints (i) ensure that each sample is on the leading edge or under the leading edge; constraints (ii) and (iii) ensure the diminishing and incremental monotony of the desired output and the undesired output, respectively, while constraint (iv) the input also has an increasing monotonic constraint; constraint (v) satisfies the transformation property of the direction distance function, and constraint (vi) is the symmetry constraint.

After estimating the parameters by the above linear programming, the first-order partial derivative of the directional distance function can be obtained, and the shadow price of the undesired output relative to the desired output can be obtained:

$$r_b = r_y \frac{\partial \bar{D}_o(x,y,b;1,1)/\partial b}{\partial \bar{D}_o(x,y,b;1,1)/\partial y} \tag{2.4}$$

Among them, the observed price of the desired output r_y is used as the standardized price, because the desired output has an observable and market-oriented price, and r_b is the absolute shadow price of the undesired output.

2.3 Variable description and estimation results

This section uses the time series data from 1995 to 2007 to estimate the carbon dioxide shadow price in China by province (city, district) through the "two inputs, two outputs" environmental production function. Among them, the two inputs are capital and labor, the good output is GDP, and the bad output is CO_2 emissions. Among the 31 provinces (cities, districts) in China, due to the lack of data in Tibet, it was not included, while Chongqing was added

36 *Emission reduction analysis*

to Sichuan Province for estimation. Therefore, 29 provinces (cities, districts) were the research objects.

Capital stock: generally use the "permanent inventory method" to estimate the actual capital stock of each year. Here, we mainly refer to the existing research results of Zhang Jun et al. (2004) and extend the capital stock sequence to 2007 according to the published method. Calculated at constant price in 2005, the unit is 100 million yuan.

Labor: foreign countries generally use working hours as a labor input variable, but limited by the availability of data. Here, the number of employed people in the current year published in the *China Statistical Yearbook* is 10,000.

GDP output data: from the *China Statistical Yearbook* from previous years, in order to facilitate comparison with the indicators published by the National Bureau of Statistics, calculated at constant prices in 2005, the unit is 100 million yuan.

CO_2 emission data: the existing research institutions do not have CO_2 emission data by province (city, district), but because CO_2 emissions are mainly from fossil energy consumption, conversion and cement production, for the sake of accuracy, energy consumption is fine here. It is divided into coal consumption, oil consumption (further subdivided into gasoline, kerosene, diesel, fuel oil) and natural gas consumption. All energy consumption and conversion data are taken from the regional energy balance sheet in the *China Energy Statistics Yearbook*. The cement production data comes from the Guotaian Financial Database. The specific calculation formula for carbon dioxide emissions from fossil energy consumption is as follows:

$$CO_2 = \sum\nolimits_{i=1}^{6} CO_{2i} = \sum\nolimits_{i=1}^{6} E_i \times CF_i \times CC_i \times COF_i \times (44/12) \qquad (2.5)$$

Here, CO_2 represents the estimated total amount of carbon dioxide emissions from various types of energy consumption; i represents various energy sources, including coal, gasoline, kerosene, diesel, fuel oil, and natural gas; E_i is the consumption of various energy sources in various provinces and cities. Total CF_i is the conversion factor, which is the average calorific value of various fuels; CC_i is the carbon content, which is the carbon content of the unit heat; COF_i is the carbon oxidation factor, which reflects the oxidation rate of the energy. Level 44/12 indicates the conversion coefficient of carbon atom mass to carbon dioxide molecular mass; the CO_2 emission coefficient of various emission sources mainly refers to IPCC (2006) and the National Climate Change Coordination Group Office and the Energy Research Institute of the National Development and Reform Commission (2007). Descriptive statistics for each of the above variables are shown in Table 2.1.

The estimated results of the average productivity of environmental factors and the average price of CO_2 shadows in China's provinces (cities, districts) from 1995 to 2007 are shown in Table 2.2. It can be seen that among the 29 provinces (cities, districts), the five provinces with the highest environmental

Interprovincial CO₂ shadow price 37

Table 2.1 Descriptive statistics of various variables

Variables	K (100 million yuan)	L (10,000 person)	GDP (100 million yuan)	CO_2 (10,000 tons)
Average	9,194.59	2,238.83	4,804.88	12,373.68
Maximum	50,421.50	6,568.20	29,400.00	59,383.50
Minimum	434.80	226.00	201.20	627.67
Standard deviation	8,443.63	1,570.28	4,523.79	8,941.19

Table 2.2 Average productivity and average CO_2 shadow price of provinces (cities, districts) in China (1995–2007)

Provinces	Efficiency	Shadow price (yuan/ton)	Rank
Beijing	0.9978	1,611	2
Tianjin	0.9257	759	8
Hebei	0.7667	468	16
Shanxi	0.9436	187	25
Neimenggu	0.8906	218	24
Liaoning	0.4948	647	10
Jilin	0.8724	323	23
Heilongjiang	0.7987	473	15
Shanghai	0.8699	1,713	1
Jiangsu	0.7610	1,169	4
Zhejiang	0.8807	1,064	5
Anhui	0.7461	355	22
Fujian	0.9992	1,008	6
Jiangxi	0.9430	452	17
Shandong	0.7634	843	7
Henan	0.8432	486	14
Hubei	0.8256	430	18
Hunan	0.8714	488	13
Guangdong	1.0000	1,426	3
Guangxi	0.9954	378	21
Hainan	0.9977	627	11
Sichuan	0.6766	598	12
Guizhou	0.5892	86	29
Yunnan	0.2179	666	9
Shaanxi	0.5644	404	20
Gansu	0.9785	136	27
Qinghai	0.8485	165	26
Ningxia	0.7670	129	28
Xinjiang	0.6022	418	19

productivity ranks are: Guangdong (1.00), Fujian (0.9992), Beijing (0.9978), Hainan (0.9977), and Guangxi (0.9954). The last five provinces listed are: Xinjiang (0.6022), Guizhou (0.5892), Shaanxi (0.5644), Liaoning (0.4948), and Yunnan (0.2179).

38 *Emission reduction analysis*

If we refer to the CO_2 shadow price of the province (city, district), the five provinces with the most expensive shadow prices are: Shanghai (¥1,713), Beijing (¥1,611), Guangdong (¥1,426), Jiangsu (¥1,169), and Zhejiang. (¥1,064), which is basically the most developed province in China, and the five provinces with the lowest shadow prices are Shanxi (¥187), Qinghai (¥165), Gansu (¥136), Ningxia (¥129), and Guizhou (¥86); these are also economically underdeveloped areas.

From the annual estimation results, it can be found that Guangdong has been at the production boundary during the period of 1995–2007. Under certain technical conditions, Guangdong's material input, economic output, and pollution level are always at the frontier efficiency, and there is no redundancy[2]; Beijing Fujian has also been in production boundary for 11 years and 12 years, respectively, and the CO_2 shadow price averages of these three provinces and cities are ranked very high, respectively, ranking third, second, and sixth, indicating the level of production efficiency and CO_2 shadow. There may be a positive correlation between price sizes. In addition, Shanghai, Jiangsu, Zhejiang, and other provinces and cities with strong economic strength have higher CO_2 shadow price averages, ranking first, fourth and fifth, respectively, while CO_2 in economically underdeveloped areas such as Qinghai, Gansu, and Ningxia average price of shadows is generally low, ranking only 26th, 27th, and 28th. From this, the level of economic development has a certain relationship with the shadow price of CO_2.

As indicated earlier, the CO_2 shadow price is a straightforward reflection of carbon abatement costs, i.e., higher CO_2 shadow prices indicate higher carbon abatement costs in the region, and vice versa. Therefore, the economic costs of reducing carbon emissions in Shanghai, Beijing, Guangdong, Jiangsu, Zhejiang, Fujian, and other places are much higher than those in Qinghai, Gansu, and Ningxia. Excessive carbon emission reduction quotas will inevitably lead to the economics of these regions. The output has been greatly reduced. On the other hand, these industrially developed regions are also the main sources of carbon emissions in China. If they are strictly controlled, China's carbon emission reduction effect will be more obvious.

Based on the analysis of the mean time sample, the book will compare the trend and characteristics of the CO_2 shadow price of 10 provinces, cities, and districts in China. In order to make the results of the comparison more significant, the top five provinces (Shanghai, Beijing, Guangdong, Jiangsu, and Zhejaing) and last five provinces (Guizhou, Ningxia, Gansu, Qinghai, Shanxi) were selected.

The CO_2 shadow price trend in Shanghai and Beijing are quite consistent. In addition to the different starting points in 1995, they experienced a sharp decline in 1995–1997, a small decline in 1997–1999, a steady increase in 1999–2006, and a fall in 2006–2007. The CO_2 shadow price trend in Guangdong, Jiangsu, and Zhejiang is significantly different from that in Shanghai and Beijing. In 1997–2000, the CO_2 shadow price gradually increased, and 2000–2004 was basically at a stable state. After 2004, the CO_2 shadow price was changed by a comparison. The low level jumped to a level similar to that of Shanghai and Beijing, especially Guangdong, surpassing the shadow price of CO_2 in Shanghai and Beijing, ranking first in the country. The provinces (cities, districts) with low CO_2 shadow prices have relatively stable fluctuations and small changes. CO_2 shadow prices have been below the high shadow price provinces (cities, districts) and lower than the high shadow price provinces (the city). The lowest historical value of the district, which experienced a small arc of rising and falling cycles in 1998–2003, and began a slow upward trend from 2004. Therefore, as far as the country is concerned, the shadow price change of carbon dioxide is mainly the result of changes in economically developed provinces and cities.

The reasons for the changes in CO_2 shadow price trends in different regions are, in the final analysis, related to the high energy-consuming industries and service-oriented industries that the regions face in their own economic development, in the process of complying with the national macro-control, and in the continuous adjustment of the industrial structure. The problem of choice, the layout of high-tech, low-pollution industries and low-tech, low-efficiency and high-pollution industries is not fully covered in this chapter, so there is no discussion here. Because the environmental production estimation method is carried out step by year, it may not fully reflect the increase in economic output caused by the improvement of production efficiency caused by technological progress during the cross-year comparison, so the actual CO_2 shadow price may be exaggerated. The level of growth needs to be viewed by the audience. The comparison results of the regions in the same year are closer to the real situation. They examine the CO_2 shadow price reflected by different levels of productivity; that is, the cost of carbon emission reduction.

2.4 Problem discussion and research conclusions

Because the estimation result of shadow price may not be comparable in a real sense to the actual price level, it reflects the high and low levels of CO_2 shadow price among different provinces (cities, districts), but is still worthy of attention. The order of magnitude of the CO_2 shadow price has a certain reference significance for the determination of the carbon tax policy. According to the preliminary plan recently released by the Ministry of Finance, the carbon tax in China is taxed at 10 yuan per ton of carbon dioxide. Compared with the estimated results, the proposed carbon tax is far less expensive than the theoretical estimate. In most of the literature on carbon tax, the carbon tax rate is often set at the level of 50–100 yuan/ton, and is much higher than the proposed price in China.

Of course, the low tax rate on carbon tax also has its rationality. The carbon tax has a role in reducing carbon emissions and improving environmental quality, and it also has a significant inhibitory effect on the economy. Its social impact will spread to employment, consumption, investment, etc. as the economic effects change, and the more impact of the high tax rate carbon

40 *Emission reduction analysis*

tax scheme on the economy is also greater. As China has just begun to try to tax carbon emissions, the low threshold is more suitable for the current situation and can mitigate the adverse impact of policy changes on the economy. With the gradual accumulation of China's carbon tax collection experience and the continuous maturity of the collection system, the future carbon tax rate will be adjusted to the optimal carbon tax level. According to the estimation results of CO_2 shadow price in Table 2.2 and its characteristics, the shadow prices of provinces (cities, districts) are not only different but also quite different; from the highest price Shanghai (¥1,713) to the lowest price Guizhou (¥86), the difference is nearly 20 times. Such a result indicates that higher requirements for the determination of the optimal carbon tax for fairness and efficiency will be imposed in the future. From the development trend of CO_2 shadow price in the country over the years, the shadow price of CO_2 will show an increasing trend, and it can be speculated that the future carbon tax rate will have a similar growth trend.

In the past, the lack of effective market price information for environmental pollutants such as carbon dioxide has caused many studies related to environmental factors to stagnate, and the government cannot accurately grasp the policy tools (such as carbon) to achieve its policy objectives, the carbon tax policy under emission control, and now the shadow price of pollutants can be estimated to make the research in the field of environmental economics more in-depth, and this chapter is a practical application of this frontier field. The article focuses on the empirical study of the shadow price of CO_2. Using the directional distance function, the environmental production theory and the parametric solution method, the CO_2 shadow price of different provinces (cities, districts) in China was measured from 1995 to 2007. We came to the following conclusions.

First, from the perspective of regional cross-section, for Guangdong, Beijing, Shanghai, Jiangsu, and Zhejiang provinces with strong economic strength, the average price of CO_2 shadows is higher than that of economically underdeveloped areas such as Qinghai, Gansu, and Ningxia. These provinces and cities have higher carbon emission reduction costs. The policy suggestion reflected in this is that the government should formulate corresponding emission reduction measures according to different policy intentions: when targeting carbon emission reduction, stricter restrictions should be imposed on high-shadow price areas, such as higher carbon. For tax level, while aiming at minimizing the economic losses caused by carbon emission reduction, low-shadow price areas should be allowed to bear more emission reduction targets, while subsidies provided by developed regions are a short-term approach.

Secondly, from the longitudinal point of view of time, the general historical trend of the CO_2 shadow price is the first to fall first, and the CO_2 shadow price is lower. Therefore, as far as the whole country is concerned, the shadow price of CO_2 is mainly driven by economically developed regions, which also indicates an increasing trend of carbon tax levels.

Thirdly, from the perspective of the actual effect of the estimation results, the estimated CO_2 shadow price and the actual price level may not be directly equated, but have important reference significance for determining the level of carbon tax; and the estimation results reflect the phenomenon of different levels of CO_2 shadow price between different economic development levels, which can be used as a reference standard for the graded carbon tax rate. It also implies that the "one size fits all" carbon tax rate will not fully realize its policy intentions.

Notes

1 This chapter is the improvement based on the Study of CO_2 Shadow Price in Different Provinces in China, *Academic Journal of Panyang Lake*, 2012, 3, co-published by Wei Chu and Huang Wenruo.
2 Frontier efficiency refers to the maximum economic output and minimum pollution emission with certain input; the existence of redundancy means that actual economic output is fewer than frontier production or actual pollution is greater than frontier pollution with certain amount of input.

3 Regional decomposition of CO_2 emission reduction potential and emission reduction targets[1]

3.1 Background of emission abatement and quota allocation

Although the Copenhagen conference failed to reach any effective emission reduction agreement, it is a solid first step for humanity to cope with climate change in the twenty-first century. The basic four countries composed of China and other large developing countries[2] successfully resisted the mandatory emission reduction targets demanded by developed countries at the meeting, and strengthened future climate change negotiations should follow the Kyoto Protocol and "Bali route" under the leadership of the UN. As China's influence in the global political, economic, and environmental fields is growing, as a rising "responsible power," China proposes an alternative target of 40–45% reduction in CO_2 emission intensity by 2020. After the Copenhagen conference, the Renewable Energy Law Amendment passed by the National People's Congress and the Climate Response Office in the vicinity of the National People's Congress can be regarded as concrete measures to deal with international challenges.[3] In the government's Twelfth Five-Year Plan, the goal of reducing carbon intensity will be integrated into various plans and policies, as well as previous energy conservation and emission reduction targets (Sustainable Development Strategy Research Group of the Chinese Academy of Sciences, 2009). The ensuing question is: How to regionally decompose the national CO_2 intensity constraint target?[4] As many scholars have disputed, due to the imbalance of economic development in China, there are great differences in the carrying capacity and acceptability of reforms between different regions and different departments (Liu Shucheng, 2008), its own level of industrial development, and energy saving. The energy structure is also inconsistent. Therefore, in the area of the CO_2 emission intensity target and the progress of the decomposition is the "one size fits all" and "step-by-step" policy, or the "differentiated" and "divide and conquer" step-by-step approach, and the basis and principle of decomposition are worthy of further discussion (Chang Xinghua, 2007; Wei Chu et al., 2010).

Previously, international research and policy recommendations for climate change were mostly dominated by the West (IPCC, 2007; Stern, 2008; UNEP,

2008), but they were often opposed by developing countries, and the focus of their debate was on how to reflect the principle of common and differentiated responsibilities, and how to ensure the fairness of the development of countries while achieving climate change mitigation. At present, the three representative programs abroad include: the Constriction and Convergence program proposed by the Global Commons Institute in 1990. The program starts from the current per-capita emission level and envisages the per-capita emission targets of different countries. After convergence to a certain level in the future, all countries will reduce emissions together and stabilize GHG concentrations to an acceptable level (Gao, 2006); the climate change framework launched by Brazil in the 1997 Kyoto Protocol negotiations. In the Summary of the Protocols of the Protocol (the "Brazil Text" program), the concept of effective GHG emissions is proposed, and the relative emission reduction obligations are set for Annex I countries. If they cannot be completed within the commitment period, they will be exceeded. Emissions penalties set up a Clean Development Fund to support adaptation and mitigation of climate change projects (Qi Yue & Xie Gaodi, 2009); in the Greenhouse Development Rights Framework proposed by the Stockholm Environment Institute (SEI) in Sweden, only rich people have the responsibility and ability to reduce emissions by setting development thresholds, The development needs of the poor with a barrier below the development threshold, the allocation of global emission reductions based on the total population capacity (purchasing GDP reduction) and total liability (cumulative historical emissions) exceeding the development threshold (Shen Gang, 2009). In the above schemes, although historical emissions are considered, most are based on national emission indicators, neglecting the principle of per-capita equity. In addition, they do not consider the development needs of countries at different stages, neglecting the distribution of demand for future emissions, and still biased from a fair perspective (Pan Jiahua & Zheng Yan, 2009).

Chinese scholars have also conducted a lot of research on global GHG distribution. The Research Group of the Development Research Center of the State Council (2009) proposed a "national emission account" program based on property rights theory and externality theory, and clearly defined the historical emission rights and future emission rights of countries; establish national emission accounts for countries, and allocate emission rights to countries according to the principle of equal per capita, so that "common but differentiated responsibilities" can be clearly defined. Jiahua and Ying (2009) proposed a "carbon budget plan" based on the theory of human development. From the basic needs of people, the corresponding carbon budget rights between 1900 and 2050 were initially allocated to countries according to the per-capita mode. Dealing with self-overdraft or surplus status not only ensures a dual goal of fairness and sustainability, but also designs a carbon budget balancing mechanism and funding mechanism. Ding Zhongli et al. (2009), also based on the "per-capita cumulative emission index" idea, calculated the per-capita cumulative emissions, deserved emission allowances,

44 *Emission reduction analysis*

and emission allowances for 2006–2050 in countries from 1900 to 2005, and calculated the deficits of countries.

China is currently committed to the goal of reducing CO_2 emission intensity by 2020. This goal can be expected to be completed in theory.[5] In the medium and long term, future CO_2 emission reduction is imperative. If more stringent energy-saving and emission reduction technologies are adopted, with effective international technology transfer and financial support, China's carbon emissions may peak in 2030–2040 and then enter a period of stability and decline (He Jiankun, 2011; He Jiankun et al., 2008; Jiang Kezhen et al., 2009; Ding Zhongli et al., 2009). Therefore, it is more meaningful to analyze the CO_2 emission reduction potential and emission reduction space of each province, and provide some reference for the future allocation of emission reduction targets.

This chapter attempts to answer the following questions. What is the potential and space for CO_2 reduction in each region? How high is the marginal cost of reducing emissions? Which provinces need to be focused on when considering the fairness and efficiency of CO_2 emission reduction targets?

This chapter considers several parameters. The fairness dimension includes the responsibility and ability to reduce climate change in different regions. The efficiency dimension includes the emission reduction potential, marginal abatement cost, emission ratio, emission reduction ratio, and emission intensity of different regions. The quantitative emission estimation and ranking of each province's emission reduction obligations have been carried out from the perspectives of emission reduction fairness and efficiency. The results show that there may be some conflicts between regional distribution fairness and efficiency of CO_2 emission reduction, and the final allocation priority and priority will depend on decision-makers' consideration of fairness and efficiency. In addition, this chapter explains the differences in provincial CO_2 emission reduction potential and finds that industrial structure, energy intensity, and energy structure have a greater impact on emission reduction potential.

The structure of this chapter is organized as follows. The first part introduces the basic ideas and models and data; the second section evaluates the regional CO_2 emission reduction potential based on China's provincial data, and estimates the marginal cost of regional CO_2 emission reduction; the third section is from fairness and efficiency, respectively. From this perspective, the province's emission reduction capacity is evaluated and ranked; the fourth section is the explanation of the difference in regional CO_2 emission reduction potential; the last is related discussion and policy implications.

3.2 Models, methods, and data

Traditional production theories cannot directly deal with undesired outputs. Indirect methods can be used to convert undesired outputs so that the transformed data can be included in the normal output function under technically unchanging conditions, including: converting undesired outputs into input factors, or performing additive inverse or multiplicative inverse transformation, as detailed in Scheel (2001); in addition, the directional distance function was developed by Färe et al. (1989), Chung et al. (1997), etc. By building environmental production technology to continue productivity and shadow price measurement, the specific application of the measurement of interprovincial technical efficiency in China can be seen in the studies of Hu Angang et al. (2008); Fu Jiafeng et al. (2010), and Tu Zhengge (2009), who examined industrial productivity and industrial SO_2 based on the measurement of shadow price; Wang Bing et al. (2010) adopted the measurement of interprovincial Malmquist–Luenberger productivity under environmental control. However, as pointed out by Fukuyama and Weber (2009), the existing direction distance function does not consider the possible redundancy, which leads to a certain bias in the final efficiency evaluation.

This chapter uses an extended Scaks-Based Measure (SBM) for estimation. The basic idea of the SBM model is to consider the efficiency of the redundancy at the input and output ends. There is no excessive investment in the optimal performance point at the leading edge, and there is no shortage of output. On this basis, Cooper et al. (2007) proposed an extended SBM model that considers undesired outputs.[6] The basic expression is as follows.

There are n decision-making units, the input vector $x \in R^m$, the production of the desired output $y^b \in R^{s2}$, and the undesired output $yb \in Rs2$, defining the corresponding matrix as $X=[x_1,...,x_n] \in R^{mxn}$, $Y^g=[y_1{}^g,...,y_n{}^g] \in R^{s1xn}$, $Y^b=[y_1{}^b,...,y_n{}^b] \in R^{s2xn}$, and suppose $X, Y^g, Y^b > 0$.

The production possible set P is defined as:

$$P = \{(x, y^g, y^b) \mid x \geq X\lambda, \ y^g \leq Y^g\lambda, \ y^b \geq Y^b\lambda, \ \lambda \geq 0\} \tag{3.1}$$

where $\lambda \in R^n$ is the intensity vector, and the production possible set P in (3.1) is equivalent to the efficiency, which is expressed as:

$$\rho^* = \min \frac{1 - \dfrac{1}{m}\sum_{i=1}^{m} \dfrac{\bar{s_i}}{x_{i0}}}{1 + \dfrac{1}{s_1 + s_2}\left(\sum_{r=1}^{s1} \dfrac{s_r^g}{y_{ro}^g} + \sum_{r=1}^{s2} \dfrac{s_r^b}{y_{ro}^b}\right)} \tag{3.2a}$$

s.t.

$$x_o = X\lambda + s^{-1}$$

$$y_o^g = Y^g\lambda - s^g$$

46 *Emission reduction analysis*

$$y_o^b = Y^b \lambda + s^b$$

$$s^- \geq, s^g \geq 0, s^b \geq, \lambda \geq o$$

where $s^- \in R^m$, $s^b \in R^{s2}$ are excessive inputs and excessive undesired outputs, respectively, and $s^g \in R^{s1}$ represents the desired output of the shortage, that is, the redundancy of inputs, unconsumed outputs, and desirable outputs. The formula (3.2a) is a strict decreasing function of s_i^-, s_r^g and s_r^b, and satisfies $0 < \rho^* \leq 1$. The sample point is at the leading edge if and only if $\rho^* = 1$, that is, it is efficient, and the redundancy value of the input, the desired output, and the undesired output is 0.

In the actual calculation, the weighting factor is often applied according to the relative importance of input and the desired output and the undesired output. Based on the objective function in (3.2a), the weighted efficiency is expressed as:

$$\rho^* = \min \frac{1 - \dfrac{1}{m} \sum_{i=1}^{m} \dfrac{w_i^- s_i^-}{x_{i0}}}{1 + \dfrac{1}{s_1 + s_2} \left(\sum_{r=1}^{s1} \dfrac{w_r^g s_r^g}{y_{ro}^g} + \sum_{r=1}^{s2} \dfrac{w_r^b s_r^b}{y_{ro}^b} \right)} \tag{3.2b}$$

where w_i, w_r^g and w_r^b are the weights of input i, desirable output r, and undesired output r, respectively, and $\sum_{i=1}^{m} w_i^- = m$, $w_i^- \geq 0$, $\sum_{r=1}^{s1} w_r^g + \sum_{r=1}^{s2} w_r^b = s_1 + s_2$, $w_r^g \geq 0$, $w_r^b \geq 0$.

3.2.1 Emission reduction potential model

For inefficient sample points, the non-conforming output corresponding to the feasible target on the leading edge is

$$\hat{y}_o^b = y_o^b - s^{b*} \tag{3.3}$$

It can be solved by (3.2b), and the actual undesired output of the sample points can be observed, so the optimal target undesired output of each sample point can be calculated, if the undesired output is defined as CO_2 emissions, which can define the feasible abatement and the abatement potential at the time t of the sample point i.

$$FA_{i,t} = s_{i,t}^{b*} \tag{3.4a}$$

$$AP_{i,t} = s_{i,t}^{b*} / y_{i,t}^{b} \tag{3.5a}$$

where $FA_{i,t}$ is the excess CO_2 emissions of sample point i at time t, indicating a reduction in CO_2 emissions compared to the leading edge effective point. $AP_{i,t}$ represents the emission reduction potential of the sample point, and its value is between 0 and 1. The higher the value of $AP_{i,t}$, the more the CO_2 emission of the sample point is excessive, and the greater the emission reduction potential of the region. If you increase the total amount of feasible emission reductions in each region, you can get the regional (national) aggregate feasible abatement and calculate the regional (national) aggregate abatement potential.

$$AFA_t = \sum_{i=1}^{n} FA_{i,t} = \sum_{i=1}^{n} s_{i,t}^{b*} \tag{3.4b}$$

$$AAP_t = \sum_{i=1}^{n} FA_{i,t} \Big/ \sum_{i=1}^{n} y_{i,t}^{b} = \sum_{i=1}^{n} s_{i,t}^{b*} \Big/ \sum_{i=1}^{n} y_{i,t}^{b} \tag{3.5b}$$

3.2.2 Shadow price model

In addition, with the method of Charnes and Cooper (1962), the dual linear programming of (3.2a) can be expressed as:

$$\max u^g y_o^g - vx_o - u_b y_o^b \tag{3.6}$$

$$\text{s.t. } u^g Y^g - vX - u^b Y^b \le 0$$

$$v \ge \frac{1}{m}\left[1/x_o\right]$$

$$u^g \ge \frac{1+u^g y_o^g - vx_o - u^b y_o^b}{s}\left[1/y_o^g\right]$$

$$u^b \ge \frac{1+u^g y_o^g - vx_o - u^b y_o^b}{s}\left[1/y_o^b\right]$$

where $s = s1 + s2$, $[1/x_o]$ represents the row vector $(1/x_{1o}, ..., 1/x_{mo})$, the dual vector $v \in R^m$, $u^b \in R^{s2}$, $u^g \in R^{s1}$ can be interpreted as input, non-consensus output and virtual price of desirable output, respectively.

48 *Emission reduction analysis*

According to the method of Färe et al. (1993) and Lee et al. (2002), the ratio of the shadow price of inconsistent output to the desired output is equal to its marginal conversion rate. In the form of parameterized distance function, it can be expressed as the distance function is not satisfactory. The ratio of the output to the first derivative of the desired output, in the non-parametric form, is the dual value of the unconstrained output and the desired output constraint in the dual linear programming, that is, the following relationship:

$$\frac{p^b}{p^g} = \frac{u^b}{u^g} \qquad (3.7a)$$

Assuming that the price p^g of the desired output is a market-oriented standardized price, the shadow price of the undesired output can be derived as:

$$p^b = p^g \cdot \frac{u^b}{u^g} \qquad (3.7b)$$

The shadow price in (3.7b) can be regarded as the marginal cost of CO_2 emissions, and the more severe the pollution emissions, the lower the shadow price (Coggins & Swinton, 1996), so for regions with lower pollutant shadow prices, the risk of opportunity costs that may result from environmental controls or the imposition of emission constraints is relatively small. For the country, it is necessary to consider the possible economic impacts of environmental policies while meeting the emission reduction targets. Therefore, the CO_2 marginal abatement costs in different regions can be used as one of the efficiency indicators for prioritizing regional emission reductions.

3.2.3 Variables and data

This chapter analyzes the capital, labor, and energy of 29 provinces in China from 1995 to 2007 as the input factors, and analyzes the GDP of each province as the desired output and the CO_2 emissions of each province as unproductive output.

Capital stock: the "permanent inventory method" is widely used to estimate the actual capital stock of each year. Here, we mainly refer to the existing research results of Zhang Jun et al. (2004) and extend its sequence to 2007 according to its published method. Calculated at constant prices in 2005, the unit is 100 million yuan.

Labor: foreign countries generally use working hours as a labor input variable, but this is limited by the availability of data. Here, the number of employed people in the current year published in the *China Statistical Yearbook* is 10,000.

Energy: the data come from the *China Energy Statistics Yearbook* over the years. Tibet lacks energy data and is not included in the sample. The unit is 10,000 tons of standard coal.

GDP output data: from the *China Statistical Yearbook* from previous years, in order to facilitate comparison with the indicators published by the National Bureau of Statistics, the unit is calculated at the constant price of 2005, the unit is 100 million yuan.

CO_2 data: existing research institutions have not yet had provincial CO_2 emission data. As CO_2 emissions are mainly derived from fossil energy consumption, conversion, and cement production, for the sake of accuracy, this chapter breaks down energy consumption into coal consumption and oil consumption (further subdivided into gasoline, kerosene, diesel, fuel oil) and natural gas consumption.[7] A large part of the primary energy consumption process is used to generate electricity and heat. Although the energy and heat generated by this part of energy consumption may not be used in the province, the resulting CO_2 does remain in the province, so this chapter, when calculating energy consumption in addition to the terminal energy consumption, also includes energy for power generation and heating. All energy consumption and conversion data in this chapter are taken from the regional energy balance sheet in the *China Energy Statistics Yearbook*. The cement production data come from the Guotaian Financial Database. The specific calculation formula for carbon dioxide emissions from fossil energy consumption activities is as follows:

$$CO_2 = \sum_{i=1}^{6} CO_{2i} = \sum_{i=1}^{6} E_i \times CF_i \times CC_i \times COF_i \times (44/12) \tag{3.8}$$

Here, CO_2 represents the estimated total carbon dioxide emissions of various types of energy consumption; i represents a variety of energy consumption, including coal, gasoline, kerosene, diesel, fuel oil and natural gas; E_i is the province's various energy consumption Total; CF_i is the conversion factor, which is the average calorific value of various fuels; CC_i is the carbon content, which is the carbon content of the unit heat; COF_i is the carbon oxidation factor, which reflects the oxidation rate of the energy. Level: 44/12 indicates the conversion coefficient of carbon atom mass to carbon dioxide molecular mass; the CO_2 emission coefficient of various emission sources mainly refers to IPCC (2006) and the National Climate Change Coordination Group Office and the Energy Research Institute of the National Development and Reform Commission (2007).

Descriptive statistics for each of the above variables can be found in Table 3.1.

3.3 Empirical research

3.3.1 Interprovincial emission reduction potential

Calculate the CO_2 redundancy of each province according to (3.2b), and obtain the CO_2 feasible emission reduction and emission reduction potential

50 *Emission reduction analysis*

Table 3.1 Descriptive statistics of various variables (1995–2007)

Variables	Capital (100 million yuan)	Labor (10,000 people)	Energy (10,000 tons standard coal)	GDP (100 million yuan)	CO_2 emission (10,000 tons)
Average	9,194.594	2,238.833	6,525.56	4,804.882	12,373.68
Standard deviation	8,443.632	1,570.283	4,676.368	4,523.785	8,941.185
Minimum	434.8	226	303	201.2	627.6658
Maximum	50,421.5	6,568.2	28,552	29,400	59,383.5

of each province according to (3.4a) and (3.5a), as shown in Table 3.2. The true meaning of "CO_2 emission reduction" in column (I) means that if the input and output of the region are operated in accordance with the most advantageous mode of the frontier, while maintaining the input and the desired output unchanged, the amount of CO_2 emission reduction that can be achieved is actually the excessive CO_2 emissions in the region. According to the province's CO_2 emission reductions, the total amount of emission reductions in the country can be obtained in the same year, and the proportion of CO_2 emission reductions in each province can be calculated as a percentage of the total amount of emission reductions in the country. See column (II). A proportional measure of the impact of the region's emission reductions on the country, the higher the proportion, indicating that the region's overall impact on the overall reduction of emissions, it should also be the area of concern for emission reduction; column (III), the "emission reduction potential," refers to the proportion of "excess CO_2 emissions" in the region to actual CO_2 emissions, which is the level of inefficiency of CO_2 emissions in the region. If the value is higher, it indicates that there is greater inefficiency, but it also shows that the region has greater potential for emission reduction through technological advancement and efficiency improvements.

In the effective areas on the cutting-edge curve, such as Beijing, Shanghai, and Guangdong, the CO_2 emission reduction and emission reduction potential are both 0, which does not mean that the area does not need environmental treatment or no CO_2 emission reduction. Space refers to the fact that compared with other inefficient provinces; these regions cannot achieve further reduction of CO_2 under the conditions of maintaining current technical conditions, input levels and desired output, that is, the region is currently in Pareto Excellent state. If you want to cut CO_2, its desirable output will also decline.[8]

It can be seen from Table 3.2 that the emission reduction potentials of different provinces are very different. In 1995–2007, Beijing, Shanghai, and Guangdong have been at the forefront of production, and their relative emission reduction potential is 0; Fujian, Guangxi, and Hainan and other provinces are also at the forefront in some years; while Guizhou, Ningxia,

Table 3.2 CO₂ emission reductions by province, accounting for the national proportion and emission reduction potential (1995–2007)

Provinces	(I) CO₂ emission reduction				(II) Proportion of national emission reduction (%)				(III) Reduction potential (%)			
	1995–1999	2000–2004	2005–2007	1995–2007	1995–1999	2000–2004	2005–2007	1995–2007	1995–1999	2000–2004	2005–2007	1995–2007
Beijing	0	0	0	0	0	0	0	0	0	0	0	0
Tianjin	1,978.9	2,421.4	1,902.7	2,131.5	1.93	1.84	0.79	1.46	42.8	42.8	24.5	38.1
Hebei	10,336.7	12,728.5	18,380.4	13,112.9	10.08	9.66	7.65	9.01	56.1	56.1	53.7	54.6
Shanxi	3,027.7	10,555.1	16,679.1	9,073.2	2.95	8.01	6.94	6.23	25.9	25.9	71.8	53.6
Inner Mongolia	5,309.8	9,008.5	19,600.8	10,030.3	5.18	6.84	8.15	6.89	67.6	67.6	75.2	70.7
Liaoning	9,197.0	9,778.9	11,871.3	10,037.9	8.97	7.42	4.94	6.89	57.0	57.0	48.4	54.5
Jilin	5,359.4	4,804.5	8,544.3	5,880.9	5.23	3.65	3.55	4.04	63.3	63.3	59.7	59.1
Heilongjiang	6,729.3	5,653.2	7,010.9	6,380.4	6.56	4.29	2.92	4.38	58.4	58.4	44.9	51.3
Shanghai	0	0	0	0	0	0	0	0	0	0	0	0
Jiangsu	4,426.5	4,226.9	11,675.8	6,022.6	4.32	3.21	4.86	4.14	24.8	24.8	30.8	23.6
Zhejiang	1,372.0	3,410.1	9,267.2	3,977.9	1.34	2.59	3.86	2.73	12.2	12.2	32.4	19.6
Anhui	5,164.9	6,597.0	8,302.8	6,439.8	5.04	5.01	3.45	4.42	52.8	52.8	49.4	51.8
Fujian	0	381.6	3,200.7	885.4	0.00	0.29	1.33	0.61	0	0	25.3	7.5
Jiangxi	1,470.0	1,698.3	3,376.2	1,997.7	1.43	1.29	1.40	1.37	30.3	30.3	34.6	30.0
Shandong	6,456.4	8,471.8	27,285.7	12,038.3	6.30	6.43	11.35	8.27	32.3	32.3	49.4	35.1
Henan	6,643.3	8,606.3	17,954.6	10,008.6	6.48	6.53	7.47	6.87	43.5	43.5	51.1	44.8
Hubei	3,676.9	6,574.4	10,108.0	6,275.4	3.59	4.99	4.21	4.31	31.1	31.1	49.3	41.5
Hunan	3,933.9	2,158.4	8,624.4	4,333.4	3.84	1.64	3.59	2.98	39.8	39.8	45.6	34.1
Guangdong	0	0	0	0	0	0	0	0	0	0	0	0
Guangxi	525.1	1,698.4	3,621.6	1,690.9	0.51	1.29	1.51	1.16	10.6	10.6	35.6	22.7
Hainan	36.6	507.1	866.2	409.0	0.04	0.38	0.36	0.28	4.0	4.0	41.1	22.4
Sichuan	8,133.8	8,243.9	8,634.6	8,291.7	7.93	6.26	3.59	5.69	47.8	47.8	34.0	42.3
Guizhou	5,132.0	7,345.2	1,2416.2	7,664.2	5.00	5.57	5.17	5.26	74.5	74.5	80.0	76.5
Yunnan	1,602.9	1,998.4	6,836.6	2,962.8	1.56	1.52	2.84	2.03	32.0	32.0	55.6	37.6
Shaanxi	3,445.6	3,703.3	7,111.2	4,390.6	3.36	2.81	2.96	3.02	52.7	52.7	55.0	51.1
Gansu	3,160.2	3,636.0	4,637.4	3,684.1	3.08	2.76	1.93	2.53	65.5	65.5	60.6	63.3
Qinghai	629.1	918.8	1,385.4	915.0	0.61	0.70	0.58	0.63	58.6	58.6	62.0	60.2
Ningxia	1,334.3	2,194.6	4,965.6	2,503.2	1.30	1.67	2.07	1.72	72.7	72.7	84.0	75.8
Xinjiang	3,474.8	4,465.0	6,105.8	4,462.8	3.39	3.39	2.54	3.07	59.4	59.4	60.2	60.9

52 *Emission reduction analysis*

Inner Mongolia, Gansu, Xinjiang, Qinghai, Jilin, Hebei, Liaoning, Shanxi, Anhui, Heilongjiang, Shaanxi, and other provinces have more than 50% reduction potential, which means that compared with the frontier areas, these provinces have large differences in factor allocation, technical level, and management efficiency, resulting in more than half of the CO_2 emissions from economic production being excessive emissions.

In terms of the scale of CO_2 emission reduction, in 1995–2007, the proportion of CO_2 emission reductions in Hebei, Shandong, Inner Mongolia, Liaoning, Henan, Shanxi, Sichuan, and Guizhou accounted for more than 5% of the total national emission reduction. The total amount of emission reductions in the above eight provinces accounts for 55% of the total national emission reduction. In the near term, in 2005–2007, the emission reductions of Shandong, Inner Mongolia, Hebei, Henan, Shanxi, and Guizhou accounted for more than 5% of the total national emission reductions. The proportion of the volume is 46.7%. In particular, Shandong and Inner Mongolia need to pay attention to the fact that the amount of CO_2 that can reduce emissions is not only higher, but also in an increasing trend.

According to (3.4b) and (3.5b), the CO_2 emission reductions and emission reduction potentials in the eastern, central, and western regions can be calculated, as shown in Figure 3.1 and Figure 3.2.

It can be seen from Figure 3.1 that the CO_2 emission reductions that can be achieved in the eastern, central, and western regions in 1995 were about 1 billion tons, and in 2007 they climbed to about 2.5 billion tons. To be specific, the proportion of emission reduction of the total national emission reduction by the eastern, central, and western regions was 33.4%, 34.6%, and 32%, respectively, between 1995 and 2007, indicating that the eastern, central, and western regions are more average in terms of the scale and proportion of emission reductions.

In addition, as can be seen from Figure 3.2, the emission reduction potentials of the eastern, central, and western regions are different. The average emission reduction potential in the eastern region is around 28%, and the central average is 48%. The western region saw the greatest emission reduction potential of 55.7%, and the emission reduction potential of the central and western regions began to increase from 2000, indicating that the excessive emissions due to inefficiency in production are increasing. The national average emission reduction potential is about 40%. Take 2007 as an example. In the same year, the national total CO_2 emissions were 5.92 billion tons. If all regions have effective areas on the frontier, such as Beijing, Shanghai, and Guangdong, goal-setting and producing through efficiency improvements and catching up with the frontier can save nearly 40% of CO_2 emissions while maintaining existing inputs and GDP. Wei Chu et al. (2010) have conducted a similar analysis on the potential of China's energy conservation and emission reduction. The conclusion is that the national energy-saving potential in 2006 and 2007 is about 39%, while the SO_2 emission reduction potential is about

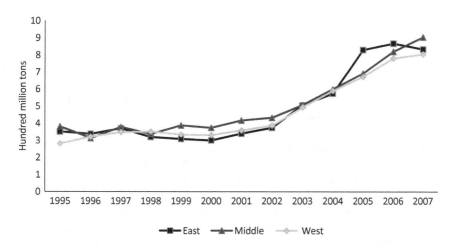

Figure 3.1 CO_2 emission reductions in the eastern, central, and western regions (1995–2007)

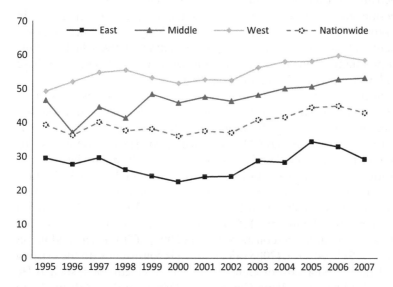

Figure 3.2 CO_2 emission reduction potential in the eastern, central, and western regions (1995–2007)

54 *Emission reduction analysis*

33–34% due to CO_2. Emissions are closely related to energy consumption. The CO_2 emission reduction potential obtained in this chapter is 40% and is consistent with its conclusion.

3.3.2 Regional marginal cost of emission reduction

According to formula (3.7), the shadow price of CO_2 emission reduction in each province can be calculated, which can be regarded as the marginal cost of reducing CO_2 in each region. Generally, if the shadow price is higher, the marginal cost of reducing emissions is greater; if the shadow price is higher, it indicates that the economic cost of reducing emissions is smaller. If environmental targets are required to be regulated in different regions and industries, from the perspective of economic costs, regions and industries with lower marginal abatement costs can be selected first. The calculation results of the average shadow price of CO_2 in each province are shown in Table 3.3.

It can be seen from Table 3.3 that between 1995 and 2007, Shanxi, Guizhou, Inner Mongolia, Ningxia, Hebei and other places have the lowest CO_2 marginal abatement costs, while marginal abatement costs in Beijing, Fujian, Guangdong, Hainan and Zhejiang. The highest, the marginal abatement cost of Beijing (266.5 yuan/ton) is nearly nine times that of Shanxi (31.1 yuan/ton), which also indicates the pollution caused by many factors such as industrial structure, energy structure, environmental control and other factors in different provinces. The cost of abatement varies widely. In general, economically efficient and economically developed regions have relatively high shadow prices for pollutants, while regions with more severe pollution emissions have lower shadow prices (Coggins & Swinton, 1996).

In the near term, in 2005–2007, the marginal abatement cost of CO_2 in Hebei, Shanxi, Inner Mongolia, Shandong, Henan, Sichuan, Guizhou and other places was even zero, indicating that CO_2 in the above provinces has serious excessive emissions and CO_2 implementation. The economic costs of emission reductions are small and can be noted in the above provinces.

In addition, based on the data from the provinces in Table 3.3, the time trend of CO_2 marginal cost reduction in the eastern, central, and western regions is calculated, as shown in Figure 3.3. It can be found that, from a national perspective, the marginal abatement cost of CO_2 between 1995 and 2007 is 94.4–139.5 yuan/ton (constant price in 2005), if it is calculated in US dollars, it is US$11.5–17/ton (2005 price), which is consistent with the existing estimate of the marginal cost of China's CO_2 emission reduction, such as He Juhuang et al. (2002) and Wang Can et al. (2005) using the CGE model to calculate China's 2010 CO_2 marginal emission reduction. The cost is \$23/ton, \$11–26.5/ton, and \$12.5–32/ton, respectively.

From a regional perspective, CO_2 abatement costs in the central and western regions showed an upward trend before 2002, declined after 2002, and rebounded in 2005. This indicates that before 2002, the GHG emissions in various regions did not surge, and the environmental quality improved.

Table 3.3 CO_2 shadow price estimates by province (1995–2007)

Provinces	Average CO_2 shadow price (yuan/ton, unchanged in 2005)				Rank (1995–2007)
	1995–1999	2000–2004	2005–2007	1995–2007	
Beijing	305.9	214.9	286.7	266.5	1
Tianjin	103.6	137.1	182.6	134.7	9
Hebei	80.8	60.1	0.0	54.2	25
Shanxi	15.9	64.9	0.0	31.1	29
Inner Mongolia	59.0	63.2	0.0	47.0	27
Liaoning	78.1	107.2	81.0	90.0	17
Jilin	67.8	100.1	97.6	87.1	18
Heilongjiang	76.1	114.7	127.8	102.9	14
Shanghai	122.1	164.2	214.1	159.5	6
Jiangsu	138.3	170.0	49.2	129.9	10
Zhejiang	160.7	182.8	156.1	168.1	5
Anhui	86.6	104.9	121.0	101.5	15
Fujian	282.2	246.8	183.1	245.7	2
Jiangxi	128.9	160.2	156.5	147.3	7
Shandong	124.2	99.7	0.0	86.1	19
Henan	103.6	103.1	0.0	79.5	22
Hubei	61.6	116.1	121.2	96.3	16
Hunan	111.9	171.8	130.2	139.2	8
Guangdong	183.1	210.9	217.1	201.7	3
Guangxi	66.2	160.4	154.0	122.7	12
Hainan	262.8	153.8	159.5	197.0	4
Sichuan	95.2	76.7	0.0	66.1	24
Guizhou	46.4	42.4	0.0	34.1	28
Yunnan	124.0	148.5	106.5	129.4	11
Shaanxi	87.2	116.1	107.8	103.1	13
Gansu	63.5	82.0	94.5	77.8	23
Qinghai	75.1	86.5	91.5	83.3	21
Ningxia	50.0	56.7	38.7	50.0	26
Xinjiang	73.8	91.0	96.1	85.6	20

Therefore, the cost of CO_2 abatement increased, and there was a certain environmental deterioration during 2003–2005. It was noted that in 2003, China experiences a high rapid expansion of energy-consuming industries and investment which have led to a rebound in energy intensity (Liao et al., 2007), which may be one of the reasons for the "richer" CO_2 emissions, which will reduce the marginal cost reduction. After 2005, the rebound in CO_2 shadow prices is due to the implementation of the energy-saving emission reduction strategy leading to further reductions in the marginal cost of CO_2. It is worth noting that there is a certain difference between the eastern region and the central and western regions. Before 1998, the marginal abatement cost increased, and then it was in a downward channel, but it rebounded in 2002 and has since declined moderately. However, in general, the marginal

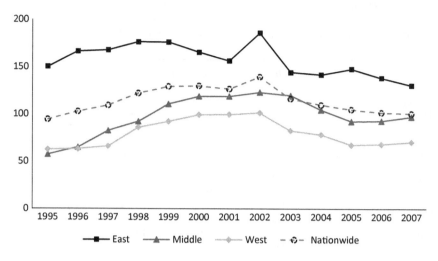

Figure 3.3 CO$_2$ marginal abatement costs in the eastern, central, and western regions (1995–2007)

abatement cost of CO$_2$ in the eastern region is always higher than that in the central and western regions, indicating that there may be a certain inverse relationship between the marginal abatement cost of CO$_2$ and the level of economic development.

3.4 Interprovincial emission reduction and emission reduction efficiency

Setting the regional emission reduction target decomposition needs to consider the two dimensions of fairness and efficiency of regional emission reduction (Qi Yue & Xie Gaodi, 2009), in which fairness should first guarantee the basic rights that everyone should enjoy (refer to Winkler et al., 2002). It can be measured by two parameters. One is to reduce the responsibility of climate change, which can be measured by per-capita CO$_2$ emissions,[9] and the other is the ability to pay, measured by per-capita GDP. The area with higher per-capita CO$_2$ emissions and per-capita GDP, should have greater responsibility for reducing emissions.

The principle of efficiency is also the principle of optimal resource allocation. Obviously, CO$_2$ emissions per unit of GDP output is an important indicator of efficiency (Winkler et al., 2002; Qi Yue & Xie Gaodi, 2009). In addition, according to Table 3.1 and Table 3.2, we can calculate the province's own emission reduction potential, marginal abatement cost, actual emissions and the proportion of emission reductions in the country, etc. If a region has high CO$_2$ emission intensity, high emission reduction potential, and a lower marginal abatement cost, while CO$_2$ emissions and emission reductions account for a higher proportion of the country, which indicates that the inefficient emissions in production in the region are large, the economic cost of achieving emission reduction is low, and the contribution to the country is high from the perspective of efficiency in terms of high emission reduction targets.

When setting the CO_2 emission reduction targets of each province, policymakers need to comprehensively consider the principles of emission reduction equity and emission reduction efficiency. Equity reduction is to ensure fair and reasonable development of all regions and appropriate emission space, and emission reduction efficiency is more focused. The real emission reduction potential, opportunity cost and impact on the whole country in different regions, in order to effectively carry out regional comparison, the CO_2 Abatement Capacity Index can be quantitatively constructed. The calculation method is as follows:

$$ACI_{i,t} = \omega \times Equality_{i,t} + (1 - \omega) \times Efficiency_{i,t} \tag{3.9}$$

$Equality_{i,t}$ is the CO_2 emission reduction fairness index, which is a standardized synthesis index based on the per-capita CO_2 emission level and the per-capita GDP level. $Equality_{i,t}$ is the CO_2 emission reduction efficiency index, according to the CO_2 emission intensity and CO_2 emission in the region. The index that combines the national weight, CO_2 emission reduction potential, CO_2 emission reduction and national CO_2 emission reduction, and the CO_2 emission reduction cost are standardized.[10] The parameter ω is the policymaker's preference for emission reduction and emission reduction efficiency. The principle of "equal importance of fairness and efficiency", if $\omega = 0.5$ is taken to calculate the final CO_2 emission reduction capacity index. The results are shown in Table 3.4.

The indicators and indices in Table 3.4 are both between 0 and 1. The higher the value, the more the emission reduction tasks should be undertaken. It can be seen from column (III) of Table 3.4 that if only the interprovincial emission reduction equity is considered, then regions with higher per-capita CO_2 emissions and higher economic development levels, including Shanghai, Beijing, Tianjin, Inner Mongolia, Ningxia Zhejiang, Liaoning, Shanxi and other provinces should undertake more emission reduction obligations; from the perspective of column (IV), if only considering the efficiency of emission reduction and the impact on national emission reduction, then there is higher emission reduction potential and CO_2 emissions. Intensity, lower marginal abatement costs, and provinces with greater impacts on CO_2 emissions and emissions reductions, such as Guizhou, Shanxi, Inner Mongolia, Hebei, Shandong, Ningxia, Liaoning, etc., should undertake more emission reduction tasks. At the same time, considering the two dimensions of fairness and efficiency, and giving the same weight as shown in the ranking of CO_2 emission reduction capacity index in column (V), it can be seen that Inner Mongolia, Shanxi, Shanghai, Ningxia, and Hebei provinces also ranked high, thus should be paid special attention to in the process of decomposing the

Table 3.4 Fairness Index, Efficiency Index, and Capacity Index (average between 1995 and 2007)

Provinces	(I) Fairness indicators		(II) CO_2 Efficiency Index					(III) Fairness Index		(IV) Efficiency Index		(V) Capability Index	
	Per-ca+pita CO_2 emission	Per- capita GDP	Emission intensity	Emission ratio	Emission reduction potential	Reduction proportion	Reduction cost	Scores	Rank	Scores	Rank	Score	Rank
Beijing	0.70	0.86	0.00	0.18	0.00	0.00	0.00	0.783	(2)	0.036	(29)	0.409	(10)
Tianjin	0.93	0.59	0.20	0.15	0.50	0.16	0.13	0.759	(3)	0.229	(22)	0.494	(7)
Hebei	0.46	0.19	0.38	0.77	0.71	1.00	0.52	0.326	(14)	0.676	(4)	0.501	(5)
Shanxi	0.71	0.14	0.75	0.48	0.70	0.69	1.00	0.429	(8)	0.726	(2)	0.578	(2)
Inner Mongolia	0.93	0.19	0.73	0.42	0.92	0.76	0.62	0.564	(4)	0.692	(3)	0.628	(1)
Liaoning	0.64	0.28	0.37	0.58	0.71	0.77	0.26	0.462	(7)	0.538	(7)	0.500	(6)
Jilin	0.49	0.17	0.46	0.29	0.77	0.45	0.27	0.328	(13)	0.449	(10)	0.389	(11)
Heilongjiang	0.40	0.19	0.35	0.38	0.67	0.49	0.21	0.298	(15)	0.420	(13)	0.359	(14)
Shanghai	1.00	1.00	0.03	0.30	0.00	0.00	0.09	1.000	(1)	0.083	(27)	0.542	(3)
Jiangsu	0.40	0.38	0.10	0.78	0.31	0.46	0.14	0.388	(9)	0.357	(17)	0.373	(13)
Zhejiang	0.48	0.45	0.08	0.54	0.26	0.30	0.08	0.466	(6)	0.251	(21)	0.359	(15)
Anhui	0.13	0.07	0.34	0.38	0.68	0.49	0.21	0.099	(23)	0.420	(12)	0.260	(22)
Fujian	0.16	0.28	0.02	0.21	0.10	0.07	0.01	0.219	(16)	0.080	(28)	0.150	(26)
Jiangxi	0.02	0.08	0.15	0.17	0.39	0.15	0.11	0.053	(28)	0.195	(23)	0.124	(27)
Shandong	0.42	0.29	0.18	1.00	0.46	0.92	0.28	0.354	(11)	0.566	(5)	0.460	(8)
Henan	0.19	0.12	0.26	0.69	0.59	0.76	0.31	0.153	(19)	0.522	(8)	0.338	(16)
Hubei	0.22	0.12	0.31	0.44	0.54	0.48	0.23	0.173	(18)	0.402	(15)	0.287	(17)
Hunan	0.08	0.10	0.20	0.35	0.45	0.33	0.12	0.092	(25)	0.289	(19)	0.190	(24)
Guangdong	0.32	0.43	0.02	0.75	0.00	0.00	0.04	0.371	(10)	0.164	(25)	0.267	(20)
Guangxi	0.00	0.07	0.15	0.18	0.30	0.13	0.15	0.035	(29)	0.181	(24)	0.108	(28)
Hainan	0.07	0.13	0.09	0.00	0.29	0.03	0.05	0.097	(24)	0.093	(26)	0.095	(29)
Sichuan	0.07	0.08	0.25	0.63	0.55	0.63	0.40	0.075	(26)	0.492	(9)	0.284	(18)
Guizhou	0.26	0.00	0.98	0.29	1.00	0.58	0.90	0.132	(21)	0.750	(1)	0.441	(9)
Yunnan	0.05	0.06	0.21	0.19	0.49	0.23	0.14	0.055	(27)	0.252	(20)	0.154	(25)
Shaanxi	0.19	0.09	0.34	0.24	0.67	0.33	0.21	0.143	(20)	0.358	(16)	0.250	(23)
Gansu	0.18	0.05	0.54	0.15	0.83	0.28	0.32	0.115	(22)	0.424	(11)	0.269	(19)
Qinghai	0.31	0.10	0.46	0.00	0.79	0.07	0.29	0.202	(17)	0.323	(18)	0.263	(21)
Ningxia	0.87	0.11	1.00	0.06	0.99	0.19	0.57	0.487	(5)	0.563	(6)	0.525	(4)
Xinjiang	0.52	0.18	0.45	0.20	0.80	0.34	0.28	0.349	(12)	0.414	(14)	0.381	(12)

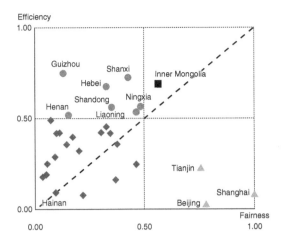

Figure 3.4 Distribution of Equity Index and Efficiency Index of emission reduction in each province (1995–2007)

targets of emission reduction areas. Before, that is, the provinces that need to be considered in the process of decomposing the targets of emission reduction areas.

Figure 3.4 shows a scatter plot of the average fairness and efficiency scores for the provinces between 1995 and 2007, and plots the 45-degree line, with the horizontal axis representing the fairness index for emissions reduction and the vertical axis representing the efficiency index for emission reductions. The metric line indicates that the efficiency weight of the point on the line is equal to the fair weight, which is the CO_2 emission reduction capacity index calculated in column (V) of Table 3.4. If the distance from the origin is further, it indicates that the emission reduction capability is higher; that is, it is needed. The provinces that focus on reducing emissions, in addition, the farther the sample is from the 45-degree moving average, the greater the gap between the efficiency index and the fairness index of the province's emission reduction, and the sample points above the 45-degree line belong to the emission reduction efficiency is higher than the reduction. The provinces with fairness and the sample points below the 45-degree line belong to the provinces with emission reduction fairness higher than emission reduction efficiency. It can be seen from the figure that Shanghai, Beijing and Tianjin are in the lower right corner, which is far from the 45-degree line. That is to say, from the perspective of emission reduction, these three regions should bear greater emission reduction obligations, but in terms of emission reduction efficiency, the marginal abatement cost may be higher than other regions; correspondingly, the provinces in the upper left corner, such as Guizhou, Shanxi, Hebei, Henan, Shandong, Ningxia, Liaoning and other provinces are reducing emissions and are more efficient provinces, but it is worth noting that

60 *Emission reduction analysis*

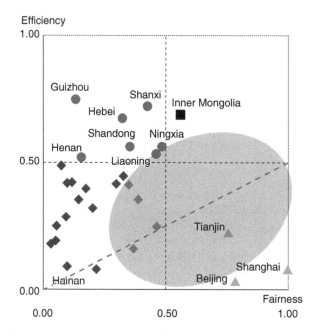

Figure 3.5 Emission reduction priority

Guizhou and Henan provinces are far from the 45-degree line, indicating that from a fair perspective, these provinces have relatively low emission reduction obligations; in addition, the only ones are high emission reductions. The provinces of the region with fairness and high emission reduction efficiency are Inner Mongolia, indicating that the province has the responsibility and obligation to undertake more emission reduction targets, both in terms of emission reduction and efficiency. Correspondingly, Hainan Province, which is in the lower left corner and close to the origin, can appropriately relax its emission reduction tasks from the perspective of fairness and efficiency, and adopt differentiated emission reduction targets.

For provinces where the fairness and efficiency rankings conflict, such as Beijing, Tianjin, Shanghai, Guizhou, etc., it is to set a reduction target or a different target equivalent to the national average, depending on the decision-makers' equity in CO_2 emission reduction. The relative weight of efficiency, if the decision-maker considers the principle of equality of emission reduction priority, it may be desirable to set the equity index weight $\omega = 1/3$. At this time, as shown in Figure 3.5, the original 45-degree line will tilt to the lower right. The key area that needs attention at this time is the sample point that is far from the origin and near the shadow range. Conversely, if the decision-makers pay more attention to energy reduction efficiency, it may be worthwhile

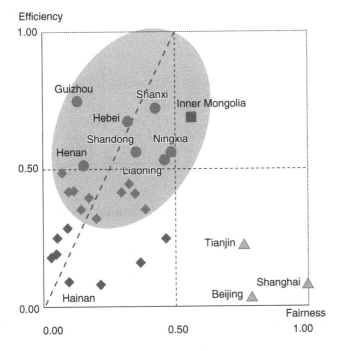

Figure 3.6 Preferred emission reduction efficiency

to set the equity index weight $\omega = 1/3$. As shown in Figure 3.6, the original 45-degree line will be closer to the efficiency axis, and the focus needs to be reduced. The row area is also a sample point that is far from the far point and is near the shadow range. Once the relative weighting factors are determined, the provinces can be ranked to identify key areas for CO_2 reduction.

According to the above discussion, according to the different weight distribution of emission reduction fairness and emission reduction efficiency, the corresponding CO_2 emission reduction capability index and ranking can be calculated. Table 3.5 lists the top and bottom five provinces, although the different weights for the allocation of emission reduction fairness and emission reduction efficiency will affect the relative ranking of the provinces (such as Beijing, Shanghai, etc.), but Table 3.5 reveals that for some provinces, whether in the principle of fairness or efficiency, the rankings of emission reduction capacity indexes are relatively consistent. For example, Inner Mongolia and Shanxi provinces are ranked high, indicating that these provinces should and can undertake larger emission reduction tasks, while Hainan, Guangxi, Jiangxi, Yunnan and other provinces rank lower. It indicates that the emission reduction tasks of these provinces should be appropriately relaxed to ensure their necessary development needs.

62 *Emission reduction analysis*

Table 3.5 CO$_2$ emission reduction capacity of major provinces under different principles (1995–2007)

	Equity is as important as efficiency ($\omega = 1/2$)	Fairness principle is prioritized ($\omega = 2/3$)	Efficiency principle is prioritized ($\omega = 1/3$)
Top 6 provinces	Neimenggu, Shanxi, Shanghai, Ningxia, Hebei, Liaoning	Shanghai, Neimenggu, Tianjin, Beijing, Shanxi, Ningxia	Neimenggu, Shanxi, Hebei, Guizhou, Ningxia, Liaoning
Last 5 provinces	Hainan, Guangxi, Jiangxi, Fujian, Yunnan	Guangxi, Hainan, Jiangxi, Yunnan, Hunan	Hainan, Fujian, Guangxi, Jiangxi, Yunnan

3.5 Further discussion on emission reduction potential and marginal cost of emission reduction

According to the above analysis, the interprovincial CO$_2$ emission reduction potential varies greatly, and the influencing factors are discussed in more depth here. Let's set up a generalized model:

$$y_{i,t} = \alpha + Z_{i,t}\beta + \eta_i + \varepsilon_{i,t} \tag{3.10}$$

where $y_{i,t}$ is the potential reduction of the tth year of the ith province; α is a constant term, η_i and $\varepsilon_{i,t}$ are individual effects and disturbance terms, respectively, β is a regression coefficient, $Z_{i,t}$ is an exogenous explanatory variable, due to subtraction, the potential of the discharge is the CO$_2$ redundancy generated by the provinces relative to the optimal production status of the frontier. Therefore, it reflects more inefficiencies in the production process due to technical level and management efficiency. According to the relevant literature and previous discussions, the following explanatory variables are as follows.

Level of economic development: as previously observed, regions with higher levels of economic development tend to be at the forefront or close to the frontier, and their production processes are more efficient. Excessive CO$_2$ emissions due to inefficiency are relatively small, and per-capita GDP is used here. Logarithmically it represents the level of economic development in each region and is expected to be negatively correlated with the emission reduction potential.

Energy intensity: the energy intensity and energy productivity are mutually reciprocal. The higher the energy intensity, the lower the energy efficiency level, indicating that the more energy is wasted in production, and the more excessive CO$_2$ emissions are generated. Therefore, the potential for emission reduction is also large, and it is expected to be positively related to the emission reduction potential.

Energy consumption structure: the difference in energy consumption structure in different regions is of great significance to the impact of actual CO_2 emissions.[11] According to Auffhammer and Carson (2008), the proportion of coal consumption in total energy consumption in each province is taken as the energy structure variable, and the higher proportion of coal consumption, the greater emission reduction potential, the higher the expected symbol is.

Industrial structure: the regional industrial structure level is measured by the proportion of the tertiary industry in each province. Because the tertiary industry is a low-energy and low-emission industry, the third industry accounts for the higher proportion of the national economy, and it "can save" CO_2 emission potential. The less, the expected sign is negative.

Factor endowment structure: according to common sense, capital deepening will promote the improvement of total factor productivity (Yang Wenju, 2006), which will reduce the inefficiency in production and reduce excessive CO_2 emissions; but at the same time, as Wei Chu, Shen Manhong (2008) discovered that excessive capital deepening may be due to the deviation from China's "resource endowment" advantage, and it is more biased towards energy-intensive industries and has a certain negative impact on economic efficiency, resulting in more ineffective CO_2 emissions, so we will use the average logarithmic term of capital to characterize and test the factor endowment structure employed by each province.

Technological progress: the development and application of low-carbon technologies is obviously an important factor affecting the potential of emission reduction. With the application of new technologies and new equipment, new emission reduction potentials will be continuously explored. Here, the logarithm of time trends is used to characterize the marginal effect of technological advancement factors on CO_2 emission reduction is characterized by a positive sign.

The above variables are all based on the data from 1995 to 2007 from the *China Statistical Yearbook*. Because the emission reduction potential is between 0 and 1, the limit Tobit model needs to be used for estimation. In addition, random effects and the fixed effects are estimated[12] and the results are shown in Table 3.6.

From the regression results in Table 3.6, the symbols of each variable are basically consistent with expectations, except that the industrial structure variables in the fixed effect model are not significant, other regression results are more significant, among which: the higher the level of economic development, the higher the proportion of the tertiary industry, the lower the emission reduction potential, while the energy intensity, coal consumption proportion, technological progress, and capital deepening are positively related to the emission reduction potential. Here, the industrial structure, energy intensity and energy consumption structure are interprovincial. The potential for emission reduction has a greater impact.

64   Emission reduction analysis

Table 3.6 Regression analysis of emission reduction potential (1995–2007)

Interpret variables	Tobit estimates	Random effect	Fixed effect
Economic development level	−0.260 ***	−0.181 ***	−0.118 *
(per-capita GDP)	(0.053)	(0.043)	(0.062)
Energy consumption intensity	0.372 ***	0.352 ***	0.382 ***
	(0.035)	(0.028)	(0.045)
Proportion of coal consumption	0.304 ***	0.221 ***	0.173 *
	(0.087)	(0.074)	(0.095)
Technological improvement	0.137 ***	0.110 ***	0.071 ***
	(0.014)	(0.011)	(0.02)
Proportion of the tertiary	−0.787 ***	−0.485 ***	0.019
industry	(0.211)	(0.153)	(0.228)
Capital deepening	0.171 ***	0.130 ***	0.133 ***
	(0.044)	(0.037)	(0.047)
Constant term	−0.171 ***	−0.092	−0.204
	(0.121)	(0.098)	(0.132)
Log likelihood	243.8		
R^2		0.80	0.71
Rho	0.43	0.37	0.58
Obs	319	377	377

Note: *, **, *** represent significance at 10%, 5% ,and 1%, respectively.

Table 3.7 EKC test of CO_2 shadow price[13]

Interpret variables	Random effect	Fixed effect
Per-capita GDP	0.514 ***	0.516 ***
	(0.072)	(0.065)
Per-capita GDP	−0.133 **	−0.126 **
Squared term	(0.064)	(0.061)
Constant term	4.760 ***	4.749***
	(0.036)	(0.089)
R^2	0.224	0.224
Rho	0.515	0.513
Obs	345	345

Note: *, **, *** represent significant at 10%, 5%, and 1%, respectively.

In addition, according to Ankarhem's (2005) research on industrial pollutants in Sweden, the relative size of shadow prices reflects the cost of reducing emissions in different regions. The more CO_2 emissions are cut, the higher the marginal cost reduction, and the higher the shadow price. Therefore, the CO_2 marginal cost reduction can be regarded as an environmental degradation indicator for the environmental Kuznets curve test. For this we have also carried out related tests, and the results are shown in Table 3.7.

Regional decomposition 65

It can be seen from Table 3.7 that the primary GDP per capita is significantly positive and the secondary term is significantly negative, indicating that the CO_2 shadow price and the per-capita GDP shows a U-shaped curve relationship with the existing environmental Kuznets curve. The hypothesis is the same, that is, in the early stage of economic development, with the increase of income and CO_2 emissions, the marginal cost of CO_2 reduction is decreasing, but with the further increase of income, the emission of pollutants shows a downward trend. At this time, the marginal cost reduction will rise, according to Table 3.6, which calculates that the per-capita GDP at the lowest shadow price (that is, the peak CO_2 emission) is 6.8–77 million yuan. At this time, the minimum marginal cost of CO_2 is 163.5–165 yuan/ton. According to the available data, some provinces have reached this turning point.

3.6 Conclusion

This chapter conducts a preliminary study on the regional decomposition target of CO_2 emission reduction. Based on the extended SBM model, the CO_2 emission reduction potential and CO_2 marginal abatement cost of 29 provinces across the country were measured during 1995–2007, considering fairness and efficiency. Based on this principle, the key provinces that need to be paid attention to when decomposing the target of emission reduction areas are proposed, and the differences between the interprovincial emission reduction potential and the marginal abatement cost are measured and interpreted. The main conclusions of this chapter include:

1. After considering the unsatisfactory output of CO_2, Beijing, Shanghai, and Guangdong are at the forefront of production; compared to the above three provinces, Guizhou, Ningxia, Inner Mongolia, Gansu, Xinjiang, Qinghai, Jilin, Hebei, Liaoning, Shanxi, Anhui, Heilongjiang, and other provinces have an emission reduction potential of more than 50%, which means that more than half of the CO_2 emissions from production in these provinces are inefficient "excessive" emissions compared to the frontier.
2. Considering the impact of CO_2 emission reductions across the province on the country, between 1995 and 2007, CO_2 emission reductions in Hebei, Shandong, Inner Mongolia, Liaoning, Henan, Shanxi, Sichuan, and Guizhou accounted for the total amount of national emission reductions. The proportions are all over 5%, and the total amount of emission reductions in the above eight provinces accounts for 55% of the total national emission reduction. In 2005–2007, the emission reductions of Shandong, Inner Mongolia, Hebei, Henan, Shanxi, and Guizhou accounted for more than 5% of the total national emission reductions. The above six provinces accounted for 46.7% of the total national emission reductions. In particular, Shandong and Inner Mongolia need to pay attention to the fact that the amount of CO_2 that can reduce emissions has a higher impact on the country, and it is on an increasing trend.

66 *Emission reduction analysis*

3. From the marginal cost of CO_2 emission reduction, Shanxi, Guizhou, Inner Mongolia, Ningxia, Hebei and other places have the lowest CO_2 marginal abatement costs, while Beijing, Fujian, Guangdong, Hainan, Zhejiang and other places have the highest marginal abatement costs. In the near term, in 2005–2007, the marginal abatement cost of CO_2 in Hebei, Shanxi, Inner Mongolia, Shandong, Henan, Sichuan, Guizhou and other places was even zero, indicating that CO_2 in the above provinces has serious excessive emissions and CO_2 implementation. The economic costs of emission reductions are small.

4. The national average emission reduction potential between 1995 and 2007 is about 40%, of which the emission reduction potentials of the eastern, central and western regions are 28%, 48%, and 55.7%, respectively, reflecting the inefficiency in production in different regions. There is a big difference in the level of excessive emissions; the scale of CO_2 that can be reduced in the country has increased from about 1 billion tons in 1995 to 2.5 billion tons in 2007, with the eastern, central, and western regions accounting for an average of 33.4%. 34.6%, and 32%; the national average CO_2 marginal abatement cost is 94.4–139.5 yuan/ton, of which the eastern marginal abatement cost is the highest, with an average of 157.6 yuan/ton, the central region is 98 yuan/ton, and the western region is the lowest at 79.9 yuan/ton.

5. When setting regional emission reduction targets, we need to consider the two dimensions of fairness and efficiency of emission reduction. If only the principle of fairness is considered, then regions with higher per-capita CO_2 emissions and higher economic development levels, such as Shanghai and Beijing, Tianjin, Inner Mongolia, Ningxia and other provinces, should undertake more emission reduction obligations; if they consider emission reduction efficiency and impact on national emission reduction, then they have greater emission reduction potential, lower marginal abatement costs, and CO_2 emissions. Provinces with major impacts on emissions reduction, such as Hebei, Shanxi, Guizhou, Inner Mongolia, Shandong and other provinces, should undertake more emission reduction tasks; if both dimensions of equity and efficiency are considered, it is necessary to focus on the decomposition of targets in emission reduction areas. The areas to be considered include Inner Mongolia, Shanxi, Hebei, Shandong, Liaoning and other provinces.

6. Analysis of the differences in interprovincial emission reduction potentials shows that the higher the level of economic development and the tertiary industry, the smaller the relative emission reduction potential, while the intensity of energy consumption, coal consumption accounts for the proportion of primary energy consumption, technological progress and capital deepening. Other factors are positively related to the emission reduction potential, and the industrial structure, energy intensity and energy consumption structure have a greater impact on the interprovincial emission reduction potential. The environmental Kuznets test on the

marginal abatement cost of CO_2 shows that with the increase of income, the marginal abatement cost of CO_2 shows a U-shaped curve with a decrease first and then an increase, and the lowest per-capita income level at the inflection point is 68,000–78,000 yuan.

The policy implications of this chapter are very clear. In the future, when decomposing regional targets for designing CO_2 emission reduction, we need to focus on the actual emissions and economic development level of the region from the perspectives of fairness and efficiency, combined with regional emission reduction potential, marginal abatement costs, and the degree of impact of emissions and emission reductions on the whole country is designed to meet the actual development of the provinces, with targeted and practical emission reduction targets. For provinces with greater emission reduction potential and affordability, they can bear more responsibility for emission reduction obligations, and for provinces with higher marginal abatement costs and lower emission reduction capacity, the emission reduction targets can be appropriately reduced. For each province, it is necessary to continue to deepen the energy conservation and emission reduction strategy in the Eleventh Five-Year Plan, seize the favorable opportunity of economic structure adjustment and optimization, and grasp the key points for the overall low level of industrial production and terminal energy efficiency. Use energy units and departments to eliminate backward production capacity, strengthen energy efficiency supervision of new projects, and vigorously improve energy efficiency; continuously optimize industrial structure, encourage the development of low-energy, low-emission service industries, and strengthen the transformation and upgrading of manufacturing industries; In the current and future fundamental position of China's energy, we strive to reach the international leading level in the field of clean coal utilization, accelerate the construction and service of renewable energy, and optimize the energy consumption structure.

Notes

1 This chapter is based on Regional Allocation of Carbon Dioxide Abatement in China, *China Economic Review*, 2012, 23(2) co-published by Wei Chu, Ni Jinlan and Du Limin.
2 Abbreviation for Brazil, South Africa, India, and China.
3 See *Amendment to the Law of Renewable Energies* taken into effect from April 1, 2010. Available online at: http://finance.sina.com.cn/roll/20100101/08167183891.shtml
4 In terms of the regional decomposition of energy reduction goals, NDRC has adopted the approach of self-declared emission reduction goals by different regions. Most of the provinces are in line with the goals of China, while some of them have set their goals lower or higher than energy conservation goal by 20% and emission reduction goal by 10%.

68 *Emission reduction analysis*

5 CO_2 emission intensity is impacted by energy consumption intensity and the energy emission coefficient. If energy can be conserved by 20%, the goal set in the Eleventh Five-Year Plan can be realized as expected with energy consumption intensity decline by 20% between 2010 and 2020, the goal of reducing CO_2 emission intensity by 40% can be achieved when energy consumption structure remains unchanged. If more renewable energies and clean energies can be adopted, CO_2 emission intensity can be further reduced.

6 This model is in fact consistent with directional distance function, which aims to ensure that desirable output can remain stable while reducing input redundancy and undesirable output redundancy, thus equivalent to $(-g_x, 0, -g_b)$ in directional distance function.

7 CO_2 emitted from fossil fuel energy consumption, transfer and cement production accounts for over 97% of the total CO_2 emissions. CO_2 is also emitted by lime, calcium carbide, and steel and iron production are not considered due to the difficulty in obtaining data and the very slight proportion.

8 If more effective sample points are included in comparison, such as Hong Kong, which is relatively more effective than Beijing, Shanghai and Guangdong, the optimal frontier will change and emission reduction potential of existing samples will also differ.

9 The original author adopted the accumulative emissions between 1915 and 1999 for consideration. Given the relative short development phase of industrialization and its lower level, per-capita emission is used for measurement.

10 The reciprocal of CO_2 emission reduction cost is reversed and all the data are conversed with the standard method of minimum – maximum, or $z_i=(x_i - MinX)/(MaxX - MinX)$ and the method of simple weighted mean is used when the value is combined into an exponent.

11 CO_2 emitted by burning of coal is 1.6 times that of natural gas, 1.2 times of oil while nuclear power, hydro power and solar power are clean energies with zero CO_2 release.

12 The Hausman test is used to determine fixed effect model and random effects model cannot reject random effects model (Prob>chi^2(6)=0.11, Chi^2(6)=10.36).

13 The Hausman test is used to examine the fixed model and the random model cannot reject zero hypotheses (Prob>chi^2(2)=0.93, Chi^2(2)=0.14).

4 Research on CO_2 marginal abatement cost in Chinese cities[1]

4.1 Urban greenhouse gas emissions

Climate change is a common challenge facing humanity. In response to climate change, China has proposed a relative emission reduction target of 40–45% reduction in CO_2 emission intensity by 2020. However, when decomposing regional carbon reduction targets, fairness and efficiency issues are faced. China has a vast territory, and there are large differences in resource endowments, industrial development, and energy structure in various regions. Regional economic development is extremely uneven (Liu Minglei et al., 2011; Liu Shucheng, 2008). In the previous provincial-level decomposition of China's "Eleventh Five-Year Plan" energy conservation and emission reduction targets, most provinces selected regional energy conservation and emission reduction targets similar to national targets, due to the lack of "bottom-up" regional emission reduction costs and emission reduction potential. Analysis by Price et al. (2011) shows that this one-size-fits-all allocation scheme is essentially contrary to the principles of fairness and efficiency (World Bank, 2009) and has led to consequences not considered by policy designers, such as individual provinces for industrial enterprises and even residents cutting power and falsified statistical data.

At the heart of the climate change issue is the allocation of carbon credits (Metz et al., 2007). A cost-effective allocation must ensure that the marginal costs of the last unit of each party's emissions are consistent, and the EU's carbon dioxide license trading market (EU-ETS) and the carbon tax system implemented in countries such as northern Europe are the two main market instruments. Under long-term equilibrium conditions, the license price in the carbon emission trading market is equal to the marginal abatement cost of the enterprise, or the government's carbon tax is equal to the marginal abatement cost of the enterprise. At this time, the total cost of emission reduction is minimized (Baumol & Oates, 1988). When designing a regional decomposition plan for carbon emission reduction targets, our government must not only consider the issue of equity between regions, but also consider the cost-effectiveness of the program; that is, the lower cost of marginal abatement

70 *Emission reduction analysis*

and greater emission reduction. Potential areas should be given more emission reduction tasks to minimize the overall cost of abatement.

How to reveal the true potential and cost of carbon emission reduction in various regions, thus avoiding the perfunctory attitude of local governments on emission reduction issues (Kousky & Schneider, 2003), is a realistic issue worthy of further discussion. Marginal abatement cost (MAC) can directly reflect the potential space and implementation cost of emission reduction in different countries and regions. In the past two decades, carbon dioxide, the World Bank, the United Nations, and other international organizations have widely used carbon dioxide marginal abatement cost information to economically assess different climate change mitigation policy sets (Kesicki & Strachan, 2011). This information is also applicable to the decomposition of carbon emission reduction targets in different regions of the country; that is, the CO_2 marginal abatement cost of each region can directly reflect the potential efficiency of regional carbon emission reduction, and at the same time, it can also be used for the carbon rights transaction to be established. The initial transaction price in the market provides a reference basis and provides a realistic basis for the government to formulate carbon taxes and other fiscal instruments (Wei et al., 2013). Because of its great practical significance, the research on the marginal abatement cost of carbon dioxide has become the focus and hotspot of theoretical research. In general, because carbon dioxide is not a normal commodity that can be traded, it cannot be reflected in market transactions to reflect its scarcity, that is, the lack of price signals for the special output of carbon dioxide; Like pollutants, there is a negative externality, and its damage to the economy, ecology, and human health is difficult to measure and aggregate through market prices, which will lead to an overestimation of the current level of economic output, and the true damage to carbon dioxide cannot be quantitatively evaluated. Therefore, the research on the marginal abatement cost of carbon dioxide has become the basis of much theoretical research and practical work such as green national economic accounting, environmental governance cost–benefit analysis, environmental policy formulation and evaluation.

Cities, as the most important gathering place for production activities, are also the concentrated source of fossil energy consumption and carbon emissions (Zhang Jinping et al., 2010). According to estimates by the World Bank, energy-related GHGs generated by Chinese cities account for 70% of total emissions. With the continuous advancement of urbanization and modernization, the Chinese population will increase to 350 million urban residents in the next 20 years (World Bank, 2012). The IEA predicts that by 2030, China's urban energy consumption will account for 83% of the country's total, and this will generate a considerable proportion of carbon emissions (IEA, 2007). Therefore, the city will become the main battlefield for controlling GHGs in China in the future.

Previous studies generally used provincial administrative divisions as the basic unit for investigation (Liu Minglei et al., 2011; Wang Qunwei et al.,

Marginal abatement cost 71

2011), and some documents based on national and industrial levels (Chen, 2005; Chen Shiyi, 2010c), but there are few studies on the city level. In fact, research by the OECD and the World Bank on China all believe that the use of cities as basic geographic units not only enables more effective implementation of environmental policies, but also contributes to the country's overall reduction in energy intensity and carbon intensity per unit of GDP (Hallegatte et al., 2011; World Bank, 2012). For urban managers, there are many specific measures that can be used to control GHG emissions: land-use decisions, residential business rulemaking, traffic control, and waste disposal; once emission reduction measures are implemented at the city level, Level 1 government learning and implementing similar policies can even affect smaller business and residential activities (Kousky & Schneider, 2003). Therefore, the consideration of carbon reduction in cities as the basic geographical unit is of great significance, and the marginal cost research of urban carbon emission reduction is a preliminary basic research, which is not only conducive to identifying the "highland" of carbon emission reduction in existing cities in China. With "squatting," it can also help to understand the drivers behind the differences in MACs in different cities.

This chapter is a study on the above background, which aims to answer the following three scientific questions. First, how high is the level of CO_2 emissions at the urban level in China? Second, what is the marginal cost of CO_2 emission reduction in China's cities? Third, what are the factors that affect the cost of CO_2 marginal abatement in cities?

The structure of this chapter is as follows: the first section summarizes the previous research literature; the second constructs the CO_2 MAC model and sets the corresponding functional formula; the third section is based on the statistical yearbook and related information on the urban level, input and output data for accounting and estimation; the fourth part calculates, compares, and analyzes the urban CO_2 MAC; the fifth section quantitatively analyzes the difference of urban CO_2 marginal abatement cost, and identifies the impact of urban carbon emission reduction and the main influencing factors of cost; finally, the relevant research conclusions are summarized, and policy implications and feasible countermeasures discussed.

4.2 Previous literature review

4.2.1 Research on urban carbon dioxide emissions

Foreign studies on urban CO_2 have been carried out previously. In addition to scientific accounting of CO_2 emissions at the urban level, different methods have been developed to identify and quantify the influencing factors. For example, Glaeser and Kahn (2010) used the 66 metropolitan cities in the USA as research samples, using the 2001 National Resident Survey and the 2000 Population and Housing Census data, according to the four energy types of gasoline, fuel oil, natural gas, and electricity consumption estimates of CO_2

72 Emission reduction analysis

emissions from households in transportation, heating, and daily energy consumption. The results show that San Diego has the lowest CO_2 emissions per household at 9 tons/year, while Memphis has the highest, reaching 32 tons/year. The CO_2 emission level is negatively correlated with population density, central aggregation degree, and winter temperature, and is positively correlated with the summer temperature of the region and the proportion of coal in the fuel of the regional power plant.

China's urban CO_2 emissions have also attracted the attention of a large number of scholars. Due to the insufficiency of urban construction and urban carbon inventory methodology in China, many scholars first calculate and estimate urban CO_2 emissions, and are committed to developing urban GHG inventory preparation methods that are consistent with China's national conditions and data characteristics. For example, Dhakal (2009) estimated and analyzed China's urban energy consumption and CO_2 emissions, and found that the city consumed 84% of the country's commercial energy, of which the largest 35 cities accommodate 18% of the population, consuming 40% of the country's energy and contribution of 40% of CO_2 emissions. In the four municipalities, per-capita energy consumption and per-capita CO_2 emissions have increased sevenfold since the 1990s, and further policy measures are urgently needed to alleviate further GHG emissions. Xie Shichen et al. (2009), based on the 2007 Shanghai Energy Balance Data and IPCC accounting method, estimated the CO_2 emissions from the burning of fossil energy in Shanghai, and plotted the CO_2 circulation map. The results show that in 1995–2007, Shanghai's energy-related CO_2 emissions were growing at an average annual rate of 5%. Among all sources in 2007, the power sector contributed the most at 35.4%, followed by the secondary industry (34.4%) and the transportation industry (23.8%), commercial and residential. Contributions to the agricultural sector are relatively small, at 4%, 2%, and 0.4%, respectively. Cai Bofeng (2011) defines the urban boundary and urban carbon emission range, and based on the GIS model, estimates the CO_2 emissions of prefecture-level cities in China in 2005, of which direct emissions reached 1.77 billion tons, while total emissions were 2.734 billion tons, accounting for 48.9% of the country's total emissions that year. Xu Cong et al. (2011) revised the CO_2 emission method caused by traditional energy consumption based on the NICE model developed by the Japan Industrial Technology Research Institute, and comprehensively examined agriculture, industry, construction, tertiary industry, and transportation, and the carbon dioxide emissions of the six major sectors of the residents' lives, and statistical data were given to estimate the city's CO_2 emissions in 2005–2008. Cai Bofeng (2012a) has a detailed comparison of the characteristics and differences between the international urban GHG inventory and the national GHG production. The former often adopts the consumption model, while the latter mainly adopts the production model. In view of the shortcomings of China's urban GHG inventory research, the paper can put forward the model of China's urban GHG inventory preparation, and use the data of Beijing and New York to make a practical comparison.

The results show that the total emissions of New York City is slightly lower than that of Beijing, and per-capita CO_2 emissions are slightly higher than those in Beijing.

Based on the scientific estimation of urban CO_2 emissions, scholars have further quantitatively analyzed the characteristics and driving factors of CO_2 emissions in China's cities. For example, Zhang Jinping et al. (2010) used the back propagation (BP) neural network method to select four municipalities of Beijing, Tianjin, Shanghai, and Chongqing as research samples, and measured and forecasted CO_2 historical emissions, emission structure and low carbon levels from 1995 to 2008. The analysis found that the CO_2 emissions of these four municipalities are increasing year by year, and the emission trend depends on the city's CO_2 emission structure. The optimization and upgrading of industrial structure have a significant effect on mitigating carbon emissions. Cai Bofeng (2012b), based on China's 0.1° large-scale CO_2 emission grid data, shows that the global Moran index is 0.27 and significant, indicating that there is a positive autocorrelation of CO_2 emissions in space, while the local Moran index reveals the key cities are the core areas of CO_2 emissions, which have significant positive spillover effects on the surrounding areas. These key cities directly determine the spatial pattern of CO_2 emissions in China. In addition, based on the analysis of 349 cities, it is found that there is a significant U-type EKC curve between economic and CO_2 emissions, that is, with the increase of per-capita GDP, the per-capita CO_2 shows a trend of rising first and then decreasing.

4.2.2 Carbon dioxide marginal abatement cost research

According to the method of deriving the MAC of carbon dioxide, the current research can be divided into three categories.

4.2.2.1 Based on expert carbon dioxide abatement costs

The basic idea is to use the most advanced available technical solutions as the reference line to conduct technical evaluations of various emission reduction measures in different countries and different industries. After summing up, calculate the emission reduction potential and abatement costs. Then, according to the order of their cost from low to high, they form a carbon dioxide MAC curve. This type of thinking is mainly based on engineering schemes for evaluation and summing up, so it is a kind of "bottom-up" research ideas. The most typical case is McKinsey's global carbon dioxide MAC curve (Mckinsey Company, 2009). Different emission reduction measures, such as nuclear power generation technology and waste water recycling technology, are ranked from low to high in terms of their emission reduction costs (CO_2 equivalent per ton). For measures with negative emission reduction costs, they are generally considered as priority measures or "regretless choices." In addition to different research institutions (such as the World Bank) and scholars

74 *Emission reduction analysis*

using carbon dioxide marginal abatement cost curve for Poland, Mexico, Ireland, etc., the country's carbon dioxide emission reduction potential and abatement costs are evaluated and analyzed (Johnson et al., 2009; Motherway & Walker, 2009; Poswiata & Bogdan, 2009).

Although the expert-based MAC curve is easy to understand and provides policy-makers with a rich set of tools and their respective priorities, the theoretical community is very controversial and believes that it has many shortcomings (Kesicki & Strachan, 2011). For example, there are differences in the boundaries and connotations of cost and benefit definitions that cause them to ignore other potential costs and benefits (Ekins et al., 2011); they do not take into account the interaction between emission reduction measures; rebound effect (Greening et al., 2000); does not evaluate the institutional barriers and transaction costs associated with implementing emission reduction measures, resulting in "negative" abatement costs (Bréchet & Jouvet, 2009), in addition, the MAC curve is mostly based on static technical characteristics and does not take into account the intertemporal dynamics and inertia characteristics of different abatement measures (Adrien & Stephane, 2011).

4.2.2.2 *Carbon dioxide abatement costs based on economic-energy models*

Such methods generally first construct a partial equilibrium or general equilibrium model, and then change the constraints; such as increasing the emission reductions to obtain the corresponding shadow price, you can get the MAC information at different emission reduction levels (Kesicki & Strachan, 2011). According to the model setting, it can be further divided into two types: one is to use a bottom-up energy system model, such as MARKAL, POLES model, etc. (Criqui et al., 1999; Gao Pengfei et al., 2004). Paying more attention to the energy sector, use non-aggregated data, and achieve optimal technology set through linear programming and set certain constraints. Most energy system models are used to analyze the situation of one country, and some can be used for international emissions trading analysis. The model uses a top-down computable general equilibrium analysis, such as EPPA, GEM-E3, and GREEN models (Ellerman & Decaux, 1998), using aggregated data from all sectors, and is subjected to simulation economic systems. The new equilibrium state after external disturbances (such as carbon taxes) derives the marginal abatement costs.

The MAC based on the economic-energy model can show the emission reduction potential of different sectors, but it is limited by the characteristics of the derived model itself, and there are some inherent defects. When using energy system models to derive marginal abatement costs, energy demand is exogenous and limited to the energy sector itself, ignoring linkages with other economic sectors; when using CGE models to derive marginal abatement costs, the impact of energy policy on other sectors and international trade can be captured, but CGE cannot accurately provide its adjustment path when calculating the new equilibrium after disturbance, and therefore may underestimate marginal abatement costs (Springer, 2003). In addition, the MACs estimated by different economic-energy models vary widely, mainly due to such economic-energy models themselves, such as setting a higher Aminton trade elasticity coefficient, or assuming alternative elasticity between elements. Higher will make the carbon dioxide marginal abatement cost lower, and the division of regions and sectors will lead to an overestimation of the carbon dioxide MAC (Fischer & Morgenstern, 2006); therefore, the assumptions imposed on the economic-energy model and the setting of the parameters will influence the final derivation of the carbon dioxide MAC distribution (Marklund & Samakovlis, 2007).

Taking different models at home and abroad as examples of China's marginal carbon abatement cost in 2010 (see Table 4.1), it can be seen that due to differences in parameter assumptions, model structure settings, and data sources of different models, the conclusions of model evaluation are often inconsistent (Gao Pengfei et al., 2004); from the current research progress of this type of model, it is not enough to provide reliable and sufficient information for decision-makers, and the theoretical model still needs to be improved.

4.2.2.3 Carbon dioxide abatement cost curve based on micro supply side

This type of model is based primarily on the micro level, defining the set of production possibilities by setting detailed production techniques and

Table 4.1 Results of China's 2010 marginal carbon abatement costs

Researchers (Institutes)	Models	Carbon emission reduction (Mt)	Marginal abatement costs (US$/t)	Emission reduction rate (%)	Marginal emission reduction costs (US$/t)
Massachusetts Institute of Technology	EPPA	100	4	10	9
Australian Bureau of Agriculture and Resource Economics	GTEM	100	8	10	18
He Juhuang et al. (2002)[a]	CGE			10.5	11
Gao Pengfei et al (2004)	MARKAL-MACRO	100	18	10	35
Wang Can et al. (2005)[a]	TED-CGE			10	12.5

Note: [a]The original text is expressed in RMB, and is converted at the current exchange rate for comparison purposes.

76 *Emission reduction analysis*

economic constraints. The derived carbon dioxide MACs can be interpreted as: carbon dioxide emissions under given market, technical conditions, and opportunity costs (De Cara & Jayet, 2011). Most of these models use production functions to quantitatively characterize the relationship between carbon dioxide MACs and emission reductions. Typical is the linear carbon dioxide MAC function defined by Nordhaus: this function can be used for research at the national level, MC is the marginal cost, r is the emission reduction rate, and the unknown parameters α and β are observed through the engineering data, such as cost-to-fit estimates (Nordhaus, 1991). Although the model can describe the trend of marginal abatement costs, it is difficult to obtain real data for countries.

This type of model has recently emerged as a new branch and development. With the expansion of production theory and the intersection with environmental economics, researchers have incorporated pollutants including carbon dioxide into production models based on the production theory framework. By constructing environmental production techniques to estimate the shadow price of carbon dioxide (Färe et al., 1993), due to the lesser theoretical assumptions of applied and realistic observations, such models have been used in a large number of carbon dioxide shadow prices at different levels. For example, Rezek and Campbell (2007) used the generalized maximum entropy to estimate the MACs of atmospheric pollutants such as carbon dioxide and sulfur dioxide in thermal power plants in the USA, and the feasibility of constructing an emissions trading market for different pollutants were discussed (Marklund & Samakovlis, 2007). The directional distance function is used to estimate the carbon dioxide abatement costs of EU member states. On this basis, the fairness and efficiency of EU carbon emission reduction target allocation are discussed in Park and Lim (2009) and are based on transcendental logarithmic form. The distance function estimates the carbon dioxide MACs of thermal power plants in Korea and discusses the costs of different abatement options; Choi et al. (2012) use non-radial redundancy-based data envelopment analysis for China's interprovincial carbon dioxide MACs. Domestic scholars have also begun to use this idea to evaluate industrial MACs. For example, Chen Shiyi (2010c, 2011) evaluated the marginal abatement cost of carbon dioxide in different sectors of China's industry, and initially discussed the issue of environmental tax; Tu Zhengge (2012) also examined the carbon dioxide abatement costs of China's eight major industrial sectors and discussed the choice of emission reduction strategies.

In summary, the above three research methods and perspectives have their scope and shortcomings. The expert-based marginal abatement cost curve is simple and easy to read, but its bottom-up analysis based on static individuals makes it difficult to dynamically evaluate the combined effects of abatement measures; the MAC results from the economic-energy model estimates. It is relatively stable, but the model construction is complex, and it is sensitive

Marginal abatement cost   77

to assumptions and parameters. The conclusion is lack of consistency. The MAC based on the production supply side is simple and intuitive, but the current research is still in a discrete "point" shape.

This chapter will focus on the third method, which uses the pollutant price model derived from the production function to estimate the marginal cost of CO_2 reduction.

4.3 Marginal abatement cost model

4.3.1 Directional distance function based on output

This chapter will use the Directional Distance Function (DDF) to derive the marginal abatement cost model for pollutants. The model is proposed by Chung et al. (1997). The basic idea is to examine the decrease in undesired output while examining the increase in desirable output, when the desired output cannot continue to expand or the undesired output fails to continue decreasing, the observation point is at the forefront of efficiency. The specific application to China can be seen in Hu Angang et al. (2008) for the measurement of China's interprovincial total factor productivity with different pollutants; Tu Zhengge (2008, 2009) and Tu Zhengge and Liu Leizhen (2011) on industrial productivity and industrial SO_2 shadow price measurement. Wang Bing et al. (2010, 2011) measure the interprovincial Malmquist–Luenberger productivity under environmental control, and Chen Shiyi (2010a, b, 2011) China's industrial CO_2 abatement costs and green productivity measurement and other literature. The model is basically expressed as follows.

Assume the input vector, the desirable output vector, the undesired output, and the production technique is defined as $P(x) = \{(y, b): x$ can produce $(y, b)\}$, which has two characteristics:

(i) Consensus output is freely disposed of, and undesired output is weakly disposed. This means
    when $y, b) \in P(x)$, $y' \leq y$, $(y', b) \in P(x)$; when $(y, b) \in P(x)$, $0 \leq \theta \leq 1$, $(\theta y, \theta b) \in P(x)$.
(ii) Consensus and undesired output are jointly produced. Its mathematical expression is $(y, b) \in P(x)$, if $b = 0$, then $y = 0$. It shows that if you want zero pollution, you can only stop production, otherwise as long as production, it will produce undesired output.

The directional distance function first needs to construct a direction vector of $g = (g_y, -g_b)$, and $g \in \mathfrak{R}^M \times \mathfrak{R}^J$, which is used to constrain the direction of change of the desired output and the undesired output. The size of the change, that is, the increase (decrease) of the desired (unintended) output on the path specified by the direction vector, the specific choice of the direction vector

78 Emission reduction analysis

depends on factors such as research needs or policy orientation preferences. The directional output distance function can be defined as:

$$D(x,y,b;g_y,-g_b) = \sup\{\beta : (y+\beta g_y, b-\beta g_b) \in P(x)\} \quad (4.1)$$

β represents the degree to which a given unit's desirable output (unsatisfactory output) can be expanded (reduced) compared to the most efficient unit on the leading-edge production surface. If β = 0, it means that this decision unit is on the leading-edge production side, which is the most efficient. The larger the value of β, the greater the potential for the desired output of the decision-making unit to continue to increase, and the smaller the space for the reduction of undesired output, so the lower the efficiency.

The directional distance function inherits the basic properties of the distance function (Färe et al., 2005), including a monotonous decrease in the desired output, a monotonous increase in the undesired output, and, in addition, a conversion attribute, namely:

$$D(x, y+\alpha, b-\alpha; g_y, -g_b) + \alpha = D(x, y, b; g_y, -g_b) \quad (4.2)$$

The DDF is a general form of Shephard's output distance function (Chung et al., 1997). When the direction vector g = (1, 0), the Shephard yield distance function is a special case of the directional distance function. Figure 4.1 depicts the relationship between the two: $P(x)$ is the set of possible production, the output distance function is along the ray determined by the origin and observation point A, and the desired output y is the same as the undesired output b. The ratio is extended to point C on the frontier surface; and the idea of the directional output distance function is: the path of the given direction vector g = (g_y, $-g_b$), the expansion of the desired output y, while reducing the

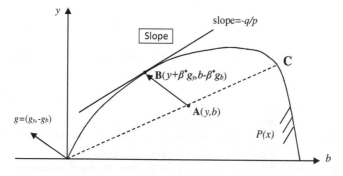

Figure 4.1 Directional distance function and shadow price

undesired production exit b to reach point B of the frontier of the output. Obviously, for the distance function, moving from the invalid point A to the C point on the leading edge, there is either an "excessive" undesired output, or a "insufficient" desirable output, while the directional distance function is not considered.

4.3.2 Shadow price model of pollutants

As pointed out by Chamber et al. (1998) and Färe et al. (2001), there is a dual relationship between the direction distance function and the income function based on the output radial direction, so if Shepard's Lemma is applied to its duality, you can get the shadow price of the output. The income function can be expressed as:

$$R(x, p, q) = \max\{py - qb : D(x, y, b; 1, -1) \geq 0\} \tag{4.3}$$

where $p = (p_1, \supset, p_M) \in \mathfrak{R}_+^M$ and $q = (q_1, \supset, q_J) \in \mathfrak{R}_+^J$, respectively, are the shadow prices of the desired output y and the undesired output b, the function $R(x, p, q)$ represents the producer, given the desired output price p and the undesired output price q, the biggest gain that can be obtained. Because the direction distance function is non-negative (Chambers et al., 1998), namely:

$$D(x, y, b; g) \geq 0 \rightarrow (y, b) \in P(x) \tag{4.4}$$

therefore, the income function (4.3) can be expressed as a direction distance function as

$$R(x, p, q) = \max\left\{py + qb : \vec{D}(x, y, b : g) \geq 0\right\} \tag{4.5}$$

Because the expansion of output cannot exceed the non-parametric frontier production surface, the relationship between the boundary benefit function and the income function can be obtained and expressed as the direction distance function in (4.5):

$$D(x, y, b : g) \leq \left\{R(x, p, q) - (py + qb)\right\} / \left\{pg_y - qg_b\right\} \tag{4.6}$$

Once the extreme points are obtained, the Shepard lemma can be applied to obtain the shadow price relationship between the output and the pollutants. Finally, the shadow price ratio of the undesired output and the desired output can be equal to the marginal conversion rate (Färe et al., 1993). In the form of parameterized distance function, it can be expressed as the ratio of the distance function to the first derivative of the undesired output and the desired

80 *Emission reduction analysis*

output. In the non-parametric form, it is the undesired output and the desired output in the dual linear programming. The dual value of the constraint is:

$$\frac{q}{p} = \frac{\partial D(x, y, b : g) / \partial b}{\partial D(x, y, b : g) / \partial y} = \frac{\partial y}{\partial b} = MRTT_{y,b} \tag{4.7}$$

In (4.7), the relative price of the output to the pollutant is equal to the relative change in the output caused by the change of one unit of pollutant, that is, the output reduced by abandoning one unit of pollution (or increasing the output of one unit of pollution) so that the shadow price model of the pollutant can be obtained. If we further assume that the shadow price of the desired output is equal to its market price (or normalized to 1), then the price q of the undesired output can be expressed as the product of the explicit price p and the marginal conversion rate of the output contaminant, which is:

$$q = p \times \frac{\partial D / \partial b}{\partial D / \partial y} \tag{4.8}$$

In Figure 4.1, the shadow price expressed by (4.8) is the tangent slope of the projection point of any point on the leading-edge production surface, which reflects the trade-off between the desired output y and the undesired output b. That is, the value of the output that is abandoned when reducing pollutants, and therefore can be used as the opportunity cost of the pollutant or the marginal abatement cost (Färe et al., 1993; Murty et al., 2007).

4.3.3 *Empirical model setting and solving*

According to the specific expression form of the directional distance function, it is mainly divided into two types: parametric and non-parametric. Among them, the parametric model mainly includes superlogarithm, quadratic and stochastic frontier models; in the environmentally sensitive productivity model with parameterized efficiency frontiers, the DEA model and the SBM model are mainly used (Wei Chu et al., 2011). Parametric models have their own strengths compared to non-parametric models. In general, non-parametric DEA does not require a-priori assumptions on the production function structure, but is sensitive to sample data. The abnormal sample value error affects the position of the production front; in addition, the non-parametric DEA method is mostly used for productivity measurement because it is difficult to obtain. The first derivative is therefore rarely used to estimate the shadow price of undesired output (Färe & Grosskopf, 1998). In comparison, the parametric method needs to preset the production frontier as a certain function expression. The advantage is that the parameter expression can be differentiated and algebraic (Hailu & Veeman, 2000), and the non-conformity of each decision unit can be calculated. The shadow price is produced, so the parametric solution method is widely used in empirical research.

In addition, in the selection of the parametric model form, the superlog (translog) and quadratic functions can generally be selected for fitting. Table 4.2 compares the similarities and differences between the model forms and assumptions of related literatures using the directional distance function to solve the parametric model at home and abroad. It can be seen that the measurement of carbon shadow price by the parametric model of directional distance function is very common in the world. The preset function forms mainly include superlogarithm and quadratic forms. Domestic research on carbon abatement costs is still relatively rare. In the existing shadow price literature based on DDF, most of them use a non-parametric distance function method (Chen Shiyi, 2010; Tu Zhengge, 2008, 2009; Liu Minglei et al., 2011); in the application of the parameter method, only Chen Shiyi (2010) measured the shadow price of CO_2 in 38 industries in China through the translog function form.

In the theoretical study of functional form selection, Färe et al. (2010) and Vardanyan and Noh (2006) used the Monte Carlo method to compare the performance of these two types of functions and found that regardless of the type of production technology, the type functions are superior to the super-logarithmic function, and the super-logarithmic function often violates the relevant assumptions required by the DDF. The result is often much lower than the quadratic function, and there is a certain deviation. Therefore, based on the comprehensive research conclusions, this chapter finally uses the parameterized quadratic function to express the DDF.

In this chapter, the direction vector $g = (1, -1)$ is set. At this time, the choice of direction vector satisfies the general environmental regulation requirements, that is, the expansion of desirable output and the reduction of undesired output are symmetrical. In the selection of input–output variables, inputs mainly include: capital (x_1), labor (x_2) and energy (x_3), the desired output is the economic output of each region (y), and the undesired output is CO_2 emissions (b), taking into account individual differences (k) and time trends (t) in cities. The specific direction distance function is set to:

$$
\begin{aligned}
D(x,y,b;g) = {} & \alpha_0 + \sum_{n=1}^{3}\alpha_n x_n + \beta_1 y + \gamma_1 b + \frac{1}{2}\sum_{n=1}^{3}\sum_{n=1}^{3}\alpha_{nn} x_n x_n + \frac{1}{2}\beta_2 y^2 \\
& + \frac{1}{2}\gamma_2 b^2 + \sum_{n=1}^{3}\delta_n x_n y + \sum_{n=1}^{3}\eta_n x_n b + \mu y b + \phi k + \varphi t
\end{aligned}
\tag{4.9}
$$

In order to solve the unknown parameters in the empirical model (4.9), a linear programming method is used for estimation (Färe et al., 1993, 2005; Hailu &

Table 4.2 Comparison of literature based on the parametric model for directional distance function at home and abroad

Authors	Samples	Variables	Function	Model assumption				
				$D\geqq0$	$D0\leqq0$	$dD/dy\leqq0$	$dD/dB\geqq0$	$dD/dx\geqq0$
Salnykov and Zelenyuk (2005)	50 countries	Input: labor/capital/ energy/land; consensus output: GNP; unsatisfactory output: $CO_2/SO_2/NO_x$	Translog_LP	√				
Färe et al. (2005)	209 US power plants 1993/ 1997	Input: labor/capital/energy; desirable output: power generation; undesired output: SO_2	Quadratic_LP Quadratic_COLS	√ √		√	√	
Färe et al. (2006)	36 US states 1960–1996	Input: labor/capital/energy/land; desirable output: livestock/ crop; undesired output: leaching/runoff	Quadratic_LP	√		√	√	√
Marklund and Samakovlis (2007)	15 EU countries 1990–2000	Input: labor/capital/energy; desirable output: GDP; undesired output: CO_2	Quadratic_LP Quadratic_COLS	√ √	√	√	√	√
Murty et al. (2007)	Five Indian power plants 1996–2004	Input: labor/capital/energy; desirable output: power generation; undesired output:SO_2/NO_x	Quadratic_ML	√				
Chen Shiyi (2010)	38 industrial sectors in China 1980–2008	Input: labor/capital/energy/ intermediate inputs; desirable output: gross industrial output; undesired output: CO_2	Translog_LP	√		√	√	

Note: Translog and Quadratic are two preset function forms of directional distance function parameters respectively; LP, COLS, and ML refer to linear program, corrected ordinary least square, and maximum likelihood, respectively.

Veeman, 2000), specifically including the following objective functions and constraints:

$$\min \sum_{k=1}^{K} \left[D\left(x_k, y_k, b_k; 1, -1\right) - 0 \right]$$

s.t.

(i) $\quad D\left(x_k, y_k, b_k; g\right) \geq 0, k = 1,\ldots, K$

(ii) $\partial D\left(x_k, y_k, b_k; g\right) / \partial b \geq 0, k = 1,\ldots, K$ $\qquad$ (4.10)

(iii) $\partial D\left(x_k, y_k, b_k; g\right) / \partial y \leq 0, k = 1,\ldots, K$

(iv) $\partial D\left(x_{n,k}, y_k, b_k; g\right) / \partial x_{n,k} \geq 0, n = 1,\ldots, N; k = 1,\ldots, K$

(v) $\beta_1 - \gamma_1 = -1, \beta_2 = \mu = \gamma_2, \delta_n = \eta_n, n = 1, 2, 3$

(vi) $\alpha_{nn'} = \alpha_{n'n}, n, n' = 1, 2, 3$

In (4.10), the objective function formula minimizes the dispersion of all samples with the leading edge (Aigner & Chu, 1968), and constraint (i) ensures that all observation points are feasible; that is, they satisfy the directional distance, the non-negative feature of the function; constraint (ii) imposes a monotonous increase in the undesired output b; i.e., if the undesired output b increases, the direction distance function value D does not decrease; (iii) is the monotonic decline of the desired output y; i.e., other conditions remain unchanged, if the desired output y increases, the inefficiency D will not increase; constraint (iv) is the monotonic constraint imposed on each input element, That is, when other conditions are constant, if the input x increases, the direction distance function does not decrease (Marklund & Samakovlis, 2007); constraints (v) and (vi) correspond to the transformation properties and symmetry of the direction distance function, respectively.

4.4 Input–output data at the city level

4.4.1 Data sources and processing

This chapter uses the "three inputs–two outputs" data for model demonstration. Among them, capital, labor, and energy are the input factors, and GDP and CO_2 emissions are taken as the desired and undesired outputs, respectively.

The selection of urban samples in China is based on the statistics of the main 354 prefecture-level cities and above published in the *China Urban Statistical Yearbook*. In order to prevent the changes in the statistical caliber caused by the change of administrative divisions, the administrative divisions have been screened over the calendar year. As the *China Urban Statistical Yearbook* does not publish energy consumption information of local cities, the only publicly available data source is the urban energy consumption data in the *China Environmental Yearbook*, but the key points in the *China*

84 Emission reduction analysis

Environmental Yearbook are selected. The city is not the same as the city covered by the *China Urban Statistical Yearbook*. Therefore, according to the availability of data, the urban sample matching the final variable is reduced to 113 prefecture-level cities. In addition, due to the lack of historical fixed capital investment data in nine cities including Sanya City, Haikou City, Lhasa City of Tibet Autonomous Region, and Xining City of Qinghai Province, the number of urban samples selected was 104 cities.

The time period selection of the sample also varies due to differences in different data sources. In estimating the capital stock, the longest possible time series is needed to eliminate the impact of the initial capital stock bias on the subsequent sequence, so the investment data of the fixed assets in the *China Urban Statistical Yearbook* goes back to 1994; *The China Environmental Yearbook* did not begin to publish more complete energy consumption data for key cities nationwide until 2001. In addition, China's prefecture-level cities have undergone many adjustments, which has led to the continuous change in the number of prefecture-level cities in the *China Urban Statistical Yearbook*, and the key cities announced in the *China Environmental Yearbook* remain basically unchanged, so in order to ensure data consistency, the final data starting and ending year sequence is determined as 2001–2008. For a list of specific cities, see Table 4.14.

4.4.2 Main variables

Labor data (*L*): foreign countries generally use working hours as the input variable of labor, but limited by the availability of data, using the number of employees in the unit at the end of the year published in the *China Urban Statistical Yearbook*, the unit is 10,000.

GDP data (*Y*): the economic output data of each city are taken from the *China Urban Statistical Yearbook* over the years, calculated at the constant price in 2001, and the unit is 100 million yuan.

Capital stock (*K*): the "permanent inventory method" can be used to estimate the actual annual capital stock, as follows:

$$K_{i,t} = I_{i,t} + (1 - \delta_i) K_{i,t-1} \tag{4.11}$$

Here, $K_{i,t}$ is the capital stock of the city i at year t, $I_{i,t}$ is the investment of the city i at year t, and δ_i is the fixed capital depreciation rate. When the base period year is selected, the above equation can be converted to:

$$K_t = K_0 1 - \delta^t + \sum_{k=1}^{t} I_k (1 - \delta)^{t-k} \tag{4.12}$$

Marginal abatement cost 85

To calculate the capital stock for each year, three important parameters need to be determined.

First, the capital depreciation rate δ_i, with reference to relevant literature, can be assumed that China's fixed capital depreciation rate is 9.7% each year (Zhang Jun et al., 2004).

The second parameter is the base period initial capital stock K_0, estimated according to the method of King and Levine (1994). Assuming that the capital-output ratio is constant under steady state conditions, it can be expressed as:

$$k_i = i_i / (\delta + \lambda g_i + (1 - \lambda)g_w) \tag{4.13}$$

Here, i_i is the investment rate of urban i in steady state, which can be expressed by the average investment rate of the city, $\lambda g_i + (1 - \lambda)g_w$, which is the economic growth rate at steady state. It is obtained by weighting the growth rate of the city and the average growth rate of the national city, where λ is a measure of the mean value of growth, and according to the literature, the value is generally 0.25 (Easterly et al., 1993); g_i is the average growth rate of the city; g_w is the average growth rate of the national city, with 1994 as the initial year. Then the initial capital stock of the year can be expressed as $K_{i,94} = k_i \times Y_{i,94}$, where Y is the real GDP of city i in 1994.

The third parameter is the fixed asset investment amount $I_{i,t}$ of each year, which can be obtained through the fixed asset investment and urban fixed asset investment price index of each city over the years, but as the *China Urban Statistical Yearbook* has not announced the investment price index, the urban GDP deflator is replaced.

Using the above method, the complete capital stock sequence can be calculated. The data used are all derived from the data published in the *China Urban Statistical Yearbook* and calculated at the constant price in 2001. The unit is 100 million yuan.

Energy consumption data (E): because the *China Urban Statistical Yearbook* has not published energy consumption data at the city level over the years, when selecting energy data, reference and use of relevant energy data from different data sources: first, the three major fossil energy consumption data of fuel coal, raw coal, and fuel oil (in 10,000 tons) in industrial energy consumption in key cities; second, the *China City Statistical Yearbook* published the household gas consumption in each city and household LPG consumption; in addition to the historical data of the cities in *China's Energy Statistics Yearbook* (in 10,000 kWh). Therefore, the city's energy consumption includes three parts: industrial energy, domestic energy, and electricity consumption. For traffic energy information, due to the inability to obtain the number of cars, fuel consumption standards and travel frequencies at various city levels, accurate accounting cannot be performed. This may also be the place to be improved in the future after having the car travel data.

86 Emission reduction analysis

Table 4.3 Various energy standard coal conversion factors and carbon emission factors

Energy products	Unit	Standard coal conversion factor	Default value of carbon content (kgC/GJ)	Average low calorific value (kcal/kg, kcal/m₃)	CO₂ emission coefficient (kg CO₂/kg, kg CO₂/m₃)
Fuel coal	Ton	0.7143	25.8	5,000	1.980
Raw coal	Ton	0.9	25.8	6,300	2.495
Fuel oil	Ton	1.4286	21.1	10,000	3.239
Gas	Ten cubic meters	5.714	12.1	4,000	0.743
Liquefied petroleum gas	Ton	1.7143	17.2	12,000	3.169
Energy used	Kilowatt hour	0.1229	–	860	–

The calculation formula for energy consumption is:

$$E_{i,t} = E^{industry} + E^{household} = \sum E_{i,t} \times coef_{i,t} \qquad (4.14)$$

In formula (4.14), E_i is the total consumption of various fossil energy sources in city i, and *coef* is the folding coefficient of different energy products. Refer to the standard coal conversion coefficient published in the *China Energy Statistical Yearbook* to convert various energy consumption values into uniform units of tons of standard coal according to the combustion heat value of different energy sources (see Table 4.3 for the energy discount coefficient).

CO_2 emission data (*b*): there are no research institutions publishing data on CO_2 emissions at the urban level. However, because CO_2 emissions are mainly derived from the consumption and conversion of fossil energy, the consumption of different fossil energy products and their carbon emissions are converted according to the above factor to estimate urban CO_2 emissions. The specific accounting formula is as follows:

$$CO_2 = \sum E_i \times CF_i \times CC_i \times COF_i \times \frac{44}{12} \qquad (4.15)$$

Here, CO_2 represents the estimated total amount of carbon dioxide emissions from various fossil energy consumption; i represents the energy consumed by various sources, E_i is the total consumption of various fossil energy in urban i, and CF_i is the conversion factor, that is, the average of various fuels. Calorific value CC_i is the carbon content, which means the carbon content of the unit heat, COF_i is the carbon oxidation factor, which reflects the

Marginal abatement cost 87

oxidation rate of the energy, and 44/12 means the carbon mass is converted to carbon dioxide, the conversion factor of molecular mass. Among them, $CF_i \times CC_i \times COF_i$ is called the carbon emission coefficient, and $CF_i \times CC_i \times COF_i \times 44/12$ is the carbon dioxide emission coefficient. The carbon emission factors of various emission sources are mainly based on the emission list coefficient of IPCC (2006) and are adjusted in conjunction with the low-calorific value of various energy products in China published in the *China Energy Statistical Yearbook*. The conversion factors and emission factors of the final urban energy products are shown in Table 4.3.

4.4.3 Data feature statistics

According to the above data accounting, the descriptive statistics of each input–output variable are shown in Table 4.4.

In order to better reflect the regional differences, the input–output variables of the eastern, central, and western regions were compared, as shown in Table 4.5. It can be seen that they show significant differences. On the input factors, the characteristics of the eastern cities are higher than

Table 4.4 Descriptive statistics of input–output variables (2001–2008)

Variables	Unit	Samples	Average	Standard deviation	Minimum	Maximum
Labor (L)	10,000 people	832	47.46	68.74	2.32	696.25
Capital stock (K)	100 million yuan	832	1,148.80	1,902.63	44.31	17,784.69
Energy consumption (E)	10,000 tons of standard coal	832	920.66	816.89	16.61	5,694.50
GDP (Y)	100 million yuan	832	825.74	1,358.56	19.29	13,560.44
CO_2 (b)	10,000 tons	832	2,219.49	1,952.49	31.58	12,825.78

Table 4.5 Comparison of output and input in terms of regions (2001–2008)

Unit	Eastern	Central	Western
Labor	62.6 (92.0)	35.8 (33.1)	33.2 (35.1)
Capital stock	1,678.1 (2,542.4)	723.8 (850.0)	664.3 (877.2)
Energy consumption	1,169.2 (962.2)	800.5 (628.4)	607.8 (530.3)
GDP	1,030.5 (1,436.8)	453.3 (514.7)	353.5 (395.7)
CO_2	2,757.1 (2,238.7)	2,004.9 (1,644.4)	1,494.2 (1,344.2)

Note: The mean value is reported and the standard deviation is shown in parentheses.

88 *Emission reduction analysis*

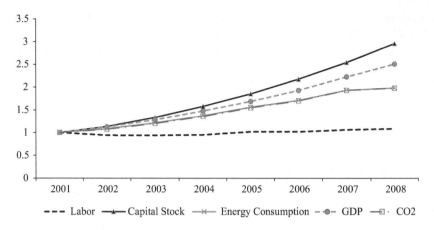

Figure 4.2 Trends of input and output variables (2001–2008)

those of the central cities, and the central cities are higher than those of the western cities. In terms of output and pollution emissions, there is also a significant decline in the east and west. Some analysis based on the provincial level is consistent.

In addition, in order to understand the time-varying trend of each input–output variable, the variables in 2001 were processed = 1, and the trend is shown in Figure 4.2. It can be seen that the labor force changes are relatively flat and the changes are small. Under the high-speed capital stock, GDP has achieved rapid growth. If it was 1 in 2001, it will increase to 2.5 in 2008, with an average annual growth rate of 14%. Energy consumption is highly consistent with the trend of CO_2 emissions, with an average annual growth rate of around 10%, and both are lower than GDP growth rate, which also indicates the energy consumption intensity (= energy consumption/GDP) and CO_2 emission intensity of these cities (= the two indicators of CO_2 emissions/GDP are declining year by year).

Table 4.6 compares the characteristics of the 2008 sample cities with all 354 prefecture-level cities. It can be seen that the selected 104 sample cities are generally better representative of China's urban entities, with a land area of 41.8% of all cities, 60% of all urban population, and labor accounts for 74% of all urban labor, creating 78% of GDP in all cities. In addition, these 104 sample cities are also the driving force for China's rapid economic growth. They are less than 3% of the country's land area. These cities have a 17% national population and 7% of the labor force, but the economic value created has reached 46%. Of course, while supporting the rapid development of the national economy, these cities also consume 44% of energy and emit 46% of CO_2. Therefore, the 104 cities selected by the Institute are not only the support points for China's economic development, but also energy-intensive consumption and pollution-intensive areas.

Marginal abatement cost 89

Table 4.6 Comparison of sample representativeness (2008)

Indicators	Sample cities	All prefecture-level cities[a]	Nationwide[b]
Land coverage (square kilometers)	261,923	626,361 (41.8%)	9,600,000 (2.7%)
Population (10,000 people)	22,773.05	37,619.34 (60.5%)	132,802 (17.1%)
Employed people (10,000 people)	5,343.48	7,186.3 (74.4%)	75,564 (7.1%)
GDP (100 million yuan)	145,001.5	186,189.7 (77.9%)	314,045.4 (46.2%)
Energy consumption (10,000 tons standard coal)	128,231	–	291,448 (44%)
CO_2 emission (10,000 tons)	31,0092.9	–	668,465.1[c] (46.4%)

Note: The proportion of 104 sample cities is reported in brackets.
(a) The data comes from the annual database of the China Economic and Trade Network, including 354 cities in all prefecture-level cities, subprovincial cities, and municipalities directly under the Central Government.
(b) The data are from the China Economic Database, which is the national aggregate data;
(c) Data from the US Energy Agency's International Energy Statistics, the carbon footprint of fossil energy (www.eia.gov).

4.5 Empirical results

4.5.1 Parameter estimation

Based on the above theoretical model and data, the MINOS 5 solver of the General Algebraic Modeling System (GAMS 22.0) software is used to first solve the unknown parameters in the model (4.9)–(4.10). To overcome the convergence problem in linear programming, all variables were normalized using the mean of input and output (Färe et al., 2005). The standardized data mean that the input–output set $(x, y, b) = (1, 1, 1)$; that is, for a representative city, it uses the average input to obtain the average output. The results of all the solved parameters are shown in Table 4.7. Due to the large number of urban samples, the individual effect estimates are shown in Table 4.15.

According to the estimated parameter values in Table 4.7, the inefficiency values and shadow prices of different cities in different years can be estimated. As the direction distance function also needs to satisfy the null-jointness hypothesis, if the contaminant $b = 0$ and $y > 0$, the DDF should not be feasible; i.e., DDF<0. The hypothesis was validated using the estimated parameters. A total of 11 observations out of all 832 observations violated this hypothesis. In addition, there are two observations in the calculation of the

90 Emission reduction analysis

Table 4.7 Direction distance function parameter estimates

Pending parameter	Variable	Estimated results	Pending parameter	Variables	Estimated results
α_0	constant	−0.62264	ϕ	Cities	See Table 4.15
α_L	L	0.09458			
α_K	K	0.48296	φ	2001	0.0000
α_E	E	0.00000		2002	−0.00203
β_y	y	−0.91111		2003	−0.00410
$\gamma_b = \beta_y + 1$	b	0.08889		2004	−0.00234
α_{LL}	L^2	−0.08220		2005	0.00000
α_{LK}	LK	0.00503		2006	0.01013
α_{LE}	LE	0.08634		2007	0.03674
α_{KK}	K^2	−0.05478		2008	0.08665
α_{KE}	KE	0.00311			
α_{EE}	E^2	−0.08944			
$\beta_{yy} = \gamma_{bb} = \mu_{yb}$	y^2, b^2, yb	0.01960			
$\delta_{Ly} = \eta_{Lb}$	Ly, Lb	0.04137			
$\delta_{Ky} = \eta_{Kb}$	Ky, Kb	0.01151			
$\delta_{Ey} = \eta_{Eb}$	Ey, Eb	0.00000	Obs	832	

Table 4.8 Descriptive statistics of eight direction distance functions and shadow prices

Variables		Unit	Sample	Average	Standard Deviation	Minimum	Maximum
Direction distance function	ddf	−	819	0.0767	0.1370	0.0000	1.5257
Shadow price	q	10,000 yuan/ton	819	0.0967	0.2992	0.0322	5.5799

shadow price, which is meaningless because the denominator is 0. Therefore, 819 observations satisfying all assumptions were finally retained for analysis.

Table 4.8 reports descriptive statistics on the direction distance function and shadow price of the sample city. It can be seen that among the 819 observations, the mean value of the directional distance function is 0.0767, which means that on average, the inefficient production of the city is 7.67%. Because the average output of representative cities is 82.574 billion yuan, the average CO_2 emissions are 221.9940 million tons, which means that if the efficiency is improved, the output can be increased to 825.74×0.0767=6.33 billion, and the emission reduction can be 2219.49×0.0767 = 17.02 million tons of CO_2.

According to the shadow price information, in order to reduce the extra unit of CO_2, the marginal abatement cost of the city is 967 yuan/ton, which is converted according to the 2001 US dollar exchange rate of 8.277 yuan.

Marginal abatement cost 91

Table 4.9 Comparison of the results of CO_2 shadow price calculation in different literatures

Authors	Year	Samples	Models	Methods	Average CO_2 shadow price
Rezek and Campbell (2007)	1998	260 US coal power plants	DF	OLS, GME	18.3–20.9 US$/ton
Salnykov and Zelenyuk (2005)		50 countries	DDF	LP	331.89 US$/ton
Marklund and Samakovlis (2007)	1990–2000	15 EU countries	DDF	LP, COLS	490–510 Euro/ton
Qin et al. (2011)	2007	19 power plants in Shanghai	DF	LP	234.2 yuan/ton
Wei et al. (2013)	2004	124 power plants in Zhejiang	DDF	LP, ML	612–2059 yuan/ton
Chen (2010b)	1980–2008	38 two-digit sectors in China	DDF	LP	3.27 (10,000 yuan/ton, unchanged price in 1990)
Liu et al. (2011)	2005–2007	30 provinces in China	DDF	DEA	1,739 yuan/ton
This book	2001–2008	104 cities in China	DDF	LP	967 yuan/ton (116.8 US$/ton, unchanged price 200)

The average abatement cost per ton of CO_2 is US$116.8/ton. Table 4.9 lists the results of this chapter compared with the literature results of recent CO_2 shadow price calculations. Due to the different model methods and data acquisition, the estimation results of CO_2 shadow price are also very different. Rezek and Campbell (2007) are mainly due to the distance function model adopted, which leads to the estimated CO_2 shadow price is lower, which is the same as Vardanyan and Noh. The finding of (2006) is consistent, that is, if the Shephard distance function model is used to estimate the shadow price, it will be significantly lower than the estimated value of the directional distance function. The shadow prices measured by Marklund and Samakovlis (2007) and Salnykov and Zelenyun (2005) are much higher than the results of this chapter. This is mainly related to sample selection. They choose Western developed countries as emission reduction samples, and compared it with their MACs.

In the study of the Chinese sample, Qin Shaojun et al. (2011) estimated the Shanghai power plant as the CO_2 marginal abatement cost was 234.2 yuan/ton; Wei et al. (2013) studied the Zhejiang thermal power plant enterprise in a similar study. For the sample, the MAC obtained by the maximum likelihood estimation method is 612 yuan/ton. If the linear programming method is used, the marginal abatement cost is 2,059 yuan/ton; and Chen Shiyi (2010b) is mainly based on the industrial industry level. To analyze, his estimated result of 32,700 yuan/ton is significantly higher than the results based on the city level. In addition, Liu Minglei et al. (2011), based on the non-parametric DEA method, the average interprovincial MAC in China from 2005 to 2007 was 1739 yuan/ton, which is similar to the conclusion of this chapter.

4.5.2 Marginal abatement cost discussion

It can also be seen from Table 4.8 that the shadow price is very different, the minimum value being 322 yuan/ton, and the maximum value 55,790 yuan/ton, which reflects the huge difference in the cost of abatement between cities. A detailed analysis will be conducted below.

First, the time series of shadow prices in eastern, central, and western cities were compared. It can be seen from Figure 4.3 that during the inspection period, the MACs of the central and western cities are close, and the trend is very consistent, showing a slow increasing trend, with the western cities slightly lower, from 502 yuan/ton in 2001 to 655 yuan/ton in 2008. That of the central city is slightly higher than the western city, from 532 yuan/ton in 2001 to 704 yuan/ton in 2008; compared with the central and western regions, the MAC fluctuated more furiously for the eastern cities, which is close to the central and western regions in 2001 at 706 yuan/ton. After 2004, there was a gathering and climbing. After a short-term decline in 2006, it reached a peak of 2,537 yuan/ton in 2007, and then fell back to 1,804 yuan/ton in 2008. Despite fluctuations, the marginal cost of CO_2 abatement in eastern cities is still growing significantly. Affected by this, the MAC of all sample cities is

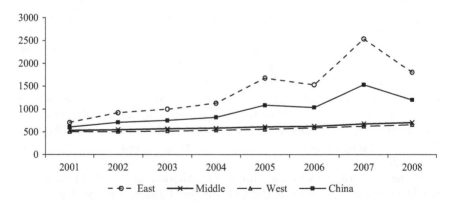

Figure 4.3 Shadow price comparison in the eastern, middle, and western regions (2001–2008)

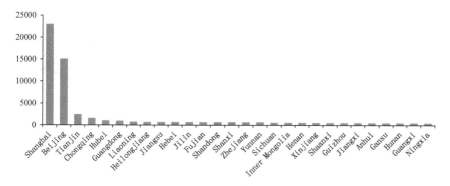

Figure 4.4 Provincial shadow price ranking (2001–2008)

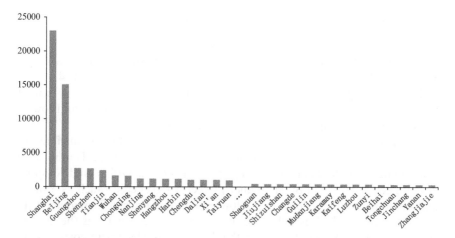

Figure 4.5 Fifteen cities with the highest marginal abatement costs and the lowest 15 cities (2001–2008)

consistent with that in the east. In 2001, the average was 603 yuan/ton. In 2007, it reached a peak of 1,529 yuan/ton. In 2008, it fell to 1,198 yuan/ton, which was still higher than the 2006 level.

Second, the MACs are evaluated at the provincial level. See Figure 4.4. It can be seen that among the 28 provinces included in the sample, Ningxia has the lowest marginal abatement cost of RMB 420/ton, in addition to Guangxi (460 yuan/ton), Hunan (465 yuan/ton), and Gansu (487 yuan/ton), Anhui (494 yuan/ton) marginal abatement costs are lower; in comparison, Shanghai's abatement costs are the highest, reaching 22,990 yuan/ton, 54 times that of Gansu, and other provinces are Beijing (15,054 yuan/ton), Tianjin

94 *Emission reduction analysis*

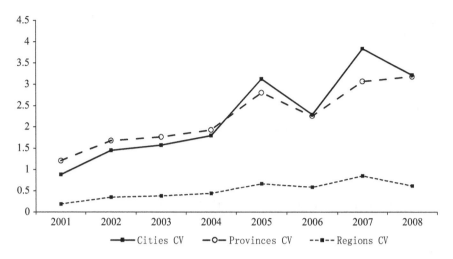

Figure 4.6 City shadow price coefficient of variation (2001–2008)

(2,413 yuan/ton), Chongqing (1,581 yuan/ton), and Hubei (1,065 yuan/ton). The annual MAC data for all 28 sample provinces is shown in Table 4.16.

Finally, the perspective is transferred to the city level, which is limited by the length. Figure 4.5 only lists the 15 cities with the highest and lowest MACs. For each sample city MAC, see Table 4.17.

It can be seen from Figure 4.5 that, except for the four municipalities directly under the central government of Shanghai, Beijing, Tianjin, and Chongqing, other large provincial capital cities, such as Wuhan and Nanjing, have higher MACs, and other smaller prefecture-level cities, such as Yan'an and Zhangjiajie, are the lowest. The lowest marginal price in Zhangjiajie City is 324 yuan/ton, which is only 1/70 that of Shanghai, which has the highest emission reduction cost. Therefore, the difference in abatement costs among cities is very large.

In order to measure the differences between cities in different years, the coefficient of variation of the MAC per year is used to measure the relative deviation. It can be seen from Figure 4.6 that the coefficient of variation between cities has declined significantly in 2006, and the other years have shown a significant increase trend, indicating that the MAC of the city is becoming more and more differentiated. Affected by this, the trend of the coefficient of variation of MAC among cities in different provinces is similar, and the relative deviation between regional cities is much more moderate.

The above analysis shows that there is a big difference in the cost of CO_2 marginal abatement in cities. This difference may be driven by a variety of factors, which will be discussed in more depth in the next chapter.

4.6 Identification of influencing factors of urban CO_2 marginal abatement costs

4.6.1 Discussion of the literature on the influencing factors

In the analysis of the MAC of common pollutants, Dasgupta et al. (2001) argued that the slope of the enterprise's MAC function becomes steeper from right to left as the pollution volume decreases, so the MAC function, location, and slope are affected by factors such as production scale and sector composition, operational efficiency of the business, available technology, and efficiency of wastewater treatment technologies. In order to obtain quantitative analysis empirically, they used the data of 370 factories provided by the Ministry of Environmental Protection and the Tianjin Environmental Protection Agency to study the abatement costs of multipollutants (suspension/COD/BOD/other pollution). The -long function finds that the emission reduction of pollutants has the characteristics of economies of scale, which will be affected by the scale of emission reduction and the degree of emission reduction. The MACs of different industries vary greatly. In addition, the impact of ownership and age-to-edge MACs of enterprises is not significant. Tu Zhenge (2009) used the non-parametric DEA method to measure the SO_2 MAC of the above-scale industrial enterprises in China. He believes that the marginal abatement cost of SO_2 depends on the level of pollutant emission and the level of productivity. Yuan Peng and Cheng Shi (2011), based on the city data from 2003 to 2008, analyzed the MAC of urban industrial pollutants, and found that it is the same as the scale of pollution discharge (pollution emissions) and the intensity of pollution supervision. There is a significant negative correlation between pollution capacity/pollution emissions and scale economy of pollution control (quantity of pollution treatment; i.e., industrial wastewater discharge scalar, industrial SO_2 removal, industrial soot removal).

There are also many theoretical and empirical tests in the literature on the marginal cost of carbon reduction. Criqui et al. (1999) and Klepper and Peterson (2006) argued that the marginal cost of carbon reduction would be affected by a number of factors, including: initial energy price levels, energy supply structure, and development of low carbon/the potential of carbon-free energy resources; Maradan and Vassiliev (2005) used the non-parametric DEA method to estimate the CO_2 shadow price based on 76 countries, and used this to verify the EKC. The curve shows that the income level is negatively correlated with the CO_2 marginal emission reduction opportunity cost, and it is considered that the high-income countries have lower output losses due to emission reduction than low-income countries. Hoeller and Coppel (1992) found that carbon prices (end-user fossil fuel consumption/carbon emissions) and carbon intensity (CO_2/GDP) in OECD countries are strongly correlated. Therefore, Bohm and Larsen (1994) put

96 *Emission reduction analysis*

forward the assumption about the MAC; that is, the marginal cost of carbon emission reduction is positively correlated with the fossil fuel consumption price, and negatively correlated with the country's CO_2 emission intensity. Murty et al. (2007) examined the monthly data of five power plants in the province of Andhra Pradesh, India, from 1996 to 2004, and measured the shadow price of pollutants in thermal power plants. The quantitative regression showed that the shadow price and unit power generation pollutant output (strengthen the indicator) is significantly negatively correlated with the amount of pollution in the power plant; that is, the dirtier the power plant, the lower the MAC.

In the analysis of China's carbon emission and abatement cost factors, Du et al. (2012) estimated and predicted China's interprovincial CO_2 emissions, and identified the factors affecting carbon emissions through the measurement model: economic development level, technological progress factors such as industrial structure, energy consumption structure, trade openness and urbanization, but they did not discuss the cost of emission reduction. Liu Minglei et al. (2011) found that in areas with low carbon emission intensity, the shadow price is higher in the region with low carbon emission intensity, which means that the CO_2 marginal abatement cost has a negative correlation with the CO_2 emission intensity. Qin Shaojun et al. (2011) studied the thermal power plant data of Shanghai and found that the CO_2 MAC of the power plant is positively related to the installed capacity of the enterprise. The explanation for this is that the power generation efficiency of the large unit is higher than that of the small unit, so the space for further reduction is small. As a result, power plants with large installed capacity will have higher MACs. Wei et al. (2013) used the stepwise regression method and model test to analyze the three main influencing factors of emission scale, power plant age, and capital depreciation rate in the analysis of CO_2 MAC of China's micro thermal power plants.

In summary, the existing literature reveals that for the marginal cost of carbon reduction: (1) there is an inverted U-type relationship with EKC at the level of economic development or per-capita income; (2) there is a negative correlation with pollution level or intensity; that is, there is a scale effect of emission reduction (Hettige et al., 1996); (3) there is a positive correlation with technical level or production efficiency (Wei et al., 2013); that is, the higher the efficiency, the greater the marginal abatement cost; (4) there is positive correlation with the fossil fuel price; (5) there is negative correlation with pollution regulation and governance intensity; and (6) other possible factors. For example, the city's public infrastructure and industrial layout will have obvious carbon lock-in effects, and the city's traffic development level, household consumption structure, and urban average temperature may also have an impact on the marginal cost of urban carbon reduction.

Table 4.10 Summary of factors affecting marginal abatement costs

Categories	Variables		Variable definition	Interpretation	Expected symbols
Variable interpreted	Marginal reduction cost	y_mac	log(marginal reduction cost)		
Interpreting variable: economy information	Per-capita income	x_rgdp	log(per-capita GDP)	The more advanced the economy, the higher the MAC	+
	Industrial structure	x_2c	Proportion of the economy of the secondary industry	The greater the proportion of the secondary industry, the lower the MAC	−
		x_3c	Proportion of the economy of the tertiary industry	The higher the tertiary industry, the higher the MAC	+
	Degree of openness	x_fdi	FDI's proportion in GDP		?
Personal information	Rate of urbanization	x_urban	Proportion of urban residents in all the residents		?
	Population density	x_popden	log(number of people in the countries land area per unit)		?
Pollutant information	CO_2 emission intensity	x_CO_2int	log(CO_2 emissions per unit GDP)	The dirtier the city, the lower the MAC	−
	Per-capita CO_2	x_rCO_2	log(per-capita CO_2 emissions)		−
	CO_2 intensity	x_CO_2den	log(CO_2 emissions per unit land area)		−
Infrastructure	Per-capita paved road area	x_rroad	log(Per-capita paved road area)	Infrastructure lock-in effect	+
	Number of public vehicles per capita	x_rbus	log(Number of buses and taxis per capita)		+
	Green coverage of built-up area	x_grecov	The proportion of the built-up green area in the country's land area	Carbon sink effect	−
	Weight of net users	x_rnet	log(the proportion of Internet users in all the residents)		?

98   *Emission reduction analysis*

Table 4.11 Descriptive statistics for explanatory variables

Variables	Samples	Mean	Standard deviation	Minimum	Maximum
x_rgdp	832	0.939	0.617	−0.968	3.169
x_2c	831	53.281	11.563	14.370	91.470
x_3c	831	42.844	11.064	8.040	73.600
x_fdi	799	0.0384	0.0363	0.000	0.2411
x_urban	811	0.706	0.178	0.191	1.000
x_popden	831	6.879	0.862	3.401	8.767
x_CO_2int	832	1.639	0.938	−1.090	4.158
x_rCO_2	832	2.577	0.828	−0.473	5.156
x_CO_2den	831	0.246	1.225	−3.958	3.568
x_rbook	831	1.984	0.773	−2.379	4.114
x_rbed	830	4.001	0.325	1.283	4.839
x_rdoc	830	3.368	0.332	2.151	4.482
x_rroad	831	2.116	0.514	0.432	4.159
x_rbus	832	3.402	0.537	1.368	5.286
x_grecov	830	35.446	8.322	4.000	70.300
x_rtel	827	−0.854	0.481	−3.912	4.038
x_rmob	825	8.607	0.778	1.787	11.372
x_rnet	717	7.000	0.881	3.339	9.628

4.6.2 *Model setting and variable selection*

In order to test the driving factors that affect the cost of urban marginal abatement, screening, and testing can be carried out according to the measurement model. A basic model is:

$$q_{i,t} = \alpha + Z\beta + \varepsilon_{i,t} \tag{4.16}$$

where q is the marginal cost of carbon reduction in urban i in t years, Z is a possible explanatory variable, β is the coefficient to be estimated, and α and ε are the intercept term and the random error term, respectively. The choice of explanatory variables depends on the discussion of the theoretical literature on the one hand, and on the other hand, depending on the data support available for the study. Each explanatory variable will be entered into the model (4.16) for estimation, and the optimal model will be based on the corresponding statistical indicators.

Based on the existing literature studies and data characteristics, the following explanatory variables are set in Table 4.10.

The descriptive statistics of the above potential explanatory variables are shown in Table 4.11.

4.6.3 *Discussion of empirical results*

First, the correlation analysis is performed on the above variables. The correlation coefficient and significance degree are shown in Table 4.18. It can be seen that there is a significant correlation between the shadow price and the set explanatory variables, but there are also strong correlations between different explanatory variables, such as the serious negative correlation between the proportion of the second production and the proportion of the three industries, and the population. There is also a strong positive correlation between density and CO_2 emission concentration. Therefore, in order to overcome multicollinearity, it is necessary to select the most representative index from the potential explanatory variables set above. To this end, first diagnose the collinearity between the explanatory variables, and use the indicators such as the variance expansion factor (*vif*) and the condition number to identify the explanatory variables that can carry the most information from each category. It can be seen from Table 4.19 that there is serious multicollinearity in the three pollutant emission indicators set. We will first retain the CO_2 emission intensity index (x_CO_2int) commonly used in the literature for analysis; in addition, due to the proportion of production of the city is relatively fixed, so the proportion of secondary production and tertiary production shows a significant correlation. In the industrial structure variables, the proportion of secondary industry (x_2c) is first selected for investigation. In order to further identify significant influencing factors from the above variables, the explanatory variables are added in turn. In addition, the Hausman test is used to identify whether the fixed effect model or the random effect model is used, and the statistical value indicates the fixed effect model estimation result is more consistent, considering that the number of sections (104 cities) is much higher than the period span (8 years), the individual fixed effects are not considered, rather than the two-way fixed model. The specific regression results are shown in Table 4.12.

First, it can be seen from Models 1 and 2 that after considering the quadratic term of per-capita income, the primary coefficient is not significant, thus indicating that there is no inverted U-shaped curve for CO_2 MAC. The first item of per-capita income is significantly positive in Model 1 and Models 3–10, indicating that the higher the urban economic level, the greater the marginal cost of emission reduction, so in the subsequent regression, the per-capita income is not retained. Second, the proportion of the second production in the industrial structure and the proportion of foreign direct investment (FDI) in the economic scale are significantly negative in all models, indicating that cities with higher proportion of secondary production and higher degree of openness have lower marginal abatement costs; the population density coefficient is negative, indicating that the degree of urban population aggregation is negatively correlated with the MAC, but this conclusion is only significant in some models; the proportion of urban population is significantly positive, indicating that the higher the level of urbanization, the greater the cost of emission reduction. The CO_2 emission intensity variable per unit of GDP is not significant in all regressions, suggesting that there may not be significant scale effects in urban emission reductions; among the infrastructure-related variables, only the number of per-capita buses and taxis is significantly

Table 4.12 Initial regression analysis results

	Model 1	Model 2	Model 3	Model 4	Model 5	Model 6	Model 7	Model 8	Model 9	Model 10
x_rgdp	0.343*** −22.59	−0.0136 (−0.48)	0.353*** −23.42	0.346*** −23.14	0.351*** −23.35	0.340*** −19.95	0.341*** −19.37	0.373*** −15.71	0.365*** −14.94	0.335*** −11.03
$(x\_rgdp)^2$		0.190*** −14.45								
x_2c			−0.00624*** (−5.09)	−0.00616*** (−4.95)	−0.00624*** (−5.03)	−0.00639*** (−5.04)	−0.00640*** (−5.04)	−0.00647*** (−5.22)	−0.00653*** (−5.23)	−0.00638*** (−4.54)
x_fdi				−1.874*** (−8.17)	−1.836*** (−8.01)	−1.899*** (−7.84)	−1.900*** (−7.83)	−1.795*** (−7.61)	−1.785*** (−7.58)	−2.256*** (−8.00)
x_popden					−0.0536* (−2.55)	−0.0613** (−2.83)	−0.0614** (−2.84)	−0.0388 (−1.81)	−0.0382 (−1.79)	−0.0226 (−0.96)
x_urban						0.150* −2.03	0.151* −2.04	0.214** −2.93	0.220** −3.02	0.188* −2.36
x_CO$_2$int							0.00705 −0.32	0.0274 −1.28	0.0274 −1.29	0.0292 −1.22
x_rroad								−0.021 (−0.87)	−0.0233 (−0.97)	−0.00336 (−0.12)
x_rbus								−0.183*** (−6.21)	−0.180*** (−6.10)	−0.174*** (−5.32)
x_grecov									0.000709 −0.9	0.00147 −1.7
x_rnet										0.0112 −1.08
_cons	−3.09*** (−208.2)	−2.99*** (−204.5)	−2.765*** (−42.50)	−2.679*** (−40.40)	−2.309*** (−14.49)	−2.339*** (−14.49)	−2.352*** (−14.17)	−1.953*** (−11.15)	−1.985*** (−11.04)	−2.214*** (−10.07)
N	830	830	829	796	795	774	774	773	772	657
Adj. R^2	0.329	0.478	0.351	0.407	0.412	0.39	0.389	0.419	0.417	0.409
AIC	−1,257.1	−1,465.4	−1,282.2	−1,277.8	−1,280.7	−1,239.8	−1,237.9	−1,282.4	−1,285.8	−1,067.5
BIC	−1,247.7	−1,451.3	−1,268	−1,259	−1,257.3	−1,211.5	−1,205.3	−1,240.5	−1,239.3	−1,018.1
Hausman chi^2	1.79	3.75	7.22**	18***	28.03***	26.75***	30.66***	33.82***	32.24***	49.72***

Table 4.13 Further study of pollutants

Interpreting variables	I	II	III	IV
x_rgdp	0.353***	0.358***	0.331***	0.360***
	(21.08)	(20.64)	(14.00)	(17.40)
x_2c	−0.00658***	−0.00662***	−0.00662***	−0.00658***
	(−5.33)	(−5.36)	(−5.36)	(−5.32)
x_fdi	−1.853***	−1.853***	−1.853***	−1.846***
	(−7.86)	(−7.86)	(−7.86)	(−7.80)
x_urban	0.198**	0.206**	0.206**	0.201**
	(2.76)	(2.86)	(2.86)	(2.79)
x_rbus	−0.188***	−0.194***	−0.194***	−0.184***
	(−6.55)	(−6.67)	(−6.67)	(−6.24)
x_CO_2int		0.0270		
		(1.26)		
x_rCO_2			0.0270	
			(1.26)	
x_CO_2den				−0.00891
				(−0.59)
_cons	−2.165***	−2.199***	−2.199***	−2.184***
	(−18.53)	(−18.34)	(−18.34)	(−17.93)
N	775	775	775	774
Adj. R^2	0.42	0.421	0.421	0.419
AIC	−1,281.4	−1,281.3	−1,281.3	−1,277.2
BIC	−1,253.5	−1,248.7	−1,248.7	−1,244.6
Hausman chi^2	45.86***	14.69**	14.69**	48.59***

negatively correlated. It indicates that cities with more developed transportation facilities have relatively lower MACs. In addition, the Hausman test results show that in Models 3–10, the fixed effect model is more appropriate.

Through the above preliminary regression, the relevant significant variables can be identified, but the regression of pollutants is not ideal. Because the CO_2 emission intensity index is selected in Table 4.12, in order to avoid the problems caused by the selection of variables based on the significant variables identified, the regression was performed again using two variables, the spatial concentration of CO_2 and CO_2 emissions per capita. The results are shown in Table 4.13. The Hausman test recommends the use of a fixed-effects model for estimation. Column I is a significant factor identified on the basis of the above table analysis. Columns II–IV add three pollutant indicators, respectively. It can be seen that either the unit CO_2 emission intensity of GDP, or the per-capita CO_2 emission, and the CO_2 emission concentration per unit area of land, the estimated coefficients are not significant, which indicates that there is no scale effect of emission reduction in urban samples. The other variables are still significant.

In summary, through the quantitative analysis of the econometric model, it is finally recognized that the urban CO_2 MAC is significantly correlated with

102 *Emission reduction analysis*

urban economic development level, industrial structure, openness, urbanization level, and public transport. Among them, the per-capita income level of the city is positively correlated with the degree of urbanization and the MAC; while the proportion of urban secondary production, the degree of openness and the number of public transportation vehicles per capita are negatively correlated with the MAC. In addition, the CO_2 emission intensity per capita, the CO_2 emission intensity per unit of GDP, and the CO_2 spatial concentration are not significantly related to the MAC.

4.7 Main conclusions and implications

In this chapter, the theory and method of urban carbon dioxide marginal abatement cost are systematically reviewed. On this basis, the direction-based distance function and the parameterized quadratic function are constructed, and the unknown parameters are solved by linear programming method. Taking 104 prefecture-level cities in China as a sample, the proportion pf labor, GDP, capital stock, energy consumption, and CO_2 emissions between 2001 and 2008 were accounted for, and the CO_2 MACs at the city level were measured. The difference in abatement costs between cities is extremely large, which further drives us to examine in more depth the possible factors that affect the MACs.

The main conclusions and revelations of this chapter mainly include two points.

The first is to find that there are huge differences in the marginal cost of input, emissions, and emission reduction in China's cities. First of all, on the various input factors, the characteristics of the eastern city>the central city>the western city are presented. In terms of output and pollution emissions, there is also a significant trend of decreasing east, middle, and west. Second, there is an average of 7.67% inefficient production and emissions in all sample cities, and the average MAC is 967 yuan/ton. From the regional perspective, the central region (604 yuan/ton) and the west (559 yuan/ton) are closer and slower, while the eastern region is higher (1,418 yuan/ton), rising in fluctuations; Shanghai's highest is 22,990 yuan/ton, followed by Tianjin and Chongqing, and the lowest, Ningxia, is only 420 yuan/ton; in all cities, the four municipalities and the larger provincial capitals have higher MACs; the lowest for Zhangjiajie City is only 324 yuan/ton, the highest cost of abatement (Shanghai) and the lowest city (Zhangjiajie) marginal abatement cost ratio of up to 70:1, there is a huge heterogeneity; except 2006, the rest of the years have shown a significant increase trend, indicating that the MAC of the city is becoming more and more differentiated, and the relative deviation between regional cities is much more moderate.

The huge difference in MACs between cities means that there is a large market trading space (Newell & Stavins, 2003); that is, under static conditions, if the city's abatement cost is higher, the more costs the market mechanism reduces, the greater the potential for cost reduction. Conversely, if the cities are more homogeneous, the advantages of market instruments will decline. Given the huge difference of 70:1 between Chinese cities, the overall cost of abatement can be reduced by means such as the emissions trading market. For example, economically developed cities with higher MACs can purchase their development from the trading market quotas required – as long as the price required to purchase an emission permit is lower than the marginal cost of its own emission reduction, and the less economically disadvantaged city benefits from the sale of emission permits due to its lower MACs. Of course, if you are in an environment where there is no set total emission reduction, you can also consider it through tax transfer payment, but at this time, in addition to the two sides of the transaction, a strong central government participation is required, namely the central government taxes are imposed on economically developed cities to allow them to increase their emissions, and then transferred to less-developed cities through fiscal transfer payments to make up for their losses, as long as the tax rate is lower than the MAC of developed cities and the transfer payment is not lower than the marginal cost of reducing emissions in less-developed cities is a welfare improvement for the whole society, and this unilateral payment method – in the absence of efficiency losses – is equivalent to the carbon trading market mechanism.

The second conclusion is to identify possible reasons for the difference in the cost of urban marginal abatement. There is a significant positive linear relationship between the level of urban economic development and the MAC. The inverted U-shaped curve hypothesis of EKC has not been verified in the sample of cities selected in this book; the level of urbanization also affects the cost of abatement. If the proportion of non-agricultural population in the urban population is higher, the cost of emission reduction will increase. Given these two main drivers, plus China's continued high-speed urbanization in the coming period, and the background of "multiple per-capita income of urban and rural residents by 2020," it can be expected that the margin of the city will be increasing for a long time to come. The cost of abatement will continue to show a growth trend. If the cities (regions) with more developed economies are forced to reduce emissions, the economic costs and costs may be increased. Therefore, the potential and cost of emission reduction between cities can be fully considered difference factors, as far as possible through the market mechanism to achieve the realization of the overall emission reduction targets, rather than imposing restrictions on individuals or a certain region.

In addition, from the analysis of influencing factors, the proportion of secondary production, openness and per-capita transportation infrastructure are significantly negatively correlated with MACs. This may become a viable field and awkward place for cities to implement emission reductions, that is, to follow the principle of "first easy and then difficult," first to implement emission reductions for industries and sectors with lower emission reduction

Table 4.14 Comparison table of sample cities

EAST	Beijing	Prefecture-level city	Beijing							
		Sample city	Beijing							
	Tianjin	Prefecture-level city	Tianjin							
		Sample city	Tianjin							
	Hebei	Prefecture-level city	Shijiazhuang	Tangshan	Qinhuangdao	Handan	Xingtai	Baoding	Zhangjiakou	Chengde
		Sample city	Shijiazhuang	Tangshan	Qinhuangdao	Handan		Baoding		
	Liaoning	Prefecture-level city	Shenyang	Dalian	Anshan	Fushun	Benxi	Dandong	Jinzhou	Yingkou
		Sample city	Shenyang	Dalian	Anshan	Fushun	Benxi		Jinzhou	
	Shanghai	Prefecture-level city	Shanghai							
		Sample city	Shanghai							
	Jiangsu	Prefecture-level city	Nanjing	Wuxi	Xuzhou	Changzhou	Suzhou	Nantong	Lianyungang	Huaian
		Sample city	Nanjing	Wuxi	Xuzhou	Changzhou	Suzhou	Nantong	Lianyungang	
	Zhejiang	Prefecture-level city	Hangzhou	Ningbo	Wenzhou	Jiaxing	Huzhou	Shaoxing	Jinhua	Quzhou
		Sample city	Hangzhou	Ningbo	Wenzhou	Jiaxing	Huzhou	Shaoxing		
	Fujian	Prefecture-level city	Fuzhou	Xiame	Putian	Sanming	Quanzhou	Zhangzhou	Nanping	Longyan
		Sample city	Fuzhou	Xiamen			Quanzhou			
	Shandong	Prefecture-level city	Jinan	Qingdao	Zibo	Zaozhuang	Dongying	Yantai	Weifang	Jining
		Sample city	Jinan	Qingdao	Zibo	Zaozhuang		Yantai	Weifang	Liaoning
	Guangdong	Prefecture-level city	Guangzhou	Shaoguan	Shenzhen	Zhuhai	Shantou	Foshan	Jiangmen	Zhanjiang
		Sample city	Guangzhou	Shaoguan	Shenzhen	Zhuhai	Shantou	Foshan		Zhanjiang
	Hainan	Prefecture-level city	Haikou	Sanya						
		Sample city								
East	Shan'xi	Prefecture-level city	Taiyuan	Datong	Yangquan	Changzhi	Jincheng	Shuozhou	Jinzhong	Yuncheng
		Sample city	Taiyuan	Datong	Yangquan	Changzhi				
	Jilin	Prefecture-level city	Changchun	Jilin	Siping	Liaoyuan	Tonghua	Baishan	Songyuan	Baicheng
		Sample city	Changchun	Jilin						
	Heilongjiang	Prefecture-level city	Harbin	Qiqihar	Jixi	Hegang	Shuangyashan	Daqing	Yichun	Jiamusi
		Sample city	Harbin	Qiqihar				Daqing		
	Anhui	Prefecture-level city	Hefei	Wuhu	Bangbu	Huainan	Maanshan	Huaibei	Tongling	Anqing
		Sample city	Hefei	Wuhu			Maanshan			
	Jiangxi	Prefecture-level city	Nanchang	Jingdezhen	Pingxiang	Jiujiang	Xinyu	Yingtan	Ganzhou	Ji' an
		Sample city	Nanchang			Jiujiang				
	Henan	Prefecture-level city	Zhengzhou	Kaifeng	Luoyang	Pingdingshan	Anyang	Hebi	Xinxiang	Jiaozuo
		Sample city	Zhengzhou	Kaifeng	Luoyang	Pingdingshan	Anyang			Jiaozuo
	Hubei	Prefecture-level city	Wuhan	Yellowstone	Shiyan	Yichang	Xiangfan	Ezhou	Jingmen	Xiaogan
		Sample city	Wuhan			Yichang				
	Hunan	Prefecture-level city	Changsha	Zhuzhou	Xiangtan	Hengyang	Shaoyang	Yueyan	Changde	Zhangjiajie
		Sample city	Changsha	Zhuzhou	Xiangtan			Yueyang	Changde	Zhangjiajie
West	Neimenggu	Prefecture-level city	Hohhot	Baotou	Wuhai	Chifeng	Tongliao	Erdos	Hulun Buir	Bayannur
		Sample city	Hohhot	Baotou		Chifeng				
	Guangxi	Prefecture-level city	Nanning	Liuzhou	Guilin	Zhangzhou	Beihai	Fangchenggang	Qinzhou	Guigang
		Sample city	Nanning	Liuzhou	Guilin		Beihai			
	Sichuan	Prefecture-level city	Chengdu	Zigong	Panzhihua	Luzhou	Deyang	Mianyang	Guangyuan	Suining
		Sample city	Chengdu		Panzhihua	Luzhou		Mianyang		

Cangzhou Langfang Hengshui

Fuxin Liaoyang Panjin Tieling Zhaoyang Huludao

Yancheng Yangzhou Zhenjiang Taizhou Suqian
Yangzhou

Zhoushan Taizhou Lishui
Taizhou
Ningde

Taian Weihai Rizhao Laiwu Linyi Dezhou Liaocheng Binzhou Heze
Taian Weihai
Maoming Zhaoqing Huizhou Meizhou Shanwei Heyuan Yangjiang Qingyuan Dong-guan Zhong-shan Chao-zhou Jieyang Yunfu

Xizhou Linfen Lvliang

Qitaihe Mudan-jiang Heihe Ruihua
Mudan-jiang
Huang-shan Chuzhou Fuyang Suzhou Chaohu Liuan Haozhou Chizhou Xuan-cheng

Yichun Fuzhou Shangrao

Puyang Xuchang Luohe Sanmenxia Nanyang Shangqiu Xinyang Zhoukou Zhuma-dian

Jingzhou Huang-gang Xianning Suizhou

Yiyang Binzhou Yongz-hou Huaihua Loudi

Ulanqab

Yulin Baise Hezhou Hechi Laibin Chongzuo

Neijiang Leshan Nanchong Meishan Yibin Guangan Dazhou Ya' ab Bazhou Ziyang

Table 4.14 (Cont.)

Chongqing	Prefecture-level city	Chongqing							
	Sample city	Chongqing							
Guizhou	Prefecture-level city	Guiyang	Liupanshui	Zunyi	Anshun				
	Sample city	Guiyang		Zunyi					
Yunnan	Prefecture-level city	Kunming	Qujing	Yuxi	Baoshan	Shaotong	Lijiang	Simao	Lincang
	Sample city	Kunming	Qujing						
Shaanxi	Prefecture-level city	Xi'an	Tongchuan	Baoji	Xianyang	Weinan	Yan'an		Yulin
	Sample city	Xi'an	Tongchuan	Baoji	Xianyang		Yan'an		
Gansu	Prefecture-level city	Lanzhou	Jiayuguan	Jinchang	silver	Tianshui	Wuwei	Zhangye	Pingliang
	Sample city	Lanzhou		Jinchang					
Qinghai	Prefecture-level city	Xining							
	Sample city								
Ningxia	Prefecture-level city	Yinchuan	Shizuishan	Wu Zhong	Guyuan	Zhongwei			
	Sample city	Yinchuan	Shizuishan						
Xinjiang	Prefecture-level city	Urumqi	Karamay						
	Sample city	Urumqi	Karamay						

Ankang   Shangluo

Jiuquan   Qingyang   Dingxi   Longnan

Table 4.15 Individual cities' effect parameters

City code	Cities	Coefficient	City code	Cities	Coefficient	City code	Cities	Coefficient	City code	Cities	Coefficient
c0101	Beijing	0	c0901	Shanghai	−2.02221	c1503	Zibo	1.13827	c1906	Foshan	0.61833
c0201	Tianjin	0.3907	c1001	Nanjing	0.77753	c1504	Zaozhuang	0.63243	c1908	Zhanjiang	0.85005
c0301	Shijiazhuang	0.53426	c1002	Wuxi	1.48579	c1506	Yantai	0.73598	c2001	Nanning	0.72123
c0302	Tangshan	0.48135	c1003	Xuzhou	0.75819	c1507	Weifang	0.70125	c2002	Liuzhou	0.69044
c0303	Qinhuangdao	0.70679	c1004	Changzhou	0.66525	c1508	Jining	0.56476	c2003	Guilin	0.69127
c0304	Handan	0.35466	c1005	Suzhou	0.95044	c1509	Taian	0.74562	c2005	North Sea	0.69205
c0306	Baoding	0.61357	c1006	Nantong	0.62124	c1510	Weihai	0.72554	c2201	Chongqing	0.47202
c0401	Taiyuan	0.26179	c1007	Lianyungang	0.58684	c1601	Zhengzhou	0.59689	c2301	Chengdu	0.94475
c0402	Datong	0.54568	c1010	Yangzhou	0.80706	c1602	Kaifeng	0.62702	c2303	Panzhihua	0.52054
c0403	Yangquan	0.57003	c1101	Hangzhou	1.68934	c1603	Luoyang	0.61916	c2304	Luzhou	0.67017
c0404	Changzhi	0.5974	c1102	Ningbo	0.55053	c1604	Pingdingshan	0.53869	c2306	Mianyang	0.84332
c0501	Hohhot	0.68878	c1103	Wenzhou	0.8999	c1605	Anyang	0.56828	c2401	Guiyang	0.54869
c0502	Baotou	0.64256	c1104	Jiaxing	0.54651	c1608	Jiaozuo	0.53136	c2403	Zunyi	0.68014
c0504	Chifeng	0.58892	c1105	Huzhou	0.70465	c1701	Wuhan	0.85296	c2501	Kunming	0.76549
c0601	Shenyang	1.28187	c1106	Shaoxing	0.63682	c1704	Yichang	0.60126	c2502	Qujing	0.5978
c0602	Dalian	1.23958	c1110	Taizhou	0.88326	c1801	Changsha	0.83302	c2701	Xi'an	0.90677
c0603	Anshan	0.99806	c1201	Hefei	0.72409	c1802	Zhuzhou	0.69862	c2702	Tongchuan	0.60781
c0604	Fushun	0.65054	c1202	Wuhu	0.66978	c1803	Xiangtan	0.67409	c2703	Baoji	0.60846
c0605	Benxi	0.59309	c1205	Ma Anshan	0.60986	c1806	Yue Yang	0.80214	c2704	Xianyang	0.59409
c0607	Jinzhou	0.67877	c1301	Fuzhou	0.82782	c1807	Changde	0.93969	c2706	Yan'an	0.61781
c0701	Changchun	1.64336	c1302	Xiamen	1.06117	c1808	Zhangjiajie	0.62659	c2801	Lanzhou	0.62504
c0702	Jilin	0.58292	c1305	Quanzhou	0.8142	c1901	Guangzhou	1.95591	c2803	Jinchang	0.62283
c0801	Harbin	0.8403	c1401	Nanchang	0.98668	c1902	Shaoguan	0.62449	c3001	Yinchuan	0.58968
c0802	Qiqihar	0.62836	c1404	Jiujiang	0.64682	c1903	Shenzhen	2.99697	c3002	Shizuishan	0.56872
c0806	Daqing	1.9518	c1501	Jinan	1.19891	c1904	Zhuhai	0.98615	c3101	Urumqi	0.73596
c0810	Mudanjiang	0.6424	c1502	Qingdao	1.12994	c1905	Shantou	0.76707	c3102	Karamay	0.69322

Table 4.16 Provincial marginal emission reduction cost (2001–2008)

	2001	2002	2003	2004	2005	2006	2007	2008	Provincial average	Rank
Beijing	5,223	6,960	8,182	1,0381	12,141	14,799	23,507	39,241	15,054	2
Tianjin	1,754	1,813	1,968	2,157	2,433	2,612	3,018	3,548	2,413	3
Hebei	579	595	618	652	711	746	800	813	689	10
Shanxi	577	578	602	613	640	676	757	760	650	14
Inner Mongolia	500	473	487	516	546	591	632	681	553	18
Liaoning	638	634	643	672	714	766	839	917	728	7
Jilin	509	512	646	671	822	741	774	802	685	11
Heilongjiang	640	687	700	677	689	713	754	777	705	8
Shanghai	–	8,312	9,406	11,526	32,989	19,908	55,799	–	22,990	1
Jiangsu	577	593	618	656	718	774	834	859	704	9
Zhejiang	514	528	561	594	639	715	788	851	649	15
Anhui	445	447	458	472	488	515	546	581	494	24
Fujian	511	554	579	618	655	709	782	823	654	12
Jiangxi	458	458	471	493	513	543	550	565	506	23
Shandong	545	558	573	603	661	704	759	803	651	13
Henan	499	510	520	537	559	570	597	615	551	19
Hubei	883	901	960	1,021	1,108	1,107	1,207	1,332	1,065	5
Hunan	420	428	431	444	458	470	524	546	465	26
Guangdong	651	701	763	826	888	1,159	1,296	1,416	962	6
Guangxi	447	423	433	444	483	476	480	497	460	27
Chongqing	1,137	1,199	1,275	1,399	1,463	1,781	2,063	2,330	1,581	4
Sichuan	514	532	540	556	579	614	641	682	582	17
Guizhou	465	477	481	497	513	542	558	569	513	22
Yunnan	544	554	582	617	618	674	733	754	634	16
Shaanxi	468	478	493	502	516	531	556	583	516	21
Gansu	461	467	474	485	491	497	505	518	487	25
Ningxia	391	393	404	421	425	431	448	448	420	28
Xinjiang	482	490	492	500	514	529	553	565	516	20

Table 4.17 Marginal emission reduction cost of cities (2001–2008)

Cities	2001	2002	2003	2004	2005	2006	2007	2008	Average	Rank
Beijing	5,223	6,960	8,182	10,381	12,141	14,799	23,507	39,241	15,054	2
Tianjin	1,754	1,813	1,968	2,157	2,433	2,612	3,018	3,548	2,413	5
Shijiazhuang City	721	728	786	829	863	909	970	986	849	22
Tangshan City	669	718	758	832	998	1,087	1,195	1,237	937	18
Qinhuangdao City	443	446	453	464	469	479	502	510	471	72
Handan	621	643	648	673	730	748	812	796	709	29
Baoding City	439	441	444	462	496	506	521	539	481	66
Taiyuan City	866	833	883	891	952	997	1,143	1,168	966	15
Datong City	551	553	560	584	573	586	609	623	580	44
Yangquan City	429	438	440	447	467	472	485	489	458	75
Changzhi City	461	487	527	529	568	650	792	761	597	43
Hohhot	455	461	471	516	549	589	609	656	538	52
Baotou City	533	544	569	603	648	732	807	895	666	34
Chifeng City	512	414	421	430	441	452	480	492	455	76
Shenyang city	977	976	980	1,038	1,134	1,300	1,491	1,707	1,200	9
Dalian	821	834	882	941	1,009	1,086	1,249	1,447	1,033	13
Anshan City	625	612	617	642	661	690	733	768	669	33
Fushun City	502	488	491	506	516	529	543	552	516	55
Benxi City	473	463	465	473	529	551	570	569	511	56
Jinzhou City	431	429	423	433	439	441	450	458	438	83
Changchun City			773	803	1,095	912	954	994	922	19
Jilin City	509	512	520	539	549	571	593	610	550	49
Harbin City	1,028	1,197	1,231	1,121	1,117	1,158	1,238	1,281	1,171	11
Qiqihar City	488	490	488	475	495	505	523	523	498	61
Daqing City	642	655	678	713	746	790	845	892	745	28
Mudanjiang City	402	405	403	399	400	400	410	412	404	95
Shanghai		8,312	9,406	11,526	32,989	19,908	55,799		22,990	1

Nanjing	951	988	1,031	1,103	1,210	1,325	1,449	1,580	1,204	8
Wuxi	643	662	705	773	847	935	1,054	1,147	846	23
Xuzhou	596	604	621	648	728	730	750	645	665	35
Changzhou	458	484	493	507	534	560	594	608	530	54
Suzhou	655	678	742	836	995	1,169	1,289	1,315	960	17
Nantong	459	465	477	495	506	521	542	561	503	59
Lianyungang	400	404	407	412	430	446	451	468	427	89
Yangzhou	454	459	465	473	494	507	547	546	493	63
Hangzhou	835	868	924	989	1,131	1,358	1,573	1,825	1,188	10
Ningbo	671	683	746	794	832	974	1,121	1,202	878	20
Wenzhou	475	497	542	567	580	626	658	671	577	45
Jiaxing	407	418	432	455	506	543	565	572	487	65
Huzhou	392	398	409	439	456	491	513	529	453	77
Shaoxing	397	402	424	448	481	512	525	537	466	74
Taizhou	421	427	447	466	486	501	562	623	491	64
Hefei	497	499	515	533	557	603	643	688	567	46
Wuhu	409	411	418	430	440	461	479	507	444	81
Maanshan	428	431	441	452	465	480	515	549	470	73
Fuzhou	589	594	607	650	679	725	811	879	692	30
Xiamen		626	668	718	782	866	963	994	802	24
Quanzhou	433	442	461	487	505	535	572	596	504	58
Nanchang	537	534	549	573	600	633	669	698	599	40
Jiujiang	379	381	394	413	426	453	430	431	413	91
Jinan	755	781	814	855	983	1,052	1,181	1,263	960	16
Qingdao	735	758	770	808	878	947	1,011	1,080	873	21
Zibo	635	653	673	709	807	879	942	995	787	26
Zaozhuang	488	490	494	514	529	557	589	604	533	53
Yantai	519	547	573	614	705	760	836	885	680	32
Weifang	466	473	484	521	566	599	639	669	552	48
Jining	472	469	484	508	536	563	634	704	546	50
Tai'an	428	431	436	456	483	506	519	530	474	71
Weihai	408	416	427	442	464	476	486	501	453	78

(continued)

Table 4.17 (Cont.)

Cities	2001	2002	2003	2004	2005	2006	2007	2008	Average	Rank
Zhengzhou	668	700	726	772	824	826	912	922	794	25
Kaifeng	393	391	392	392	397	402	399	395	395	97
Luoyang	537	547	547	562	610	635	652	697	598	42
Pingdingshan	489	496	507	518	538	563	582	617	539	51
Anyang	465	470	483	499	498	509	542	554	502	60
Jiaozuo	445	457	467	482	485	487	494	506	478	69
Wuhan	1,309	1,337	1,455	1,567	1,727	1,719	1,921	2,162	1,650	6
Yichang	457	464	465	475	490	495	492	503	480	67
Changsha	586	610	618	651	687	727	773	844	687	31
Zhuzhou	422	421	429	448	460	463	474	478	449	79
Xiangtan	412	414	416	425	439	450	464	484	438	84
Yueyang	394	411	408	417	429	439	462	471	429	87
Changde	380	390	392	397	408	420	445	454	410	93
Zhangjiajie	324	323	322	326	326	324			324	104
Guangzhou	1,734	1,887	2,159	2,431	2,721	3,015	3,550	4,064	2,695	3
Shaoguan	400	401	402	418	423	443	467	460	427	90
Shenzhen						2,373	2,671	2,957	2,667	4
Zhuhai	483	507	539	574	607	646	698	734	599	41
Shan Tou	431	430	469	480	485	505	511	521	479	68
Foshan	445	566	579	608	636	673	707	701	614	39
Zhangjiang	414	416	432	444	453	459	468	474	445	80
NanNing	476	490	498	527	647	588	609	639	559	47
Liuzhou	477	469	493	498	513	536	517	546	506	57
Guilin	390	396	400	406	412	416	422	421	408	94
Beihai		338	341	346	361	365	370	382	358	100
Chongqing	1,137	1,199	1,275	1,399	1,463	1,781	2,063	2,330	1,581	7
Chengdu	822	890	909	954	1,008	1,104	1,224	1,369	1,035	12
Panzhihua	449	450	456	466	488	502	486	493	474	70

Quzhou	371	375	378	383	389	403	408	421	391	98
Mianyang	416	412	418	421	433	446	445	445	429	86
Guiyang	567	581	594	621	645	662	701	721	636	36
Zunyi	362	372	367	372	380	422	415	418	389	99
Kunming	686	692	725	720	749	831	882	892	772	27
Qujing	402	417	439	513	487	516	585	615	497	62
Xi'an	841	882	916	953	1,022	1,082	1,183	1,264	1,018	14
Tongchuan	346	352	352	351	352	352	356	376	355	101
Baoji	408	410	442	446	448	449	459	472	442	82
Xianyang	414	414	424	428	424	432	443	459	429	85
Yan'an	328	329	330	331	335	338	339	342	334	103
Lan'Zhou	578	590	604	619	633	643	657	674	625	38
Jinchang	343	343	345	350	349	351	354	361	349	102
Yinchuan	398	400	425	430	433	441	445	453	428	88
Shizuishan	384	385	383	411	416	422	452	444	412	92
Urumqi	576	593	596	606	w625	648	686	704	629	37
Karamay	388	387	389	394	404	410	421	426	402	96

Table 4.18 Relative coefficients of variables (relative coefficient and significance of Spearman)

	y_mac	x_rgdp	x_2c	x_3c	x_fdi	x_urban	x_popden	x_CO_2int	x_rCO_2	x_CO_2den	x_rroad	x_rbus	x_grecov	x_rnet
y_mac	1													
x_rgdp	0.5378	1												
	0													
x_2c	−0.1128	0.0424	1											
	0.0038	0.278												
x_3c	0.2633	0.1186	−0.9362	1										
	0	0.0023	0											
x_fdi	0.3662	0.5102	−0.0747	0.1641	1									
	0	0	0.0558	0										
x_urban	0.2366	0.3273	0.04	0.1398	0.1082	1								
	0	0	0.3065	0.0003	0.0055									
x_popden	0.247	0.1791	0.02	0.1253	0.2578	0.3834	1							
	0	0	0.6097	0.0013	0	0								
x_CO_2int	−0.3579	−0.4759	0.3499	−0.3833	−0.4103	−0.0466	−0.0172	1						
	0	0	0	0	0	0.2331	0.6605							
x_rCO_2	−0.0555	0.1143	0.4476	−0.3774	−0.1565	0.164	0.0909	0.7903	1					
	0.1557	0.0034	0	0	0.0001	0	0.0197	0						
x_CO_2den	0.0915	0.2165	0.3169	−0.1649	0.102	0.3312	0.687	0.5229	0.7418	1				
	0.0189	0	0	0	0.0089	0	0	0	0					
x_rroad	0.2597	0.6502	0.0856	0.0361	0.449	0.3025	0.1812	−0.2162	0.1987	0.2785	1			
	0	0	0.0283	0.3557	0	0	0	0	0	0				
x_rbus	0.3307	0.3568	−0.195	0.3548	0.0778	0.5302	0.1296	−0.161	0.0501	0.0975	0.2516	1		
	0	0	0	0	0.0462	0	0.0009	0	0.1992	0.0124	0			
x_grecov	0.0973	0.3436	0.0915	−0.0514	0.2961	0.2006	0.0933	−0.0745	0.1539	0.1759	0.3834	0.0116	1	
	0.0125	0	0.019	0.1884	0	0	0.0168	0.0562	0.0001	0	0	0.7661		
x_rnet	0.5128	0.6789	−0.1392	0.3075	0.4469	0.3611	0.3488	−0.367	0.0209	0.2442	0.4994	0.3712	0.2654	1
	0	0	0.0003	0	0	0	0	0	0.5927	0	0	0	0	

Table 4.19 Multicollinearity of explanatory variables

Variable	VIF	VIF	VIF	VIF
x_rgdp	4.95E+13	4.95E+13	3.96	3.84
x_2c	19.95	1.99E+01	19.94	1.44
x_3c	20.17	20.14	20.14	
x_fdi	1.4	1.38	1.38	1.38
x_urban	1.97	1.97	1.97	1.78
x_popden	4752.33	1.49	1.49	1.34
x_CO_2int	1.16E+14	1.16E+14	1.78	1.75
x_rCO_2	9.26E+13	9.26E+13		
x_CO_2den	11,340.83			
x_rroad	2.16	2.15	2.15	2.15
x_rbus	1.98	1.97	1.97	1.84
x_grecov	1.25	1.25	1.25	1.22
x_rnet	2.33	2.33	2.33	2.29
Mean VIF	1.99E+13	2.15E+13	5.3	1.9

costs. For example, for cities with a higher proportion of the secondary industry, priority can be given to reducing emissions in this area. Similarly, public transportation is also a viable and worthy sector. In addition, the negative correlation between the degree of openness and the MAC may be due to the higher degree of openness, the more available and available abatement technology options and means, so that the cost of abatement will be relatively lower, this also provides other feasible and economical ways to reduce emissions for city managers.

This chapter is limited to time and energy. There are deficiencies in the following aspects: first, in terms of data, because the sources of urban data-related variables are more scattered, only 104 representative cities are included, and the data are updated to 2008; given more information sources, such as fossil energy consumption, urban private car numbers, and urban average temperature, we will be able to more accurately estimate the amount of energy and carbon emissions, and identify the impact of natural conditions such as temperature on MACs. In the research method, the linear programming method is used to solve the model. Although the relevant constraints can be directly applied, the statistic cannot be obtained for solving the parameters. In the future, other methods such as maximum likelihood estimation or maximum entropy estimation could be considered to get a more robust estimate of the parameters.

Note

1 This chapter is based on Marginal CO_2 Emission Reduction Cost and its Influential Factors in Chinese Cities, *World Economy*, 2014 (7) published by Wei Chu with some of the content edited, revised or deleted.

Part II
Strategic response

5 Industrial restructuring strategy to mitigate and control CO_2 emissions

5.1 Major research findings

Based on the perspective of industrial structure, this book quantitatively analyzes the characteristics of CO_2 emissions, CO_2 emission reduction potential and abatement costs in China from the macro and meso levels, and examines the direction and strength of industrial structure on CO_2 emissions and emission reduction, and thus provides theoretical support and scientific basis for China to control and slow down greenhouse gases (GHGs) through industrial restructuring strategies. Overall, the book has the following four main findings.

First, the book theoretically clarifies the relationship between industrial structure changes and CO_2 emissions, and answers the basic theoretical questions of whether industrial structure can affect CO_2 emissions.

Theoretical model analysis shows that different industrial sectors have significant differences in carbon emission levels due to differences in energy use and structure, that is, different "carbon productivity" among industrial sectors. Therefore, the change in the relative proportion between different industrial sectors – that is, the change in industrial structure – will affect the overall carbon emission quantity and emission scale through the change of carbon productivity. Therefore, it is theoretically confirmed that the industrial structure change is the change of GHG emissions. One of the important reasons is that it provides realistic and feasible means and methods for mitigating GHG emissions, and also provides theoretical evidence for industrial restructuring.

In addition, from the relevant domestic and international practical experience and the actual situation in China, the coal-based energy structure in China cannot be adjusted in the short term, the alternative energy cannot be applied in a short period of time, and the space for continued improvement of energy efficiency is shrinking. It should be considered to reduce GHG emissions by adjusting the industrial structure of high-energy consumption and high emissions, and this adjustment is not limited to the adjustment between the three industries, but more should be reflected in the adjustment and upgrading of the secondary and tertiary industries. However, it should

120 *Strategic response*

be noted that the structural adjustment of low-carbon industrialization that has occurred in certain periods has also increased economic inefficiency. Therefore, when industrial restructuring is needed to address climate change, it should conform to the basic laws of industrial development and fully consider the stability of economic growth. Even if there are significant differences in carbon productivity between different industries, it does not mean that industries with low carbon productivity need to be the target of industrial restructuring, but need to consider the carbon emissions impact and industrial influence of each industry.

Second, this book systematically analyzes and summarizes the emission characteristics of CO_2 in China, identifies the main influencing factors of CO_2 emissions in China, key industries and regions, and examines the role of industrial structure in CO_2 emissions.

From the regional perspective, the total carbon dioxide emissions of Shandong, Hebei, Guangdong, Jiangsu, Sichuan, Henan, and Liaoning provinces accounted for 46% of the national total. From the perspective of per-capita CO_2 emissions, the non-equilibrium characteristics of the eastern>central>western regions are presented. Coal, oil, and cement production is the main source of emissions; by 2015, per-capita emissions may exceed 7 tons, and in 2020 it will reach 9 tons, but still far below the 2007 US per-capita emissions (19.4 tons), and the EU level was basically flat in 2007 (8.6 tons); from the total emissions, China's total CO_2 emissions in 2015 and 2020 reached 10 billion tons and 12 billion tons, respectively. The proportion of heavy industry is significantly positively correlated with the per-capita carbon dioxide emissions. In addition, the level of economic development, energy consumption structure, urbanization level, and technological progress are also the main factors affecting China's carbon dioxide emissions.

In terms of industries and sectors, the CO_2 generated by fossil energy consumption and conversion in China's six major production industries of agriculture, industry, construction, transportation, commerce and energy increased from 2.813 billion tons in 1996 to 7.303 billion tons in 2011. The average annual growth rate is 6.5%. Especially since entering the accelerated phase of heavy chemical industry in 2002, CO_2 emissions have also accelerated. In terms of emission scale, CO_2 emissions from six production industries in China accounted for 91% of the national fossil energy-related CO_2 emissions in that year, accounting for 23% of global stone energy-related CO_2 emissions. The main sources of CO_2 in China are energy, industry, and transportation. In 2011, these three sectors accounted for 97% of CO_2 emissions from all industries. In the industrial sector, metal products, non-metal products and chemical industries are the main sources of industrial CO_2 emissions, accounting for 71% of the total industrial CO_2 emissions. China's CO_2 emissions from different industries and different periods have similar patterns, namely: the expansion of output scale is the main reason for the increase of CO_2 emissions. The adjustment of industrial structure

Industrial restructuring strategy 121

and the improvement of energy efficiency of the sector are the main ways to inhibit CO_2 emissions, but the inhibitory effect is still not enough to offset the growth effect of the scale of output, the energy structure and carbon emissions of energy products have also slowed down CO_2 emissions, but the impact is small.

Third, this book quantitatively evaluates China's CO_2 emission reduction potential and marginal abatement cost, and further examines the relationship between industrial structure and CO_2 emission reduction.

The average emission reduction potential of CO_2 in China is about 40%, and there are regional differences in the eastern<central<western regions. Beijing, Shanghai, and Guangdong are at the forefront of efficiency, while Guizhou, Ningxia, Inner Mongolia, Gansu, Xinjiang, Qinghai, Jilin and the emission reduction potentials of Hebei, Liaoning, Shanxi, Anhui, Heilongjiang, Shaanxi and other provinces all exceed 50%; the analysis of the differences in interprovincial emission reduction potential shows that the higher the level of economic development and the tertiary industry, the relative emission reduction potential The smaller the energy intensity, the proportion of coal consumption in primary energy consumption, technological progress and capital deepening are positively related to the emission reduction potential, among which the industrial structure, energy intensity and energy consumption structure have greater impact on interprovincial emission reduction potential.

China's average interprovincial CO_2 marginal abatement cost is 94.4–139.5 yuan/ton; the region is characterized by eastern>central>western. Shanxi, Guizhou, Inner Mongolia, Ningxia, Hebei and other places have the lowest CO_2 marginal abatement costs. The marginal abatement costs of Beijing, Fujian, Guangdong, Hainan, and Zhejiang are the highest. The average marginal abatement cost (MAC) of China's cities is 967 yuan/ton. From the regional point of view, it also shows the characteristics of the east>middle>west. In all cities, the ratio of the MAC of the highest abatement cost (Shanghai) to the lowest (Zhangjiajie) is as high as 70:1, and there is huge heterogeneity. And this difference shows a significant increase trend. The MAC of CO_2 may have a U-shaped relationship with income. The level of urbanization is positively related to the MAC, while the proportion of the secondary industry, the degree of openness and the per-capita transportation infrastructure are significantly negatively correlated with the MAC.

Finally, based on the principles of fairness and efficiency, this book simulates the regional emission quota allocation scheme and proposes two market instruments that can be adopted in the future.

When setting regional emission reduction targets, we need to consider the two dimensions of fairness and efficiency of emission reduction. If only the principle of fairness is considered, then regions with higher per-capita CO_2 emissions and higher economic development levels, such as Shanghai, Beijing, Tianjin, Inner Mongolia, Ningxia, and other provinces

122 *Strategic response*

should undertake more emission reduction obligations; if considering the efficiency of emission reduction and the impact on national emission reduction, then have greater emission reduction potential, lower MACs, and CO_2 emissions and emission reductions. For provinces with greater influence in the country, such as Hebei, Shanxi, Guizhou, Inner Mongolia, Shandong, and other provinces, they should undertake more emission reduction tasks; if both dimensions of equity and efficiency are considered, it is necessary to consider them when decomposing targets in emission reduction areas. The regions include Inner Mongolia, Shanxi, Hebei, Shandong, Liaoning, and other provinces.

Considering the future of China's rapid urbanization process and the background of "double the per-capita income of urban and rural residents by 2020," it can be expected that the cost of slowing or controlling CO_2 emissions in China's interprovincial/urban areas is becoming more and more expensive, if the economy is forced to develop. Provincial/ urban emission reductions may result in greater economic costs and costs. Therefore, the interprovincial/intercity emission reduction potential and cost difference factors should be fully considered, and the market mechanism should be used to achieve emission reduction targets and reduce overall abatement costs. Two options can be considered. First, the emission trading system, which reduces the cost of abatement through mutual trading between regions with higher and lower MACs; second, taxation that can be considered for unilateral payments. The system is that the central government imposes a tax on carbon emissions in areas with higher MACs, and transfers part of the tax to the lower MAC to compensate for its emission reduction losses. In the complete case of information, the welfare of these two social systems is equivalent.

5.2 Basic ideas for industrial structure adjustment

5.2.1 Current domestic and international situation in controlling greenhouse gas emissions

The formulation and introduction of any policy needs to fully consider the changes in the external environment. At present, the international and domestic situations facing China's control of GHGs and implementation of energy conservation and emission reduction mainly include the following.

From the perspective of the international situation, there are mainly three profound and major changes.

First, the global economy is uncertain and energy prices are fluctuating. Since the 2008 financial crisis, the global economy has been full of uncertainty. Economic uncertainty is also transmitted to the international energy market. From 2000 to 2008, the world's three major energy prices continued to rise; after the 2008 financial crisis, total energy demand fell sharply, energy prices fell sharply, but with the adjustment of macroeconomic policies and the recovery of emerging countries' demand, energy prices entered a new round. Since 2011, affected by the US shale gas revolution, the global economic slowdown and the overcapacity of major oil producers, energy prices have once again entered a downward channel, and the fluctuations have increased, which has intensified the uncertainty of energy investment, production and consumption.

Second, the international climate agreement can be expected, and the pressure on GHG emission reduction will increase. The international community is fully aware of the importance of the coordinated control of GHG emissions and has conducted numerous international negotiations. In 2014, in the UN Lima Climate Agreement, countries achieved an international consensus for the first time and promised to decide their own emission reduction plans. Overall, the international community has reached a broadly acceptable climate agreement. As a responsible big country and the largest emitter of GHGs, China will undoubtedly undertake more energy conservation and emission reduction tasks.

Third, the low-carbon approach has become a trend, and low-carbon economy, low-carbon life, and low-carbon energy have become the development trend. This is first manifested in the low carbonization of economic development. Developed countries such as the United Kingdom and Japan have taken the lead in achieving low-carbon economic transformation through breakthroughs in low-carbon energy-saving technologies and institutional innovation and industrial transformation. Second, the lifestyle is low-carbon. Through energy demand management and low-carbon education, more and more residents choose low-carbon lifestyles and try to reduce domestic energy and carbon emissions. Finally, it is reflected in the low carbonization of the energy structure. Countries are committed to the development of renewable energy and clean energy to achieve the goal of low carbonization of the energy structure.

Predicated on the domestic situation, there are three main changes and characteristics.

First, the concept of governing the country according to law has won the consensus of the whole society. The Fourth Plenary Session of the 18th CPC Central Committee clearly stated that it is necessary to "govern the country according to law and govern by the constitution." The broad recognition and implementation of the concept of governing the country according to law will further improve the laws and regulations for energy conservation and emission reduction and climate change management, and emphasize the implementation of the system at the same time; the implementation of the concept of governing the country according to law will form a good institutional environment, and further promote the operation of market mechanisms to promote GHG emission reduction and other energy conservation and emission reduction work. In addition, the popularization of the rule of law will form a good atmosphere for energy conservation and emission reduction in the whole society.

124   *Strategic response*

Second, positive progress has been made in economic restructuring. China's economic restructuring has made positive progress and the industrial structure has been optimized. After 2008, the proportion of the secondary industry has also declined due to the continuous decline in the proportion of the industry. The proportion of the tertiary industry has gradually increased. By 2013, the proportion of the tertiary industry in China has reached 46%, surpassing the proportion of the secondary industry (43%) for the first time. However, the proportion of China's tertiary industry is still lower than that of the United States (80%) and other developing countries (50%).

Third, energy security, energy efficiency, energy structure and environmental pollution are still outstanding. For example, the energy supply and demand gap continues to threaten national energy security. In 2012, China's import dependence on crude oil and natural gas was as high as 58% and 29%, respectively. At the same time, China's energy import method is relatively simple, and its source is relatively concentrated, mainly through sea transportation; energy security is extremely vulnerable to threats; energy efficiency is still low, and between 1990 and 2011, China's energy intensity fell by 52%. Although energy efficiency has been greatly improved, there are still large differences compared with developed countries. In 2011, China's energy consumption per unit of GDP was 2.5 times the world average, 5.4 times that of Japan, and 3.4 times that of the USA. In addition, coal-based energy structure and environmental pollution are difficult to reverse in the short term. Oil, less gas, coal accounted for about 70% of the primary energy for a long time, and the coal-based energy structure is difficult to fundamentally change in the short term. The coal-based energy structure has also brought about a large number of environmental problems, causing serious pollution and ecological damage to the atmosphere, water bodies and soils, and thus affecting the health of residents.

5.2.2 Main challenges in controlling current greenhouse gas emissions

The main challenges facing China's current energy conservation and emission reduction and control of GHG emissions are as follows.

First, under the background of the new economic normal, investment funds are under pressure. At present, China has entered a new economic normality from the transition to a high-speed growth period. As shown in Figure 5.1, the economic growth rate and the fiscal revenue and expenditure growth rate have gradually shifted from high-level to low-level operation, and the corresponding investment funds are also facing greater financial pressure. For example, in 2007, the total amount of local government finance and energy conservation expenditures was 96.1 billion yuan, accounting for 0.36% of the GDP in the same period. By 2012, the proportion was only 0.56%.

It can be expected that as China's reform enters the deep water area and the macro economy enters the deceleration shift period, controlling GHG

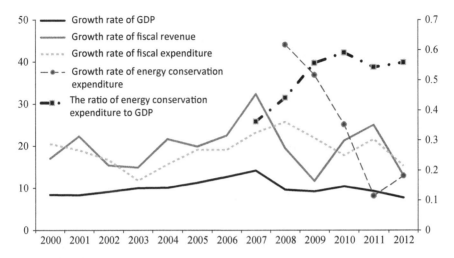

Figure 5.1 China's GDP, fiscal revenue and expenditure and local energy conservation protection expenditure trends (2000–2012)

emissions and implementing energy conservation and emission reduction may face the following three challenges. First, the requirements of "adjusting structure and promoting transformation" are energy-saving. The platoon work puts forward higher standards and requirements. Second, under the new normal state, the financial funds available to the government may also decrease or even decrease the total amount. The financial expenditures required for energy conservation and emission reduction may face greater pressure; in the period of economic slowdown or even decline, local governments in order to stabilize growth, under the actual pressure of reducing the original local fiscal revenue sources, the demand for investment is large, and it is inevitable that the energy conservation and emission reduction work will be placed in a secondary position. Therefore, the difficulty in controlling GHGs and implementing energy conservation and emission reduction will be greatly enhanced.

Second, the potential for energy conservation and emission reduction will decrease in the future, and the cost will increase. During the Eleventh Five-Year Plan and the Twelfth Five-Year Plan period, China's energy conservation and emission reduction has made great achievements. A large number of equipment and projects have been put into production successively. A considerable part of the backward production capacity with high energy consumption, high pollution, and low output has been eliminated. Starting from the Twelfth Five-Year Plan, energy conservation and emission reduction work has been carried out in terms of capacity replacement, mergers and acquisitions, environmental protection relocation, upgrading and transformation. During the Thirteenth Five-Year Plan period, the space for relying on new projects and large-scale elimination of backward production capacity has been small,

126 *Strategic response*

and the potential for energy conservation and emission reduction will decline in the future. In addition, the cost of energy conservation and emission reduction is also rising. Taking thermal power generation as an example, during the Eleventh Five-Year Plan period, many small thermal power plants have been shut down, and a large number of ultra-supercritical units have been launched. The thermal efficiency of power generation is close to the world advanced level. Under such conditions, the economic cost of thermal power efficiency is further improved. It will be very high.

Third, the goal of controlling GHG emissions conflicts with local performance assessments and other short-term goals. In China, some local governments and officials still regard economic growth as the top priority, lacking understanding of the urgency and arduousness of controlling GHG emissions, energy conservation and emission reduction, and paying insufficient attention to transforming development methods and adjusting industrial structure. The promotion of emission reduction work failed to handle the relationship between the two. Moreover, the interests of the central and local governments are inconsistent, which also leads to the partial implementation of some policies. In addition, short-term policy objectives often contradict policy objectives and long-term policy objectives for responding to emergencies. For example, the government needs to recover the economy by guaranteeing GDP growth targets, but the recovery economy often increases the difficulty of achieving energy conservation and emission reduction targets.

Fourth, the non-marketization distortion of energy prices is not conducive to the control of GHGs. The formation mechanism of China's existing energy prices mainly includes government pricing and monopolistic prices formed by monopoly. Due to factors such as single pricing entity and information asymmetry, the market has not played its due role in the allocation of energy resources. The price of energy cannot reflect the scarcity of its resources and the externalities generated during the consumption process. The overall price level is low, which not only causes huge waste, but also adjusts the economic structure of China, the development of energy conservation and emission reduction work and the ecological environment. The improvement has created a huge obstacle.

Fifth, infrastructure and support capabilities are relatively weak. China's GHG emission reduction management institutions and management systems are in the initial stage of development, and the level of supervision, coverage, and supervision are all constrained, and the capacity building of grassroots teams is weak. In addition, there are many shortcomings in the energy and GHG emissions statistical accounting system, monitoring and early warning, energy auditing, technology research and development and promotion and application. The relevant energy conservation and environmental protection industries have not been fully developed and cannot meet the current GHG emission reduction work.

Sixth, China's enterprises and citizens have weak awareness of energy conservation and need to be popularized. Enterprises generally pay insufficient attention to GHG emission reduction work. Due to insufficient policy coverage, low energy prices, lack of market mechanisms, and insufficient government supervision, enterprises lack the inherent motivation and incentives for spontaneous energy conservation and emission reduction, which has caused enterprises to pay less attention to their work and internal management systems are not perfect. In addition, there is a gap between the awareness of energy conservation and environmental protection of Chinese citizens compared with developed countries. This is mainly due to the lack of public participation mechanism and low level of citizen participation. In addition, the level of education and publicity related to GHG emission reduction in China still needs to be improved, which also hinders the popularization of citizens' awareness of energy conservation and environmental protection.

5.2.3 Basic ideas of industrial restructuring in the short and medium term

In summary, in the short and medium term, maintaining a certain rate of economic growth will remain one of the main goals of China's national economic development. The economic restructuring will also take a certain period of time to complete, so GHG emissions will increase further in the future. As a major driving force for curbing GHG emissions energy efficiency, there is also a great improvement in resistance, because the Eleventh Five-Year Plan energy conservation and emission reduction binding target requires a 20% reduction in energy intensity. For this reason, all parts of the country have already been launched. A large number of more energy-efficient and economical infrastructures and various energy-saving policies have been applied adequately. Then, in the Twelfth Five-Year Plan and Thirteenth Five-Year Plan periods, the space for reducing energy intensity through equipment renewal and administrative control has been further limited, so industrial restructuring in the short to medium term will become another major way to control GHG emissions.

The adjustment of industrial structure has its own evolutionary law. There are also interrelated relations between industries. It is impossible to force the transformation of a certain industry/industry due to its high level of GHG emissions. At the same time, it is necessary to maintain economic stability while controlling GHGs. Rapid growth, guaranteeing urbanization and industrialization processes, energy conservation and emission reduction strategies, and other strategic objectives are mutually connected and cannot be ignored. Therefore, adjusting the industrial structure to control GHG emissions requires the consideration of other strategies and planning from a global perspective.

The basic ideas of China's industrial restructuring in the short and medium term can be summarized as follows: comprehensively implement the scientific development concept, accelerate the transformation of economic development mode as the main line, adhere to the basic national policy of conserving resources and protecting the environment, so as to

128 *Strategic response*

slow down and control GHG emissions and enhance with the goal of industrial sustainable development, we will vigorously develop low-carbon industries that save energy, clean development and sustainable development, promote the optimization and upgrading of traditional high-carbon industries, vigorously develop circular economy, optimize energy structure, and strictly control high-energy consumption, high-emissions industry, accelerate the elimination of backward production capacity; promote the healthy and coordinated development of the primary, secondary and tertiary industries, and gradually form an industrial structure based on agriculture, high-tech industries as the forerunner, basic industries and manufacturing industries, and comprehensive development of the service industry, and further optimize the spatial layout of the industry, improve its ability to cope with climate change, and make new contributions to protecting the global climate.

5.2.5 Basic principles of industrial restructuring in the short to medium term

The basic principles of industrial restructuring in China in the short to medium term include the following five points.

First, we must adhere to the principle of organically combining industrial policies, climate change policies and other relevant policies. Actively responding to and adapting to climate change is the direction and goal of industrial restructuring. Industrial restructuring is the main way and means to reduce and control GHG emissions. It is necessary to adjust the industrial restructuring strategy with China's climate change policy and the successful implementation of energy-saving emission reduction policies, ecological protection and construction policies and other organic integration, so as to achieve the overall consideration and coordination between different policies.

Second, we must adhere to the combination of market mechanisms and government guidance. It is necessary to give full play to the role of the main body of the enterprise, follow the characteristics and laws of the industry itself, give full play to the basic role of market allocation of resources, strengthen market supervision to promote fair competition and efficient development; the government is fulfilling its basic public service responsibilities and ensuring basic needs. At the same time, the operation of non-essential services will be given more to the market regulation, and comprehensive use of fiscal, tax, price, financial and other policy measures will be used to guide the development of the industry and achieve optimal resource allocation.

Third, we must adhere to the principle of relying on scientific and technological progress and technological innovation to drive industrial upgrading. Scientific and technological progress and technological innovation are effective ways to reduce GHG emissions and improve the adaptability of climate change. They are also a favorable support for upgrading industrial technology and realizing industrial transformation and upgrading. We must vigorously develop new energy, renewable energy technologies and new energy-saving technologies to promote the development of carbon absorption technology and various adaptive technologies will promote its application in the industry and enhance the overall technical level of the industry.

Fourth, we must adhere to the principle of combining industrial restructuring with energy efficiency and optimizing energy structure initiatives. Industrial restructuring is only one of the factors affecting climate change. In order to comprehensively and effectively control GHG emissions, it is necessary to adopt multiple approaches. While actively adjusting the industrial structure, it will vigorously promote the improvement of internal energy efficiency, and develop and promote the use of renewable clean energy and optimize energy structure.

Fifth, we must adhere to the principle of scientific layout of industrial structure. The adjustment of industrial structure is not only the change of relative proportion between different industries, but also the adjustment of different geographical distribution. It is necessary to follow the division requirements of the main functional areas, optimize the industrial structure and layout between urban and rural areas, and optimize the domestic market and international market industrial structure layout.

5.3 Strategic conception of industrial structure adjustment

In order to control the speed and scale of GHG emissions, China's industrial restructuring can follow the four strategic ideas of "plus," "subtract," "lift," and "transfer."

5.1.1 Addition strategy: vigorously develop low-carbon and carbon-fixing industries

The addition strategy consists of two levels. One is to develop low-carbon industries and promote the development of the overall industrial structure by promoting the development of low-carbon sectors with low energy consumption, low emissions and high output, while improving the overall industry carbon emissions productivity. The second level is the development of carbon-fixing industries, which promotes the development of industries with carbon sequestration properties, sequestering carbon dioxide from existing atmospheres, thereby forming carbon sinks and directly reducing carbon emissions. Its specific strategic content includes:

(1) Promote the scale and proportion of the development of service industries with low energy consumption and low emissions. Put the modern service industry in a priority position, expand the total scale of the

130   *Strategic response*

service industry, and increase the proportion of the service industry in the three industrial structures. Adhere to the equal emphasis on production service industry and life service industry, modern service industry and traditional service industry, and vigorously develop various service formats that support production, benefit the people and increase employment, and focus on cultivating modern logistics, design consulting, e-commerce, health services, etc. The new service format will promote the development of the service industry, increase its proportion, and increase its level, ensuring that the value added of the service industry will reach 47% of GDP at the end of the Twelfth Five-Year Plan.

(2) Cultivate and strengthen strategic emerging industries. To strengthen and expand the high-tech industry that plays a major role in economic and social development, accelerate the cultivation and development of emerging industries such as information, biology, new materials, new energy, aerospace and other industries that meet the requirements for energy conservation and emission reduction, and actively develop new materials industries to ensure that by 2015, the added value of strategic emerging industries will increase to about 8% of GDP.

(3) Develop ecologically efficient agriculture. Significantly reduce the use of chemical fertilizers and pesticides, promote the use of organic fertilizers, improve soil carbon sequestration capacity, make full use of agricultural and sideline residues as biomass energy and organic fertilizer raw materials, promote solar energy and biogas technology, improve farmers' health and living environment, and protect food safety.

(4) Promote the development of forestry and related biological carbon sequestration industries. Continue to implement forestry key ecological construction projects such as afforestation, returning farmland to forests and grassland, natural forest resources protection, and shelter forest systems, curb the increasing trend of grassland desertification, restore grassland vegetation and grassland coverage, and build on existing forest and grassland carbon sequestration. Increase forestry carbon sinks. At the same time, cultivate other biological carbon sequestration industries, such as the development of economic algae and oil-producing energy algae farming. By 2015, we will strive to achieve a forest coverage rate of 21.66%.

(5) Explore the development of marine carbon sequestration industry. About 13% of the carbon dioxide produced by fossil fuels on the earth is absorbed by terrestrial vegetation, and 35% is absorbed by the ocean. At present, countries are in the starting stage in this field. When implementing the plan for marine economic development, China should combine Hong Kong's industrial characteristics, actively explore and develop marine low-carbon technologies, tap the potential of marine carbon sequestration, form relevant industrial chains such as research and development of marine carbon sequestration technologies, carbon-fixing equipment

Industrial restructuring strategy 131

manufacturing, and carbon-fixing technology applications, and form an international community as soon as possible.

(6) Increase research on carbon capture and storage technologies. CO_2 capture and storage (CCS) technology has been listed as a frontier technology in China's medium- and long-term science and technology development plan. Because the technology is still in the preliminary research stage, China should pay close attention to the progress of CCS technology and carry out related technology and project cooperation with developed countries. Carry out carbon-capture experimental projects in the thermal power, coal chemical, cement and steel industries, and build a demonstration project of carbon dioxide capture, oil displacement and storage for large-scale practical applications in the future.

5.3.2 Subtraction strategy: contain heavy chemical industry, shut down the backward industry

The subtraction strategy also includes two levels. One is to curb the scale and speed of expansion of high-energy, high-emission, low-output, high-carbon sectors at a relative level, so that the proportion of these sectors has declined, or to maintain relative Stable state, thus relatively reducing the scale and speed of GHG emissions of the entire industry, to achieve the goal of relative emission reduction; second, in the absolute level, eliminate backward production capacity, thereby directly reducing the GHG emissions brought by this part of production activities. Specifically includes the following:

(1) To curb the scale and growth rate of heavy chemical industry with high energy consumption and high emissions. Strictly control new heavy chemical industry projects with high energy consumption, high emissions and overcapacity, further improve industry access standards for high energy consumption, high emissions and overcapacity, improve energy efficiency and environmental protection barriers, and strengthen energy conservation, environmental protection, land and safety. Such as index constraints, establish and improve project approval, approval, and record responsibility system, and strictly control new projects.

(2) Accelerate the elimination of backward production capacity. In accordance with the principle of "controlling the total amount, eliminating backwardness, mergers and acquisitions, and independent innovation," we will coordinate industrial, environmental protection, land and financial policies, improve the exit mechanism of backward production capacity, strictly implement the "two high" industry elimination standards, and implement the state's production capacity reduction in some industries' excessive and redundant construction policies and measures to strictly control the new capacity of high-energy industries such as cement, steel, electrolytic aluminum, and coke.

132 *Strategic response*

5.3.3 Upgrade strategy: upgrade traditional industries and improve resource efficiency

The addition strategy is mainly to increase low-carbon industries. The subtraction strategy is mainly to reduce high-carbon industries, and the improvement strategy is mainly for stocks, that is, to maintain the scale of existing industrial sectors, through industrial transformation and upgrading, resource recycling, and energy efficiency. Improve the way to achieve the same input, increase output, or output to reduce energy and other factors, thereby improving the economic efficiency of GHG emissions, reducing the GHG emission intensity per unit of output, and achieving indirect emission reduction. Specifically include the following strategic content:

(1) Promote the transformation and upgrading of traditional manufacturing. For China's traditional equipment manufacturing sector, the focus is on improving the level of localization of technical equipment and improving the overall level of R&D, processing, manufacturing and system integration through independent innovation, introduction of technology, cooperative development, and joint manufacturing; the department should use industrialization to promote industrialization, use high-tech and advanced practical technologies to transform, promote the in-depth integration of information and industrialization, and increase the proportion of independent intellectual property rights, independent brands and high-end products. According to energy, resource conditions and environmental capacity, we will focus on adjusting the product structure, enterprise organization structure and industrial layout of the raw material industry to improve product quality and technical content.

(2) Actively explore and develop circular economy. In accordance with the requirements of the new industrialization road, we will actively promote the reduction of clean production and resource utilization in the industrial sector, reuse and resource utilization, and form a more mature model of circular economy development within enterprises, enterprises and parks, and reduce cement as much as possible. The use of lime, steel, calcium carbide and other products to reduce GHG emissions from the source and production processes. At the same time, it researches and promotes advanced waste incineration and landfill gas recycling technologies, promotes the industrialization of waste treatment, and reduces GHG emissions such as methane during waste disposal. By 2015, the comprehensive utilization rate of industrial solid waste will reach over 72%.

(3) Strive to improve energy efficiency in key industries. Improve the concentration of key industries such as steel, cement, non-ferrous metals, machinery, and automobiles, reduce the energy consumption level of energy-consuming products in key industries, and improve energy efficiency. Implement energy-saving key projects and strengthen energy-saving management. Implement energy-saving renovation projects such as

boiler kiln renovation, motor system energy conservation, energy system optimization, energy-saving technology industrialization demonstration project, contract energy management promotion project, etc., and promote energy conservation in industries, construction, transportation and other fields and industries.

5.3.4 Transfer strategy: transfer high-carbon product production and replace high-carbon energy

The transfer strategy has three main meanings. The first is to reduce the production of productive carbon sources through the transfer of industrial structure in spatial layout. Developed countries have transferred the production of a large number of high-carbon products industries to developing countries. At the same time, they have also constrained developing countries through international negotiations. Under the premise that they cannot temporarily change the basic framework of international climate negotiations, they can consider part of the developed regions in China in due course. The geographical transfer of carbon industry to other neighboring countries; the second is to reduce carbon through the carbon product trade strategy; that is, to form a trade deficit of high-carbon products through international trade, thereby indirectly reducing domestic energy consumption and carbon emissions. It is the transfer of energy between different carbon sources in the energy production conversion sector; that is, the replacement between clean energy and traditional fossil energy. Specific strategic content includes:

(1) Optimize industrial layout for domestic and international markets, and promote capacity transfer and overseas investment. In the process of industrial transformation and upgrading, the central and western regions will undertake a large number of industrial transfer in the east. The central and western regions should adhere to the requirements of the main functional zoning, adhere to high standards according to the resource and environmental carrying capacity and development potential, and ban high-energy consumption and high pollution industries and backwardness. Transfer of production capacity. Support qualified enterprises to go abroad to invest overseas, and transfer some industries that do not have labor advantages, resource and energy consumption, carbon emissions and other serious pollution to other countries.
(2) Strictly control the export of high-carbon products and increase the import of energy-intensive products to replace domestic production. We will adopt measures such as adjusting export tax rebates and tariffs to strictly control the export of high-energy, high-emission and resource-based products, and increase the import scale of corresponding resource-based raw materials, energy-intensive and carbon-intensive processed products. In addition, the use of fiscal and taxation means to encourage the import of equipment, instruments and technical materials for clean

134 *Strategic response*

production, and to ban the production technology, equipment and products that are explicitly eliminated by the state.

(3) Develop renewable energy sources to replace traditional fossil energy sources. Under the premise of environmental protection and resettlement, we will develop hydropower in an orderly manner, strive to build a large-scale wind power industry and wind power base, promote the development and utilization of biomass energy, and actively support solar power, solar heat, geothermal energy, and ocean. We can develop and utilize such resources, actively and steadily promote the construction of nuclear power, and replace traditional fossil energy with clean renewable energy. By 2015, non-fossil energy accounts for 11.4% of total primary energy consumption, of which commercialized renewable energy accounts for more than 9.5% of total energy consumption.

5.4 Key fields and links of industrial structure adjustment

According to previous empirical studies, the most important areas of concern for the impact of GHGs on various sectors are: the energy sector, the industrial sector, and the transportation sector. The three sectors account for the national economy. More than 97% of GHG emissions from fossil energy are consumed in the sector.

From the perspective of the direction and size of the various factors affecting GHG emissions, the expansion of production scale is the main cause of the increase in GHG emissions, and the adjustment of industrial structure and the improvement of energy efficiency have played a positive role in mitigating GHGs. The industry, the optimization of energy consumption structure and the carbon emission coefficient effect also inhibited the growth of GHGs to some extent.

5.4.1 Energy sector

The energy sector, especially the electric power and heat production industries, is one of the main sources of GHG emissions. The expansion of its output scale has led to an increase in GHG emissions, and its annual decline in the proportion of the economy has slowed down CO_2 emissions. In addition, energy intensity effect and energy structure effects within the department are also greatly affected; therefore, the structural adjustment of the energy sector is mainly concentrated in three aspects.

First, we must focus on controlling the scale and speed of power production expansion mitigating GHG emissions from energy production and conversion processes. Under the premise of ensuring economic production and energy use, rationally arrange new investment to avoid redundant construction. New energy projects must meet the relevant access standards for energy conservation and environmental protection, and small power plants and small coal mines that do not comply with national industrial policies. Wait for the shutdown and transfer to eliminate backward production capacity.

The second is to vigorously optimize the energy structure. On the basis of protecting the ecology, we will develop hydropower in an orderly manner, actively promote nuclear power construction on the basis of ensuring safety, and appropriately develop small-scale distributed power sources using natural gas and coal-bed methane as fuel, and use biomass to generate electricity, biogas, biomass solid fuel and liquid fuel. Focusing on the development and utilization of biomass energy, we will develop renewable energy such as wind energy, solar energy, biomass energy and geothermal energy according to local conditions.

The third is to continue to improve energy efficiency. Vigorously develop high-efficiency and clean power generation technologies such as supercritical units and large combined cycle units with a single machine of 600,000 kW and above, develop cogeneration and combined heat and power gas technologies to improve power generation efficiency and strengthen the power grid construction, using advanced transmission, transformation, distribution technology and equipment to reduce energy consumption.

5.4.2 Industry

The industrial sector is also the main source of GHG emissions, and its most influential sectors include: metal products, non-metal products and petroleum processing, while equipment manufacturing has low emissions and high output; production scale expansion is the main factor leading to an increase in industrial CO_2 emissions, and the improvement of energy efficiency within the industrial sector and the adjustment of sectoral structure are the two main ways to reduce GHG emissions. The improvement of energy structure and the low carbonization of fuel carbon emission coefficient have a relatively small contribution to industrial CO_2 emissions. Therefore, the structural adjustments to the industrial sector are mainly concentrated in three areas.

First, we must vigorously curb the excessive growth of heavy-duty industries with high energy consumption and high emissions. Especially for steel, non-ferrous metals, petrochemicals, building materials and other high-energy-consumption and high-emission departments, we must strengthen existing industrial policies, strict market access standards for high-energy-consuming industries, improve energy-saving and environmental protection thresholds, and adopt export tax rebates. Measures such as tariffs will curb the export of "two high and one capital" (high energy consumption, high emission, resource type) products, adjust the scale of high energy consumption and high pollution industries, and reduce the proportion of high energy consumption and high pollution industries; industrial policies, severely polluting ironmaking, steelmaking, cement and chemical production capacity.

The second is to accelerate the development of equipment manufacturing and other high-tech industries. In particular, the development of advanced manufacturing industries with the focus on revitalizing the equipment manufacturing industry, encourage the use of high-tech and advanced applicable

136 *Strategic response*

technologies to transform and upgrade the manufacturing industry, accelerate the development of high-tech industries and information industries, and increase the proportion of "low-carbon" industries in industrial development.

In addition, it is necessary to promote cleaner production and circular economy models in the industrial sector to improve resource utilization. In accordance with the principles of reduction, reuse, and resource utilization, we will vigorously promote the construction of comprehensive recycling and reuse systems for resources, and focus on promoting technological transformation of energy conservation and consumption reduction in industries such as iron and steel, non-ferrous metals, electric power, petrochemicals, construction, coal, building materials, and papermaking. For metallurgy, building materials, chemical and other industries, strengthen measures such as nitrous oxide emission control to control GHG emissions from industrial production processes.

5.4.3 Transportation industry

The expansion of the transportation industry is the main driver of the increase in GHGs, and the main factors that mitigate GHG emissions are energy intensity effects and energy structure effects. If we only focus on the transportation sector itself, its internal structural adjustment mainly focuses on three aspects. First, we must control the scale of the transportation industry infrastructure, optimize the transportation structure of railways, highways, waterways, civil aviation, and pipelines, and focus on urban and intercity development. The rapid transportation network will give priority to the development of urban public transportation, increase the proportion of rail transit in urban transportation, and properly control the growth rate of private transportation. The second is to improve the fuel efficiency of vehicles. Accelerate the elimination of old vehicles with high energy consumption, promote the implementation of the national standard for the "fuel consumption limit of passenger cars," control the development of high-fuel-consuming vehicles from the source, adopt the fuel-saving model, and improve the load rate, passenger load factor and transportation. Turnover capacity, improve fuel efficiency and reduce fuel consumption. The third is to accelerate the development of electrified railways, develop high-efficiency electric locomotives, and encourage enterprises to develop and produce hybrid vehicles, pure electric vehicles, and other vehicles that use renewable alternative energy sources.

In addition, another factor in the surge of GHGs in the transportation industry is China's accelerating urbanization process. Therefore, controlling the GHG emissions of the transportation sector requires not only the adjustment of the internal structure of the transportation sector, but also the multichannel solution of urban planning and other measures. For example, to control the scale of development of megacities, scientifically formulate urban spatial planning, and adhere to the group-type urban pattern. On the one

Industrial restructuring strategy 137

hand, intercity transportation is called connecting large and medium-sized cities, and on the other hand, within the city, it is necessary to break through the circulation between buildings. The passage unblocks the city's microcirculation system.

5.4.4 Agriculture

The agricultural GHGs are mainly methane and nitrous oxide. The GHG emissions of agricultural sources in China account for about 17% of the total GHG emissions in the country. In the agricultural production process, not only are GHGs released, but also the carbon sink function of agriculture can be effective. To offset the GHG emissions caused by production processes and energy consumption; in addition, the agricultural sector not only needs to slow down GHGs, but more importantly, it needs to adjust the ability of the agricultural sector to adapt to climate change through structural adjustment, thus promoting the structural adjustment of the agricultural industry. There is a need to consider the mitigation and adaptation of climate change capabilities in the agricultural sector from the two levels of GHG emissions and GHG absorption. The focus can be on the following.

First, we must strengthen the construction of agricultural infrastructure and improve the ability of agriculture to adapt to climate change. Accelerate the implementation of large-scale irrigation districts with water-saving transformation as the center, focus on the construction of field projects, update and rebuild aging mechanical and electrical equipment, improve irrigation and drainage systems; eliminate backward agricultural machinery, promote less tillage and no-tillage, joint operations, etc., mechanized agronomic technology, the use of electric motors in fixed work sites, the development of renewable energy such as water, wind and solar energy in agricultural machinery. Vigorously develop rural biogas, promote the application of rural renewable energy technologies such as solar energy, fuel-saving and coal-saving stoves.

Second, we must strengthen the construction of ecological agriculture, optimize the structure of agricultural products, and slow down GHG emissions from agriculture. Implement agricultural non-point source pollution prevention and control projects, continue to promote low-emission high-yield rice varieties and semi-dry cultivation techniques, adopt scientific irrigation and soil testing and formula fertilization techniques, scientifically apply chemical fertilizers, guide the application of organic fertilizers, and reduce nitrous oxide emissions from farmland; promote conservation tillage with straw cover and no-tillage as the main content, develop straw to raise livestock, return to the abdomen and increase soil organic carbon content; at the same time expand the cultivation of economic crops and forage crops, cultivate high yield potential and good quality, comprehensive varieties of excellent animals and plants with outstanding resistance and wide adaptability, systematically cultivate and select drought-resistant, anti-caries, high-temperature resistant, pest-resistant

138 *Strategic response*

and other resistant varieties, research and development of excellent ruminant breed technology and large-scale feeding management techniques, etc.

Finally, we must actively develop forestry, increase carbon sinks, and reduce GHG emissions. Strictly control the reclamation of land in areas with fragile ecological environment, promote the further development of afforestation work, and continue to promote forestry key ecological construction projects such as natural forest resource protection, returning farmland to forests and grasslands, shelter forest systems, wildlife protection and nature reserve construction. We will do a good job in the construction of biomass energy forestry bases, and further increase the capacity of land carbon storage and carbon sinks to reduce GHG emissions on the basis of protecting existing forest carbon storage.

5.4.5 *Construction industry*

Broad-based urban building energy consumption includes housing construction, water supply and drainage, heating, ventilation, lighting, air conditioning, household appliances, cooking and other fields. The construction industry's own GHG emissions are small, but the building-related heating and other energy consumption and GHG emissions from the use of the building are considerable. According to statistics, the energy consumed in the construction and use of buildings worldwide accounts for about 50% of total energy consumption, and China is about 47%. However, the life expectancy of buildings in China is generally short, plus the average insulation level of building exterior walls. It is one-third of the European countries in the same latitude, thus resulting in a total lifetime comprehensive energy consumption per unit of building area is 2–3 times that of developed countries.

In general, in the early planning, design and construction of China's construction industry, energy conservation concepts and standards are lacking, and supervision is weak, and the efficiency of the construction process is paid more attention, but the long-term use and energy-saving efficiency of the use process are less considered. The structural adjustment of the construction industry needs to be carried out in three aspects. First, it is necessary to develop green buildings, promote green construction, and strengthen energy conservation and emission reduction throughout the construction of the project to achieve low-cost, environmentally friendly and efficient production. Second, for new buildings, strict implementation of building energy-saving standards, the use of advanced energy-saving emission reduction technology, vigorously promote the application of high-strength steel and high-performance concrete; promote the application of high-performance, low-material consumption, renewable recycling of building materials, and actively carry out recycling and utilization of construction waste and waste products; making full use of straw and other products to produce plant fiberboard; promoting residential full-renovation and assembly construction, and promoting renewable energy, such as the application of solar water heaters in buildings. Third, on the existing stock buildings, on the one hand, we must promote the urban heating measurement reform in the northern regions, and on the other hand, increase the energy-saving renovation of large public buildings and ordinary houses.

5.4.6 Service industry

The scale of GHG emissions in the service industry is much lower than that in the industrial sector, but there is still a large potential for emission reduction and space. The main focus should be on increasing the proportion of the service industry, while optimizing the internal structure of the service industry and providing services to other productive sectors. The consulting services for energy conservation and emission reduction mainly focus on the following three aspects.

First, we must promote the accelerated development of the service industry and increase the proportion of the service industry. We will vigorously develop modern service industries such as finance, insurance, logistics, information and legal services, accounting, intellectual property, technology, design, and consulting services, and actively develop industries with high demand potential such as culture, tourism, and community services, and accelerate education, training, and aged care services reform and development in areas such as health care. Standardize and upgrade traditional service industries such as commerce, catering, accommodation, etc., and promote organizational forms and service methods such as chain operations, franchising, agency, multi-modal transport, and e-commerce.

The second is to vigorously optimize and improve the internal energy efficiency of the service industry. Promote the implementation of energy standards and labels in public institutions such as hotels, restaurants, office buildings, schools, hospitals, etc., promote the use of high-efficiency energy-saving appliances and electric lamps, and implement the transformation of systemic energy-saving projects such as lighting, air conditioning, water pumps, and top heat utilization. Strengthen the management of overpackaging of goods, reduce the use of disposable articles, strictly enforce the restrictions on plastics, rationally plan and construct efficient and convenient modern logistics networks, vigorously develop third-party logistics, implement urban common distribution and centralized distribution, and improve logistics distribution efficiency.

The third is to vigorously develop energy-saving service industries and energy-saving consulting services. Vigorously develop energy-saving service industries that use contract energy management and power demand side management mechanisms, establish a vibrant, distinctive and standardized energy-saving service market, and establish a relatively complete energy-saving service system.

140 *Strategic response*

5.5 Safeguard measures for the implementation of industrial structure adjustment strategy

In order to ensure that the GHG emission binding targets can be achieved through effective industrial restructuring in the coming period, it is necessary to comprehensively utilize various government means and market-based means. To this end, it is recommended to ensure the adjustment of industrial structure through the following measures.

5.5.1 Strengthening the target responsibility assessment system

The central government has decomposed the target of carbon dioxide emissions per unit of GDP and established a statistical monitoring and evaluation system. In order to achieve this strategic goal, by 2015, the value-added of service industry will increase to 47%, and the proportion of added value of strategic emerging industries will increase to 8%. This is an important way to achieve this. From the central to the provincial level, two industrial structure indicators, as well as other indicators (such as the proportion of the first two or three industries are regularly monitored and evaluated the proportion of heavy chemical industry, etc.); at the provincial level, there is no strict industrial structure adjustment targets, but also according to the province's own industrial structure characteristics and related industrial structure development plans, formulate corresponding industrial structure adjustment targets and measures to promote GHG emission reduction targets in various regions and the realization of national industrial restructuring targets.

5.5.2 Implementation of the existing industrial restructuring policies

Strictly implement and implement the Guidance Catalogue for Industrial Structure Adjustment issued by the State, the Catalogue of Guidance for Foreign Investment Industries, and the Catalogue of Regional Industry Guidance; continuously improve the access threshold for industries with high energy consumption, high emissions and overcapacity, and improve project approval, approval and filing system, strictly control new and backward production capacity; resolutely eliminate and dismantle outdated production capacity, according to the list of "eliminating backward production capacity enterprises," smelting and lead in iron making, steel making, coke, ferroalloy, calcium carbide, copper (recycled copper) (including recycled lead) smelting, zinc (including regenerative zinc) smelting, cement (clinker and mill), flat glass, paper, alcohol, leather, printing and dyeing, chemical fiber, lead storage batteries and other high-energy consumption, high-pollution industries, backward production capacity resolutely eliminated.

5.5.3 *Accelerate the pace of market-oriented reforms and increase industrial concentration*

It is necessary to further increase the pace of market-oriented reforms, break the situation of regional administrative monopoly and market segmentation, and use assets as a link to achieve reintegration of resource elements through acquisitions, mergers, and reorganizations, to avoid duplication of construction and formation of backward production capacity between regions. Enterprises will become stronger and bigger, continuously increase industrial concentration and form economies of scale.

5.5.4 *Form a price mechanism that reflects the cost of resources and the environment*

It is necessary to rationalize the relationship between factor prices and price factors (such as coal, oil, natural gas, etc.) to form a price mechanism that reflects resource costs and environmental costs, thereby guiding low carbonization and new carbon industry through price adjustment leverage low-carbon production capacity.

5.5.5 *Comprehensive use of fiscal and taxation means to support the transformation and upgrading of traditional industries*

The fundamental driving force for the transformation and upgrading of traditional industries is to improve product quality through innovation, such as fiscal interest subsidies, tax reductions, equipment loans, subsidies for conversion, accelerated equipment depreciation, high carbon product export tax increases, low carbon products export tax rebates, etc. Measures to support traditional enterprises to carry out technological transformation and equipment upgrades, thereby enhancing the competitiveness of traditional industries, improving the technical content and added value of products, and at the same time forming new industrial growth points.

5.5.6 *Providing public welfare support for technology, management, and training for the elimination industry*

For declining industries, shutting down and transferring industries and other backward industries, it is necessary to provide corresponding technical and operational guidance, consulting and employee skills training and other public services, and incorporate them into the government's public welfare social service system, thereby reducing social and economic shocks caused by production capacity.

References

Articles published in Chinese

Cai Bofeng. (2012a). China's urban greenhouse gas inventory study. *China Population, Resources and Environment*, *22*(1), 21–27.

Cai Bofeng. (2012b). Analysis of CO_2 emissions in Chinese cities based on 0.1° grid. *China Population, Resources and Environment*, *22*(10), 151–157.

Cao Jing. (2009). The design of China coal tax and CGE model. *Financial Research*, *12*, 19–29.

Chang Xinghua. (2007). SWOT analysis of Jing-Jin-Ji metropolitan region. *Review of Economic Research*, *8*, 2–27.

Chen Ru & Lu Jinyong. (2010). A restudy on efficiency of China's commercial banks: Based on directional distance function. *South China Finance*, *12*, 42–46.

Chen Shiyi. (2010a). China's green industrial revolution: An interpretation based on environmental total factor productivity (1980–2008). *Economic Research*, *45*(11), 21–34.

Chen Shiyi. (2010b). Shadow prices of industrial carbon dioxide: Parametric and non-parametric methods. *World Economy*, *33*(8), 93–111.

Chen Shiyi. (2010c). Energy-saving emission reduction and win–win development of Chinese industry: 2009—2049. *Economic Research*, *45*(3), 129–143.

Chen Shiyi. (2011). Marginal emission reduction costs and China's environmental tax reform. *Chinese Social Sciences*, *3*, 85–100.

Chen Zhaorong. (2011). Empirical study on the relationship between the advanced industrial structure and carbon emissions in China. *Journal of Hubei University of Economics*, *9*(4), 77–81.

Dong Feng, Tan Qingmei, Zhou Dequn, & Li Xiaohui. (2010). The effect of technology progress to energy efficiency: Based on total factor productivity index including environment factor and panel econometric analysis. *Science of Science and Management of S. & T.*, *6*, 53–58.

Feng Fei. (2011). Cultivate new competitive advantage and promote industrial structure adjustment and upgrading – "The 12th Five-Year Plan" and the study of China's industrial structure change in 2020. *China Development Watch*, 42–44.

Fu Jiafeng, et al., 2008. An empirical study of the CO_2 environment Kuznets curve from the perspective of production and consumption. *Progress in Climate Change Research*, *6*, 376–381.

Gao Guangsheng. (2006). Climate change and allocation of carbon emission rights. *Progress in Climate Change Research*, *2*(6), 301–305.

References 143

Gao Pengfei & Chen Wenying. (2002). Carbon tax and carbon emission. *Journal of Tsinghua University*, *42*(10), 1335–1338.

Gao Pengfei, Chen Wenying, & He Jiankun. (2004). Costs of carbon dioxide marginal abatement in China. *Journal of Tsinghua University (Science Edition)*, *44*(9), 1192–1195.

He Jiankun, Zhang Xiliang, Li Zheng, & Chang Shiyan. (2008). Some issues of China's energy development under CO_2 emission reduction scenarios. *Science and Technology Review*, *26*(2).

He Jiankun. (2011). Low carbon development in Twelfth Five-Year Plan period: Trends and policies. *China Opening Journal*, *4*, 9–12.

He Juhuang, Shen Keting, & Xu Songling. (2002). Carbon tax and carbon dioxide mitigation: A CGE approach. *Journal of Quantitative & Technical Economics*, *10*, 39–47.

Hu Angang, Zheng Jinghai, Gao Yuning, Zhang Ning, & Xu Haiping. (2008). Provincial technical efficiency ranking considering environmental factors (1999–2005). *Economics Quarterly*, *3*, 933–960.

Li Yanmei & Fu Jiafeng. (2010). Structural decomposition analysis of the implied carbon emission growth in China's export trade. *China Population, Resources and Environment*, *8*, 53–57.

Liu Minglei, Zhu Lei, & Fan Ying. (2011). China's provincial carbon emission performance evaluation and marginal abatement cost estimation: Based on non-parametric distance function methods. *China Soft Science*, *3*, 106–114.

Liu Shucheng. (2008). Progressive, a road to reform in line with China's national conditions. *Guangming Daily*, Beijing.

Liu Zaiqi & Chen Chun. (2010). Research on the adjustment of low-carbon economy and industrial structure. *Foreign Social Sciences*, *3*, 21–27.

National Development and Reform Commission. (2004). *People's Republic of China initial national information on climate change*. Beijing.

National Development and Reform Commission. (2007). *China's National Climate Change Program*. Beijing.

Pan Jiahua & Zheng Yan. (2009). Responsibility and individual equity for carbon emissions rights. *World Economics and Politics*, *10*, 6–17.

Qi Yue & Xie Gaodi. (2009). The carbon emission permits allocation and its impact on regional functions in China. *Resources Science*, *4*, 590–597.

Qin Dahe. (2008). Recent developments in the science of climate change. *Science and Technology Review*, *26*(7), 1–3.

Qin Shaojun, Zhang Wenkui, & Yin Haitao. (2011). Cost estimation of carbon dioxide emissions reduction in Shanghai thermal power enterprises based on output distance function. *Journal of Engineering Management*, *25*(6), 704–708.

Shen Gang. (2009). The global gaming of GHG emission reduction. *China Development Observation*, *6*, 16–18.

State Council Development Research Center on Climate Change Task Force. (2009). Current key issues and policy recommendations for developing a low-carbon economy. *China Development Watch*, *8*, 13–15.

Su Ming, Fu Zhihua, Xu Wen, Wang Zhigang, Li Xin, & Liang Qiang. (2009). *Review of Economic Research*, *72*, 8–18.

The Chinese Academy of Sciences Sustainable Development Strategy Research Group. (2009). *2009 China Sustainable Development Strategy Report – Exploring low-carbon roads with Chinese characteristics*. Beijing: Science Press.

144 *References*

Tu Zhengge. (2008). Coordination of environment, resources, and industrial growth. *Economic Research, 2*, 93–105.

Tu Zhengge. (2009). The shadow price of industrial SO_2 emissions: A new analysis framework. *Economics Quarterly, 9*(1), 259–282.

Tu Zhengge. (2012). China's carbon emissions reduction path and strategic choice: An index decomposition analysis of carbon emissions in eight industries sectors. *Chinese Social Sciences, 3*, 78–94, 206–207.

Tu Zhengge & Liu Leiyi. (2011). Evaluation of China's industrial efficiency considering energy and environmental factors: Provincial data analysis based on SBM model. *Economic Review, 2*, 55–65.

Wang Bin & Yu Dongxi. (2004). Analysis of the economic structure effect of China's informatization: Empirical research based on the econometric model. *China's Industrial Economy, 7*, 21–28.

Wang Bing, Wu Yanrui, Yan Pengfei. (2008). Environmental regulation and total factor productivity growth: An empirical study of the APEC economies. *Economic Research, 5*, 19–23.

Wang Bing, Wu Yanrui, & Yan Pengfei. (2010). China's regional environmental efficiency and environmental total factor productivity growth. *Economic Research, 45*(5), 95–109.

Wang Bing, Zhang Jihui, & Zhang Hua. (2011). Empirical study of provincial total factor energy efficiency under environmental constraints. *Economic Review, 4*, 31–43.

Wang Qunwei, Cui Qinjun, & Zhou Dequn. (2011). Marginal abatement costs of carbon dioxide in China: A nonparametric analysis. *Energy Procedia, 5*, 2316–2320.

Wang Yirong. (2006). Sensitivity of grain and oil production to climate warming in Gansu Province. *Agricultural Research in Arid Regions, 24*(5).

Wang Yueping. (2009). Study on China's industrial structure adjustment strategies and policies during the Twelfth Five-Year Plan period. *Macroeconomic Research, 11*, 3–8.

Wei Chu, Huang Wenruo, & Shen Manhong. (2011). A review of environmental sensitivity productivity research. *World Economy, 5*, 136–160.

Wei Chu & Shen Manhong. (2008). Can structural adjustment improve energy efficiency: A study based on Chinese provincial data. *World Economy, 31*(11), 77–85.

Wei Chu & Xia Dong. (2010). Per capita CO_2 emission decomposition in China: A cross-country comparison. *Management Review, 22*(8), 114–121.

Wei Taoyuan & Romslod. (2002). The impact of coal tax on Chinese economy and GHG emission. *World Economy and Politics, 8*, 47–49.

Wei Yue & Xie Gaodi. (2009). Spatial allocation of carbon emissions and its impact on regional functions in China. *Resources Science, 31*(4), 590–597.

World Bank. (2012). *Sustainable low-carbon urban development in China*. Beijing: World Bank.

Wu Jun. (2009). TFP growth and convergence across China's industrial economy considering environmental protection. *Journal of Quantitative and Technical Economics, 11*, 17–27.

Wu Jun, Da Fengyuan, & Zhang Jianhua. (2010). Environmental regulation and regional TFP growth of China. *Statistical Research, 27*(1), 83–89.

Xie Shichen, Chen Changhong, Li Li, Huang Cheng, Cheng Zhen, Dai Pu, & Lu Jun. (2009). Shanghai CO_2 emissions inventory and carbon distribution chart for energy consumption. *China Environmental Science*, *29*(11), 1215–1220.

Xinhuanet. (2011). Significant achievements in energy conservation and emission reduction – One of the "Eleventh Five-Year" energy-saving and emission reduction review. Beijing: Xinhuanet.

Xu Dafeng. (2010). Research on industrial structure adjustment under the guidance of low-carbon economy: An empirical study based on Shanghai's industry linkage. *East China Economic Management*, *24*(10), 6–9.

Xu Dafeng. (2011). Carbon productivity, industrial linkages and adjustment of low-carbon economic structure – Empirical analysis based on China's input–output table. *Soft Science*, *25*(3), 42–46.

Xu Cong, Wei Baoren, Tahara Kiyotaka, Kobayashi Kensuke, & Sagisaka Masayuki. (2011). A preliminary review of urban CO_2 emissions auditing. *Environmental Science Guide*, *30*(2), 19–21.

Yang Jun & Shao Hanhua. (2009). Empirical study on China's industrial growth under the binding of environment. Economic Research Journal, *9*, 64–78.

Yang Wenju. (2006). Technology efficiency, technology progress, capital deepening and economic growth: An empirical analysis based on DEA. *Journal of World Economy*, *5*, 73–84.

Yuan Peng & Cheng Shi. (2011). Shadow price estimation of industrial pollutants in China. *Statistical Research*, *28*(9).

Yue Shujing & Liu Fuhua. (2009). The industrial efficiency and its determinants considering environmental protection. *Journal of Quantitative and Technical Economics*, *5*, 94–106.

Zhang Jinping, Qin Yaochen, Zhang Yan, & Zhang Lijun. (2010). Measurement of urban CO_2 emission structure and low carbon level: Taking Beijing, Tianjin, Shanghai and Anhui as an example. *Geography Science*, *30*(6), 874–879.

Zhang Jun, Wu Guiying, & Zhang Jipeng. 2004. Inter-provincial material capital stock estimation in China: 1952–2000. *Economic Research*, *10*, 35–44.

Zhou Jian & Gu Liuliu. (2009). Transformation of industrial growth mode under energy and environment constraint: Empirical analysis of Shanghai data based on nonparametric production frontier model. *Journal of Finance and Economics*, *35*(5), 94–103.

Zhou Li'an. (2004). Incentives and cooperation of government officials in the promotion game. *Economic Research*, *6*, 33–40.

Zhou Rongshun & Jia Zhen. (2012). Shandong Zibo saves 1.7 million tons of coal by saving energy and low carbon. *Zibo Daily*, Zibo.

Zhou Yean. (2003). Local government competition and economic growth. *Journal of Renmin University of China*, *1*, 97–103.

Articles published in English

Adrien, V.-S. & Stéphane, H. (2011). When starting with the most expensive option makes sense: Use and misuse of marginal abatement cost curves. World Bank Policy Research Working Paper.

Aigner, D. J. & Chu, S. F. (1968). On estimating the industry production function. *American Economic Review*, *58*(4), 826–839.

146 *References*

Aigner, D., Lovell, C. K., & Schmidt, P. (1977). Formulation and estimation of stochastic frontier production function models. *Journal of Econometrics, 6*(1), 21–37.

Alcantara, V. & Roca, J. (1995). Energy and CO_2 emissions in Spain: Methodology of analysis and some results for 1980–1990. *Energy Economics, 17*(3), 221–230.

Anderson, T. W. & Hsiao, C. (1981). Estimation of dynamic models with error components. *Journal of the American Statistical Association, 76*, 598–606.

Ang, B. W. (2004). Decomposition analysis for policymaking in energy: Which is the preferred method? *Energy Policy, 32*(9), 1131–1139.

Ang, B. W. & Pandiyan, G. (1997). Decomposition of energy-induced CO_2 emissions in manufacturing. *Energy Economics, 19*(3), 363–374.

Ang, B., Zhang, F. Q., & Choi, K.-H. (1998). Factorizing changes in energy and environmental indicators through decomposition. *Energy, 23*(6), 489–495.

Ankarhem, M. (2005). Shadow prices for undesirables in Swedish industry: indication of environmental Kuznets curves? Umeå Economic Studies, working paper No. 659.

Arellano, M. & Bond, S. (1991). Some tests of specification for panel data: Monte Carlo evidence and an application to employment equations. *Review of Economic Studies, 58*(2), 277–297.

Atkinson, S. E. & Dorfman, J. H. (2005). Bayesian measurement of productivity and efficiency in the presence of undesirable outputs: Crediting electric utilities for reducing air pollution. *Journal of Econometrics, 126*(2), 445–468.

Auffhammer, M. & Carson, R. T. (2008). Forecasting the path of China's CO_2 emissions using province-level information. *Journal of Environmental Economics and Management, 55*(3), 229–247.

Ball, V. E., Lovell, C. A., Nehring, R. F., & Somwaru, A. (1994). Incorporating undesirable outputs into models of production: An application to US agriculture. *Cahiers d'Economie et de Sociologie Rurales, 31*, 59–74.

Baumol, W. J. & Oates, W. E. (1988). *The theory of environmental policy*. Cambridge: Cambridge University Press.

Bohm, P. & Larsen, B. (1994). Fairness in a tradeable-permit treaty for carbon emissions reductions in Europe and the former Soviet Union. *Environmental and Resource Economics, 4*(3), 219–239.

Boyd, G., Molburg, J., & Prince, R. (1996). Alternative methods of marginal abatement cost estimation: Non-parametric distance functions (No. ANL/DIS/CP-90838; CONF-9610179-3). Argonne National Laboratory, IL, USA, Decision and Information Sciences Division.

Brännlund, R. & Ghalwash, T. (2008). The income–pollution relationship and the role of income distribution: An analysis of Swedish household data. *Resource and Energy Economics, 30*(3), 369–387.

Bréchet, T. & Jouvet, P. A. (2009). Why environmental management may yield no-regret pollution abatement options. *Ecological Economics, 68*(6), 1770–1777.

Chambers, R., Chung, Y., & Färe, R. (1998). Profit, directional distance functions, and Nerlovian efficiency. *Journal of Optimization Theory and Applications, 98*(2), 351–364.

Charnes, A. & Cooper, W. W. (1962). Programming with linear fractional functionals. *Naval Research Logistics Quarterly, 15*, 333–334.

Chen, W. (2005). The costs of mitigating carbon emissions in China: Findings from China MARKAL-MACRO modeling. *Energy Policy, 33*(7), 885–896.

Choi, Y., Zhang, N., & Zhou, P. (2012). Efficiency and abatement costs of energy-related CO_2 emissions in China: A slacks-based efficiency measure. *Applied Energy*, *98*(10), 198–208.

Chung, Y. H., Färe, R., & Grosskopf, S. (1997). Productivity and undesirable outputs: A directional distance function approach. *Journal of Environmental Management*, *51*(3), 229–240.

Coelli, T. & Perelman, S. (1996). Efficiency measurement, multiple-output technologies and distance functions: With application to European railways. CREPP Working Paper, 96/05, University of Liege, Belgium.

Coggins, J. S. & Swinton, J. R. (1996). The price of pollution: A dual approach to valuing SO allowances. *Journal of Environmental Economics and Management*, *30*(1), 58–72.

Cooper, W. W., Seiford, L. M., & Tone, K. (2007). *Data envelopment analysis: A comprehensive text with models, applications, references and DEA-solver software*. New York: Springer Verlag.

Criqui, P., Mima, S., & Viguier, L. (1999). Marginal abatement costs of CO_2 emission reductions, geographical flexibility and concrete ceilings: an assessment using the POLES model. *Energy Policy*, *27*(10), 585–601.

Dasgupta, S., Huq, M., Wheeler, D., & Chang, Z. (2001). Water pollution abatement by Chinese industry: Cost estimates and policy implications. *Applied Economics*, *33*(4), 547–557.

de Boo, A. J. (1993). Costs of integrated environmental control. *Statistical Journal of the United Nations Economic Commission for Europe*, *10*(1), 47–64.

De Cara, S. & Jayet, P.-A. (2011). Marginal abatement costs of greenhouse gas emissions from European agriculture, cost effectiveness, and the EU non-ETS burden sharing agreement. *Ecological Economics*, *70*(9), 1680–1690.

Denison, E. F. (1967). *Why growth rates differ: Postwar experience in nine western countries*. Washington, DC: Brookings Institution.

Dhakal, S. (2009). Urban energy use and carbon emissions from cities in China and policy implications. *Energy Policy*, *37*(11), 4208–4219.

Dinda, S. (2004). Environmental Kuznets curve hypothesis: A survey. *Ecological Economics*, *49*(4), 431–455.

Du, L.-M., Wei, C., & Cai, S. (2012). Economic development and carbon dioxide emissions in China: Provincial panel data analysis. *China Economic Review*, *23*(2), 371–384.

Easterly, W., Kremer, M., Pritchett, L., & Summers, L. H. (1993). Good policy or good luck? *Journal of Monetary Economics*, *32*(3), 459–483.

EIA. (2011). *International energy statistics*. US Energy Information Administration.

Ekins, P., Pollitt, H., Barton, J., & Blobel, D. (2011). The implications for households of environmental tax reform (ETR) in Europe. *Ecological Economics*, *70*(12), 2472–2485.

Ellerman, A. D. & Decaux, A. (1998). *Analysis of post-Kyoto CO_2 emissions trading using marginal abatement curves*. MIT Joint Program on the Science and Policy of Global Change.

Ellerman, A. D., Joskow, P. L., Schmalensee, R., Bailey, E. M., & Montero, J. P. (2000). Markets for clean air: The US acid rain program. New York: Cambridge University Press.

Fan, Y., Liu, L.-C., Wu, G., Tsai, H.-T., & Wei, Y.-M. (2007). Changes in carbon intensity in China: Empirical findings from 1980–2003. *Ecological Economics*, *62*(3–4), 683–691.

148   References

Färe, R. (1988). *Fundamentals of production theory*. Berlin: Springer-Verlag.

Färe, R., Grosskopf, S., Lovell, C. K., & Pasurka, C. (1989). Multilateral productivity comparisons when some outputs are undesirable: A nonparametric approach. *Review of Economics and Statistics, 71*(1), 90–98.

Färe, R., Grosskopf, S., Lovell, C. K., & Yaisawarng, S. (1993). Derivation of shadow prices for undesirable outputs: A distance function approach. *Review of Economics and Statistics, 75*(2), 374–380.

Färe, R., Grosskopf, S., & Roos, P. (1998). Malmquist productivity indexes: A survey of theory and practice. In *Index numbers: Essays in honour of Sten Malmquist* (pp. 127–190). Dordrecht: Springer.

Färe, R., Grosskopf, S., & Leber, W. L. (2001). Shadow prices of Missouri public conservation land. *Public Finance Review, 29*(6), 444–460.

Färe, R., Grosskopf, S., Noh, D.-W., & Leber, W. (2005). Characteristics of a polluting technology: Theory and practice. *Journal of Econometrics, 126*(2), 469–492.

Färe, R., Grosskopf, S., & Weber, W. L. (2006). Shadow prices and pollution costs in US agriculture. *Ecological Economics, 56*(1), 89–103.

Färe, R. & Grosskopf, S. (2006). *New directions: Efficiency and productivity* (Vol. 3). New York: Springer Science and Business Media.

Färe, R., Grosskopf, S., & Pasurka Jr, C. A. (2007). Environmental production functions and environmental directional distance functions. *Energy, 32*(7), 1055–1066.

Färe, R., Martins-Filho, C., & Vardanyan, M. (2010). On functional form representation of multi-output production technologies. *Journal of Productivity Analysis, 33*(2), 81–96.

Färe, R. & Grosskopf, S. (1998). Shadow pricing of good and bad commodities. *American Journal of Agricultural Economics, 80*(3), 584–590.

Färe, R. & Zelenyuk, V. (2003). On aggregate Farrell efficiencies. *European Journal of Operational Research, 146*(3), 615–620.

Ferrier, G. D. & Lovell, C. K. (1990). Measuring cost efficiency in banking: Econometric and linear programming evidence. *Journal of Econometrics, 46*(1–2), 229–245.

Fischer, C. & Morgenstern, R. D. (2006). Carbon abatement costs: Why the wide range of estimates? *Energy Journal, 27*(2), 73–86.

Fisher-Vanden, K., Jefferson, G. H., Liu, H., & Tao, Q. (2004). What is driving China's decline in energy intensity? *Resource and Energy Economics, 26*(1), 77–97.

Friedl, B. & Getzner, M. (2003). Determinants of CO_2 emissions in a small open economy. *Ecological Economics, 45*(1), 133–148.

Fukuyama, H. & Weber, W. L. (2009). A directional slacks-based measure of technical inefficiency. *Socio-Economic Planning Sciences, 43*(4), 274–287.

Galeotti, M. & Lanza, A. (1999). Richer and cleaner? A study on carbon dioxide emissions in developing countries 1. *Energy Policy, 27*(10), 565–573.

Gallop, F. M. & Roberts, M. J. (1985). Cost-minimizing regulation of sulfur emissions. *Review of Economics and Statistics, 67*(1), 81–90.

Garbaccio, R. F., Ho, M. S., & Jorgenson, D. W. (1999). Controlling carbon emissions in China. *Environment and Development Economics, 4*(4), 493–518.

Ghorbani, M. & Motallebi, M. (2009). The study on shadow price of greenhouse gases emission in Iran: Case of dairy farms. *Research Journal of Environmental Sciences, 3*(4), 466–475.

Glaeser, E. L. & Kahn, M. E. (2010). The greenness of cities: carbon dioxide emissions and urban development. *Journal of Urban Economics, 67*(3), 404–418.

References 149

Greening, L. A., Greene, D. L., & Difiglio, C. (2000). Energy efficiency and consumption – The rebound effect – A survey. *Energy Policy*, *28*(6–7), 389–401.

Grossman, G. M. & Krueger, A. B. (1991). *Environmental impacts of a North American free trade agreement*. Cambridge, MA: National Bureau of Economic Research.

Grosskopf, S. & Hayes, K. (1993). Local public sector bureaucrats and their input choices. *Journal of Urban Economics*, *33*(2), 151–166.

Guo, X.-D., Zhu, L., Fan, Y., & Xie, B.-C. (2011). Evaluation of potential reductions in carbon emissions in Chinese provinces based on environmental DEA. *Energy Policy*, *39*(5), 2352–2360.

Hailu, A. & Veeman, T. S. (2000). Environmentally sensitive productivity analysis of the Canadian pulp and paper industry, 1959–1994: An input distance function approach. *Journal of Environmental Economics and Management*, *40*(3), 251–274.

Hallegatte, S., Henriet, F., & Corfee-Morlot, J. (2011). The economics of climate change impacts and policy benefits at city scale: A conceptual framework. *Climatic Change*, *104*(1), 51–87.

Hatzigeorgiou, E., Polatidis, H., & Haralambopoulos, D. (2008). CO_2 emissions in Greece for 1990–2002: A decomposition analysis and comparison of results using the Arithmetic Mean Divisia Index and Logarithmic Mean Divisia Index techniques. *Energy*, *33*(3), 492–499.

Hetemäki, L. (1996). *Essays on the impact of pollution control on a firm: A distance function approach*. Helsinki: Helsinki Research Centre.

Hettige, H., Huq, M., Pargal, S., & Wheeler, D. (1996). Determinants of pollution abatement in developing countries: Evidence from South and Southeast Asia. *World Development*, *24*(12), 1891–1904.

Hoeller, P. & Coppel, J. (1992). *Energy taxation and price distortions in fossil fuel markets: Some implications for climate change policy*. Paris: Organisation for Economic Co-operation and Development.

Holtz-Eakin, D. & Selden, T. (1995). Stoking the fires? CO_2 emissions and economic growth. *Journal of Public Economics*, *57*(1), 85–101.

IEA. (2007). *World energy outlook 2007 – China and India insights*. Paris: OECD/IEA.

IEA. (2009). *CO_2 emissions from fuel combustion*. International Energy Agency.

IEA. (2010). *Key world energy statistics 2010*. Paris: OECD.

IPCC. (2006). *2006 IPCC guidelines for national greenhouse gas inventories*. Geneva: Intergovernmental Panel on Climate Change.

IPCC. (2007). *Climate change 2007: Impacts, adaptation and vulnerability*. Cambridge: Cambridge University Press.

İpek Tunç, G., Türüt-Aşıc, S., & Akbostancı, E. (2009). A decomposition analysis of CO_2 emissions from energy use: Turkish case. *Energy Policy*, *37*(11), 4689–4699.

Jiahua, P., & Ying, C. (2010). Carbon budget proposal: A framework for an equitable and sustainable international climate regime. *Social Sciences in China*, *31*(1), 5–34.

Johnson, T. M., Alatorre, C., Romo, Z., & Liu, F. (2009). *Low-carbon development for Mexico*. Washington, DC: World Bank.

Kaya, Y. (1989). Impact of carbon dioxide emission control on GNP growth: interpretation of proposed scenarios. Paper presented to the Energy and Industry Subgroup, Response Strategies Working Group. Intergovernmental Panel on Climate Change, Paris, France.

Ke, T. Y., Hu, J. L., Li, Y., & Chiu, Y. H. (2008). Shadow prices of SO_2 abatements for regions in China. *Agricultural and Resources Economics*, *5*(2), 59–78.

150 References

Kesicki, F. & Strachan, N. (2011). Marginal abatement cost (MAC) curves: Confronting theory and practice. *Environmental Science and Policy*, *14*(8), 1195–1204.

Kumbhakar, S. C. & Lovell, C. A. K. (2000). *Stochastic frontier analysis*. Cambridge: Cambridge University Press.

King, R. G. & Levine, R. (1994). Capital fundamentalism, economic development, and economic growth. *Carnegie-Rochester Conference Series on Public Policy*, *40*, 259–292.

Klepper, G. & Peterson, S. (2006). Marginal abatement cost curves in general equilibrium: The influence of world energy prices. *Resource and Energy Economics*, *28*(1), 1–23.

Kolstad, C. D. & Turnovsky, M. H. (1998). Cost functions and nonlinear prices: Estimating a technology with quality-differentiated inputs. *Review of Economics and Statistics*, *80*(3), 444–453.

Kousky, C. & Schneider, S. H. (2003). Global climate policy: Will cities lead the way? *Climate Policy*, *3*(4), 359–372.

Kumar, S. (1999). Economic evaluation of development projects: A case analysis of environmental health implications of thermal power projects in India. Delhi.

Kumar, S. (2006). Environmentally sensitive productivity growth: A global analysis using Malmquist–Luenberger index. *Ecological Economics*, *56*(2), 280–293.

Lantz, V. & Feng, Q. (2006). Assessing income, population, and technology impacts on CO_2 emissions in Canada: Where's the EKC? *Ecological Economics*, *57*(2), 229–238.

Lee, J.-D., Park, J.-B., & Kim, T.-Y. (2002). Estimation of the shadow prices of pollutants with production/environment inefficiency taken into account: A nonparametric directional distance function approach. *Journal of Environmental Management*, *64*(4), 365–375.

Lee, K. & Oh, W. (2006). Analysis of CO_2 emissions in APEC countries: A time-series and a cross-sectional decomposition using the log mean Divisia method. *Energy Policy*, *34*(17), 2779–2787.

Lee, M. (2005). The shadow price of substitutable sulfur in the US electric power plant: A distance function approach. *Journal of Environmental Management*, *77*(2), 104–110.

Liao, H., Fan, Y., & Wei, Y.-M. (2007). What induced China's energy intensity to fluctuate: 1997–2006? *Energy Policy*, *35*(9), 4640–4649.

Liu, L.-C., Fan, Y., Wu, G., & Wei, Y.-M. (2007). Using LMDI method to analyze the change of China's industrial CO_2 emissions from final fuel use: An empirical analysis. *Energy Policy*, *35*(11), 5892–5900.

Lu, I. J., Lin, S. J., & Lewis, C. (2007). Decomposition and decoupling effects of carbon dioxide emission from highway transportation in Taiwan, Germany, Japan and South Korea. *Energy Policy*, *35*(6), 3226–3235.

Ma, C. & Stern, D. I. (2008). Biomass and China's carbon emissions: A missing piece of carbon decomposition. *Energy Policy*, *36*(7), 2517–2526.

Maddison, A. (1987). Growth and slowdown in advanced capitalist economies: Techniques of quantitative assessment. *Journal of Economic Literature*, *25*(2), 649–698.

Magnus, L. (2002). An EKC-pattern in historical perspective: Carbon dioxide emissions, technology, fuel prices and growth in Sweden 1870–1997. *Ecological Economics*, *42*(1–2), 333–347.

References   151

Maradan, D. & Vassiliev, A. (2005). Marginal costs of carbon dioxide abatement: Empirical evidence from cross-country analysis. *Revue Suisse D Economie et de Statistique, 141*(3), 377–410.

Marklund, P.-O. & Samakovlis, E. (2007). What is driving the EU burden-sharing agreement: Efficiency or equity? *Journal of Environmental Management, 85*(2), 317–329.

McKinsey & Company. (2009). *Pathways to a low-carbon economy: Version 2 of the Global Greenhouse Gas Abatement Cost Curve.*

Metz, B., Davidson, O. R., Bosch, P. R., Dave, R., & Meyer, L. A. (2007). *Contribution of Working Group III to the Fourth Assessment Report of the Intergovernmental Panel on Climate Change.* Cambridge: Cambridge University Press.

Motherway, B. & Walker, N. (2009). Ireland's low carbon opportunity: An analysis of the costs and benefits of reducing greenhouse gas emissions. Sustainable Energy Ireland.

Muradian, R. & Martinez-Alier, J. (2001). Trade and the environment: From a 'Southern' perspective. *Ecological Economics, 36*(2), 281–297.

Murty, M. N. & Kumar, S. (2003). Win–win opportunities and environmental regulation: Testing of porter hypothesis for Indian manufacturing industries. *Journal of Environmental Management, 67*(2), 139–144.

Murty, M., Kumar, S., & Dhavala, K. K. (2007). Measuring environmental efficiency of industry: A case study of thermal power generation in India. *Environmental and Resource Economics, 38*(1), 31–50.

Newell, R. G. & Stavins, R. N. (2003). Cost heterogeneity and the potential savings from market-based policies. *Journal of Regulatory Economics, 23*(1), 43–59.

Nordhaus, W. D. (1991). To slow or not to slow: The economics of the greenhouse effect. *Economic Journal, 101*(407), 920–937.

Park, H. & Lim, J. (2009). Valuation of marginal CO_2 abatement options for electric power plants in Korea. *Energy Policy, 37*(5), 1834–1841.

Peng, Y. & Shi, C. (2011). Determinants of carbon emissions growth in China: A structural decomposition analysis. *Energy Procedia, 5*, 169–175.

Pittman, R. W. (1983). Multilateral productivity comparisons with undesirable outputs. *Economic Journal, 93*(372), 883–891.

Poswiata, J. & Bogdan, W. (2009). *Assessment of greenhouse gas emissions abatement potential in Poland by 2030.* Warsaw: McKinsey & Company.

Price, L., Levine, M. D., Zhou, N., Fridley, D., Aden, N. T., Lu, H., ..., Yowargana, P. (2011). Assessment of China's energy-saving and emission-reduction accomplishments and opportunities during the 11th Five Year Plan. *Energy Policy, 39*, 2165–2178.

Reig-Martínez, E., Picazo-Tadeo, A., & Hernandez-Sancho, F. (2001). The calculation of shadow prices for industrial wastes using distance functions: An analysis for Spanish ceramic pavements firms. *International Journal of Production Economics, 69*(3), 277–285.

Repetto, R., Rothman, D., Faeth, P., & Austin, D. (1996). *Has environmental protection really reduced productivity growth? We need unbiased measures.* Washington, DC: World Resources Institute.

Rezek, J. P. & Campbell, R. C. (2007). Cost estimates for multiple pollutants: A maximum entropy approach. *Energy Economics, 29*(3), 503–519.

Richmond, A. K. & Kaufmann, R. K. (2006). Is there a turning point in the relationship between income and energy use and/or carbon emissions? *Ecological Economics, 56*(2), 176–189.

152   References

Salnykov, M. & Zelenyuk, V. (2005). *Estimation of environmental efficiencies of economies and shadow prices of pollutants in countries in transition.* EERC Research Network, Russia and CIS.

Scheel, H. (2001). Undesirable outputs in efficiency valuations. *European Journal of Operational Research, 132*(2), 400–410.

Shepard, R. N. & Chipman, S. (1970). Second-order isomorphism of internal representations: Shapes of states. *Cognitive Psychology, 1*(1), 1–17.

Springer, U. (2003). The market for tradable GHG permits under the Kyoto Protocol: A survey of model studies. *Energy Economics, 25*(5), 527–551.

Steckel, J. C., Jakob, M., Marschinski, R., & Luderer, G. (2011). From carbonization to decarbonization? – Past trends and future scenarios for China's CO_2 emissions. *Energy Policy, 39*(6), 3443–3455.

Stern, D. I. (2004). The rise and fall of the environmental Kuznets curve. *World Development, 32*(8), 1419–1439.

Stern, D. I. & Common, M. S. (2001). Is there an environmental Kuznets curve for sulfur? *Journal of Environmental Economics and Management, 41*(2), 162–178.

Stern, N. (2008). The economics of climate change. *American Economic Review, 98*(2), 1–37.

Sunil, M. (2009). CO_2 emissions from electricity generation in seven Asia-Pacific and North American countries: A decomposition analysis. *Energy Policy, 37*(1), 1–9.

Swinton, J. R. (1998). At what cost do we reduce pollution? Shadow prices of SO_2 emissions. *Energy Journal, 19*(4), 63–83.

Time. (2009). *Lessons from the Copenhagen Climate Talks.*

Torvanger, A. (1991). Manufacturing sector carbon dioxide emissions in nine OECD countries, 1973–87: A Divisia index decomposition to changes in fuel mix, emission coefficients, industry structure, energy intensities and international structure. *Energy Economics, 13*(3), 168–186.

Tucker, M. (1995). Carbon dioxide emissions and global GDP. *Ecological Economics, 15*(3), 215–223.

Tyteca, D. (1997). Linear programming models for the measurement of environmental performance of firms – Concepts and empirical results. *Journal of Productivity Analysis, 8*(2), 183–197.

UNEP. (2008). Green jobs: Towards decent work in a sustainable, low-carbon world. Report produced by Worldwatch Institute and commissioned by UNEP.

Unruh, G. C. & Moomaw, W. R. (1998). An alternative analysis of apparent EKC-type transitions. *Ecological Economics, 25*(2), 221–229.

Van Ha, N., Kant, S., & Maclaren, V. (2008). Shadow prices of environmental outputs and production efficiency of household-level paper recycling units in Vietnam. *Ecological Economics, 65*(1), 98–110.

Vardanyan, M. & Noh, D.-W. (2006). Approximating pollution abatement costs via alternative specifications of a multi-output production technology: A case of the US electric utility industry. *Journal of Environmental Management, 80*(2), 177–190.

Wagner, M. (2008). The carbon Kuznets curve: A cloudy picture emitted by bad econometrics? *Resource and Energy Economics, 30*(3), 388–408.

Wang, C., Chen, J., & Zou, J. (2005). Decomposition of energy-related CO_2 emission in China: 1957–2000. *Energy, 30*(1), 73–83.

Wei, C., Löschel, A., & Liu, B. (2013). An empirical analysis of the CO_2 shadow price in Chinese thermal power enterprises. *Energy Economics, 40*, 22–31.

References 153

Winkler, H., Spalding-Fecher, R., & Tyani, L. (2002). Comparing developing countries under potential carbon allocation schemes. *Climate Policy*, *2*(4), 303–318.

World Bank. (2009). *Mid-term evaluation of China's 11th five year plan*. Washington, DC: World Bank.

World Bank. (2010). *Development and climate change, World Development Report 2010*. Washington, DC: World Bank.

WRI. (2011). *Climate analysis indicators tool*. Washington, DC: World Resource Institute.

Wu, L., Kaneko, S., & Matsuoka, S. (2005). Driving forces behind the stagnancy of China's energy-related CO_2 emissions from 1996 to 1999: The relative importance of structural change, intensity change and scale change. *Energy Policy*, *33*(3), 319–335.

Yaisawarng, S. & Klein, J. D. (1994). The effects of sulfur dioxide controls on productivity change in the US electric power industry. *Review of Economics and Statistics*, *76*(3), 447–460.

Zha, D., Zhou, D., & Ding, N. (2009). The contribution degree of sub-sectors to structure effect and intensity effects on industry energy intensity in China from 1993 to 2003. *Renewable and Sustainable Energy Reviews*, *13*(4), 895–902.

Zha, D. L., Zhou, D., & Zhou, P. (2010). Driving forces of residential CO_2 emissions in urban and rural China: An index decomposition analysis. *Energy Policy*, *38*(7), 3377–3383.

Zhang, M., Mu, H., Ning, Y., & Song, Y. (2009). Decomposition of energy-related CO_2 emission over 1991–2006 in China. *Ecological Economics*, *68*(7), 2122–2128.

Zhang, Y., Zhang, J., Yang, Z., & Li, S. (2011). Regional differences in the factors that influence China's energy-related carbon emissions, and potential mitigation strategies. *Energy Policy*, *39*(12), 7712–7718.

Index

Note: Page numbers in **bold** refer to tables and in *italics* to figures.

agriculture 72, 120, 128, 130, 137–138
Aigner, D. 8
Aigner, D. et al. (1977) 11
Ankarhem, M. 64
Atkinson, S. E. **18**
Auffhammer, M. 63
Australian Bureau of Agriculture and
  Resource Economics **75**

backward production capacity 67, 125,
  131, 134, 140, 141
Bali roadmap 42
Beijing: carbon marginal abatement
  cost 54, 66, 93, 94, **109**, **110**; carbon
  shadow price 38–39, 40, **55**; emission
  reduction potential 50, 121; emissions
  51, **58**, 59, *60*, *61*, **62**, 65, 73
Bohm, P. 95–96
Boyd, G. et al. (1996) **16**, 24

Cai Bofeng 72, 73
Campbell, R. C. 76, 91
"carbon budget plan" 43
carbon capture and storage *see* CCS
carbon emissions, marginal abatement
  costs (MAC) 69–115: economic-
  energy models 74–75; expert-based
  73–74; influencing factors 95–102;
  micro supply side 75–77; provincial
  109; urban 71–73, **110–113**
carbon emissions, reduction potential
  42–67: challenges to 125–127;
  emission reduction potential model
  46–47; interprovincial 49–54, 56–62;
  reduction capacity index 57–59, 61;
  regional marginal cost 54–56; shadow
  price model 47–48

carbon emissions, shadow price:
  directional distance function 6–8,
  33–35; distance function 4–6;
  evidence-based studies **16**, **18**, **20**, **22**;
  index method 4; provincial 30–41, 45,
  47–48, 54–56, 64–65; theory 24–26
carbon sequestration 129–130
carbon sinks 129, 130, 137, 138
carbon tax 30, 39–41, 69, 70
Carson, R. T. 63
Caves, D. W. 28n7
CCS (carbon capture and storage) 131
CGE (Computable General
  Equilibrium) model 54, 74, 75
Chamber, R. et al. (1998) 79
Charnes, A. 47
Chen et al. (2010) **22**
Chen Shiyi (2010) 32, 76, 77, 81, **82**, 92
Cheng Shi 95
China Environmental Yearbook 83–84
China Statistical Yearbook 36, 48, 49
China Urban Statistical Yearbook 83–84,
  85
Chipman, S. 5
Choi, Y. et al. (2012) 76
Christensen, L. R. 28n7
Chung (1996) 34
Chung (1997) 14
Chung, Y. H. et al. (1997) 4, 6, **16**, 32,
  33, 45, 77
circular economy 132, 136
Clean Development Fund 43
CO_2 *see* carbon emissions
coal consumption: industrial restructuring
  119–120, 121, 124, 134–135; marginal
  abatement cost (MAC) 85–86, **87**, **89**;
  regional 48, 49, **50**, 63, **64**, 66, 72

Coelli, T. 11
Coggins, J. S. **16**, 32
"complete efficiency" 24
Computable General Equilibrium model *see* CGE
construction industry 120, 138–139
contaminant disposal modeling 3–27: data envelope analysis (DEA) 13–15; parameterized distance function method 8–9; quadratic direction distance function 9–11; stochastic frontier analysis (SFA) 11–13
Cooper, W. W. 47
Cooper, W. W. et al. (2007) 45
Copenhagen conference 42
Coppel, J. 95
Criqui, P. et al. (1999) 95

Dasgupta, S. et al. (2001) 95
DDF (directional distance function) 6–8, 23–25, 31–35, 45, 68n6, 76–83, 89–91
DEA (Data Envelopment Analysis) model 8, 13–15, 24–25, 32, 80, 92, 95
deterministic linear programming 25
Dhakal, S. 72
Diewert, W. 28n7
Ding Zhongli et al. (2009) 43–44
directional distance function *see* DDF
distance function 4–6, 8–15, 23–25, 32, 48, 76
Dong Feng et al. (2010) **22**, 23
Dorfman, J. H. **18**
Du, L.-M. et al. (2012) 96

economic restructuring 124–125, 127
efficiency boundary 3
Efficiency Index **58**–59
Eleventh Five-Year Plan 23, 67, 69, 125–126, 127
emerging industries 130, 140
emission reduction efficiency 56–62, 66
emission reduction potential 44, 46–47, 49–54, 56–**58**, 62–67, 73–74, 121–122
energy conservation 52, 67, 69, 122–127, 133, 134, 138
energy consumption per unit of GDP 124
energy efficiency 62, 67, 119–120, 124, 129, 132–133, 135, 139
energy prices 122–123, 126
energy sector 74, 134–135
energy security 124
equipment manufacturing sector 132, 135–136

EU-ETS (greenhouse gas emissions trading) 69
external damage price 4

fairness 43–44, 56–**62**, 66, 69, 76, 121
Fairness Index **58**–59
Färe, R. et al. (1989) 45
Färe, R. et al. (1993) 5, 8, 32, 48
Färe, R. et al. (2001) 79
Färe, R. et al. (2005) 12, **18**, 32
Färe, R. et al. (2007) **19**
Färe, R. et al. (2010) 81
Ferrier, G. D. 11
forestry 130, 138
fossil energy: carbon emissions 36, 49, 95–96, 120, 130; urban consumption 70, 72, 85–86
frontier production function 5
Fu Jiafeng et al. (2010) 45
Fujian: carbon marginal abatement cost (MAC) 54, **109**; carbon shadow price 37–38, **55**; emission reduction potential 50, **58**, 66, 121; emissions **51**
Fukuyama, H. 24, 45

Gallop, F. M. **16**
Gansu: carbon marginal abatement cost (MAC) 93, **109**; carbon shadow price 37–38, **55**; emission reduction potential 52, **58**, 65, 121; emissions **51**
Gao Pengfei et al. (2004) **75**
gas 85, **86**, 124 *see also* natural gas
GHG (greenhouse gas) emissions: industrial restructuring and 119, 122–129, 131–132, 134–140; regional 43, 54; urban 69–73
Ghorbani, M. **20**
Glaeser, E. L. 71
Global Commons Institute 43
global economy 122–123
government role 31, 40, 71, 102, 122–128, 140
greenhouse gas emissions *see* GHG emissions
Grosskopf, S. 11, 28n17
Gu Liuliu **21**
Guangdong: carbon marginal abatement cost 54, **109**; carbon shadow price **37**, 38–39, 40, **55**; emission reduction potential 50, **58**, 66, 121; emissions 40, **51**, 65, 120
Guangxi: carbon marginal abatement cost (MAC) 93, **109**; carbon shadow

price 37, **55**; emission reduction potential 50, **58**, 61, **62**; emissions **51**

Guizhou: carbon marginal abatement cost (MAC) 54, **109**; carbon shadow price 37–38, 40, **55**; emission reduction potential 50, **58**, 60, *61*, **62**, 65, 66, 121; emissions **51**, 52, 65

Hailu, A. **17**, 32

Hainan: carbon marginal abatement cost 54; carbon shadow price **37**, **55**; emission reduction potential 50, **58**, *59*, 60, 61, **62**, 66, 121

Hayes, K. 11, 28n17

He Juhuang et al. (2002) **75**

heavy chemical industry 120, 131

heavy industry 120, 135

high-carbon transfer 133–134

Hirschberg, J. 28n17

Hoeller, P. 95

Hu Angang et al. (2008) **20**, 23, 45, 77

hydropower 68n11, 134, 135

IEA (International Energy Agency) 70

imports 124, 133

India 96

industrial restructuring 119–141: agriculture 137–138; carbon-fixing industries 129–131; construction industry 138–139; domestic and international situation 122–124; energy sector 134–135; existing policies 140; industrial concentration 141; industrial sector 135–136; low-carbon industries 129–131; market-oriented reforms 141; price mechanism 141; public welfare support 141; service industry 139; target responsibility assessment system 140; transportation industry 136–137; upgrading of traditional industries 141

industrial sector 23, 119, 76, 120, 132, 135–136: secondary 72, **97**, 99, 124; tertiary 63, 66, **97**, 99, 119, 121, 124

infrastructure 96, **97**, 99, 103, 121, 126, 127

International Energy Agency *see* IEA

Japan 124

Jiahua, P. 43

Jiangsu **37**, 38, 40, **51**, **55**, **58**, **109**, 120

Kahn, M. E. 71

Ke, T. Y. et al. (2008) **19**, 23

King, R. G. 85

Klepper, G. 95

Kolstad, C. D. **17**

Kumar, S. 11, **17**, **19**

Kumbhakar, S. C. 12

Kyoto protocol 42, 43

Larsen, B. 95–96

Lee, J.-D. et al. (2002) **18**, 24, 32, 48

Lee, M. **18**

Levine, R. 85

Liaoning: carbon marginal abatement cost **109**, **110**; carbon shadow price 37, **55**; emission reduction potential 121; emissions **51**, 57, **58**, 59, *60*, *61*, **62**, 65, 120

Lim, J. 76

Liu Fuhua **21**

Liu Leiyi 77

Liu Minglei et al. (2011) **91**, 92, 96

Lovell, C. K. 11, 12

low-carbon approach 63, 120, 123, 129–131

Malmquist index of productivity 4, 32

Malmquist–Luenberger index of productivity 32, 45, 77

Maradan, D. 95

marine carbon sequestration 130–131

market mechanisms 122, 123, 127, 128

Marklund, P.-O. **82**, 91

Massachusetts Institute of Technology **75**

McKinsey & Company 73

methane 137

Monte Carlo method 81

Motallebi, M. **20**

multiproductivity index 28n7

Murty, M. 11, **17**

Murty, M. et al. (2007) **82**, 96

national emission account 43

natural gas 36, 49, 68n11, 124, 135

New York City 72–73

Ningxia: carbon marginal abatement cost 93, 102, **109**; carbon shadow price **37**, 38, **55**; emission reduction potential 50, 57, **58**, *59*, *60*, *61*, **62**, 66, 121; emissions **51**, 65

nitrogen oxides (NOx) 32

nitrous oxide 137

"no redundancy" 24, 38

Noh, D.-W. 29n19, 81, 91

non-fossil energy 134

Index   157

non-parametric method 25, 32, 34
nuclear power 68, 134, 135

OECD (Organisation for Economic Co-operation and Development) 71, 95
oil consumption 36, 49, 85, **86**, 120, 124

parameter estimation method 11, 32–33
Park, H. 76
Perelman, S. 11
Peterson, S. 95
petroleum gas **86**
Pittman, R. W. 4, 28n7, 32
Price, L. et al. (2011) 69
private car ownership 85, 136
productivity of environmental factors, average 36–37

Qin Shaojun et al. (2011) 91, 96
Qinghai **37, 51, 55, 58**, 65, 121

Reig-Martinez, F. et al. (2001) **18**
renewable energy 68n5, 123, 129, 134, 135, 137
Renewable Energy Law Amendment 42
Repetto, R. et al. (1996) 28n8
resource efficiency 132–133
resource utilization 132, 136
Rezek, J. P. 76, 91
Roberts, M. J. **16**

Salnykov, M. **18, 82**, 91
Samakovlis, E. **82**, 91
SBM (Scaks-Based Measure) model 45, 80
Scheel, H. 45
scientific development 127, 128–129, 131, 137
SEI (Stockholm Environment Institute), Greenhouse Development Rights Framework 43
service industries 129–130, 139, 140
SFA (stochastic frontier analysis) 11–13, 24
Shaanxi 37, **51, 55, 58, 109**, 121
shale gas 122
Shanghai: carbon marginal abatement cost 91, 93, 94, 96, 102, **109, 110**; carbon shadow price **37**, 38–39, 40, **55**, 91; emission reduction potential 50, 121; emissions **51**, 57, **58**, 59, *60*, *61*, **62**, 65, 72
Shanghai Energy Balance 72
Shanxi: carbon marginal abatement cost **109**; carbon shadow price 37, 38, **55**;

emission reduction potential 52, 54, 121–122; emissions **51**, 57, **58**, 59, *60*, *61*, **62**, 65–66, 72
Shao Hanhua **21**
Shen Manhong 63
Shepard, R. N. 5
Shephard output distance function 7
SO_2 *see* sulfur dioxide
State Council Development Research Center 43
stochastic frontier analysis *see* SFA
Stockholm Environment Institute *see* SEI
subtraction strategy 131–132
sulfide (SO_x) 32
sulfur dioxide (SO_2) 15, **16–22**, 23, 26, 32, 45, 52, 77, 95
sustainability 43, 128
Sweden 43, 64
Swinton, J. R. **16, 17**, 32

target responsibility assessment system 140
TFP (total factor productivity) 15
Thirteenth Five-Year Plan 125–126, 127
total factor productivity *see* TFP
total suspended particulate matter *see* TSP
traditional industries, upgrading of 132–133
traditional productivity analysis 3–27: Data Envelopment Analysis (DEA) 8, 13–15, 24; directional distance function 4–14; index method 4; transportation industry 136–137
TSP (total suspended particulate matter) 32
Tu Zhenge **20, 21**, 23, 45, 76, 77, 95
Turnovsky, M. H. **17**
Twelfth Five-Year Plan 42, 125, 127, 130

UN Lima Climate Agreement 123
upgrading strategy 132–133
urban carbon dioxide emissions 70–73, **108, 110–113**
urbanization 70, 99, 102, 103, 121, 122
USA 32, 71–72, 122, 124

Van Ha, N. et al. (2008) **19**, 24
Vardanyan, M. 29n19, 81, 91
Vassiliev, A. 95
Veeman, T. S. **17**, 32

Wang Bing et al. (2008) **20**
Wang Bing et al. (2010) **22**, 23, 45, 77

158   *Index*

Wang Bing et al. (2011) 77
Wang Can et al. (2005) **75**
Weber, W. L. 24, 45
Wei, C. et al. (2013) 91, 96
Wei Chu 63
Wei Chu et al. (2010) 52
World Bank 70, 71
Wu Jun **21**, 23
Wu Jun et al. (2010) **22**

Xie Shichen et al. (2009) 72
Xinjiang 37, **51**, **55**, **58**, 65, **109**, 121
Xu Cong et al. (2011) 72

Yang Jun **21**
Ying, C. 43
Yuan Peng 95
Yue Shujing **21**
Yunnan 37, **51**, **55**, **58**, **62**, **109**

Zelenyun, V. **18**, **82**, 91
Zhang Jinping et al. (2010) 73
Zhang Jun et al. (2004) 36, 48
Zhejiang: carbon marginal abatement cost 91, **109**; carbon shadow price **37**, 38, 40, **55**; emission reduction potential 121; emissions **51**, 54, **58**, 66
Zhou Jian **21**